# PRAISE FOR ...
## AN INSIDER SHARES HIS STORY

*HOLLYWOOD'S CHOSEN* IS THE STORY of a film buyer. The job has existed for as long as there have been movies, yet hardly anyone outside the motion picture industry has heard of it.

For over twenty years, Larry Vaughn negotiated with Hollywood studios to book their films into theatres. Blessed with a love of movies and a shrewd instinct for judging popular taste, this talented yet humble man came to regard choosing films as both a calling and a privilege.

In chronicling his career, Larry pulls back the curtain to provide a look at a largely undocumented aspect of the film industry. And in the process, he shares stories from his remarkable life that, were they to be filmed, would make one heck of a good movie.

So grab a bag of popcorn, find a comfortable seat, and get ready . . . the show is about to begin.

—**JOHN H. HERSKER**
President and CEO, Movie Tavern
Former Executive VP of Distribution, Paramount Pictures

RARELY IN OUR LIVES DO we get a chance to meet a man like Larry Vaughn. I was lucky enough to meet Larry and his family in 1985, and I can say without a shadow of a doubt that not only are he and his entire family people you would want to know, love, respect, and remain close with always, but simply knowing them makes one feel like a better person.

I implore you: read Larry's story. You won't be able to put it down. And it is all true; Larry is as honest and loyal as the day is long. I believe you will understand what I'm saying as you turn every page. When you finish reading, you will thank me—no, thank God for Larry Vaughn and his wife Doneata, for their beautiful daughter, Mentora, and for their combined inspiration in the writing of *Hollywood's Chosen*.

—**BERT LIVINGSTON**
Former Senior VP of Distribution and
General Sales Manager West, 20th Century Fox

I'VE KNOWN LARRY VAUGHN FOR over thirty years, and I can honestly say I've never known anyone more comfortable in their own skin.

Larry's journey not only gives you a better understanding of what is *truly* important in life, but it helps you find the strength and courage to redefine yourself. I really enjoyed reading *Hollywood's Chosen*, as I remember many of the stories from my years of working with Larry.

*Hollywood's Chosen* has something for everyone. It's a fast and entertaining read; I found it enlightening, as well as inspirational. Enjoy!

—**MARK GAINES**
Executive VP, General Sales Manager
Universal Pictures Distribution

LARRY VAUGHN MAKES THE SKILL set needed to be a top film buyer come to life. Film buying is a curious mix of art and science that results in which movies you get to see and which theatres you see them in.

Larry's courage and determination leap off the page. This is the story of a life well lived.

—**BRUCE SNYDER**
Former President of Distribution
20th Century Fox

IT HAS BEEN MY PRIVILEGE to know Larry Vaughn for over thirty-five years. Our careers paralleled each other. We both started in the theatre business as ushers, were promoted to manager, and then climbed the corporate ladder to become vice president / head film buyer for major theatre companies.

Do yourself a favor and read this entertaining and true story of a truly remarkable man. You will be enlightened and inspired as you get to know Larry and his family.

—**TONY RHEAD**
Former Senior Vice President / Head Film Buyer
Carmike Cinemas

A FASCINATING AND ENTERTAINING ACCOUNT of one man's lifelong love affair with the movie business.

—**LEE ROY MITCHELL**
Founder and Chairman
Cinemark Theatres

NOT SO LONG AGO MOVIES were bought and sold—and fortunes made or lost—using a little inside information, a gambler's hunch, and a personal relationship. The deal was sealed with nothing more than a handshake.

*Hollywood's Chosen* is Larry Vaughn's personal story about where the business of the motion picture industry meets the glamour of Tinsletown.

A must read for all who enjoy tales of the movie industry.

—**CLARK WOODS**
Former President of Distribution
MGM

# HOLLYWOOD'S CHOSEN

## AN INSIDER SHARES HIS STORY

Holly,

What a blessing you are to so many
People. You will always have a
Special place in our heart.

Enjoy my Story —
Your brother in Christ, Larry
Vaughn

To my mentor and friend —
So thankful for your ministry
in my life. With much love,
Mentora

# AUTHORS' NOTE

THE NAMES OF A FEW people have been changed as a courtesy to them, but all the stories are true and happened as described, to the best of our memory.

ADMIT ONE

# HOLLYWOOD'S CHOSEN

AN INSIDER SHARES HIS STORY

# LARRY VAUGHN
## & MENTORA VAUGHN GRATRIX

AMBASSADOR INTERNATIONAL
GREENVILLE, SOUTH CAROLINA & BELFAST, NORTHERN IRELAND

www.ambassador-international.com

# Hollywood's Chosen
## An Insider Shares His Story

ISBN: 978-1-62020-252-4
eISBN: 978-1-62020-352-1


Cover Design & Page Layout: Hannah Nichols
E-book conversion: Anna Raats

AMBASSADOR INTERNATIONAL
Emerald House
427 Wade Hampton Blvd.
Greenville, SC 29609, USA
www.ambassador-international.com

AMBASSADOR BOOKS
The Mount
2 Woodstock Link
Belfast, BT6 8DD, Northern Ireland, UK
www.ambassadormedia.co.uk

*The colophon is a trademark of Ambassador*

*To my friends and loved ones who are no longer living, and yet whose influence still lives on in my life today. Your lives made my story rich and full.*
*L.V.*

*Jack Vaughn*                 *Walter Powell*
*Mary Vaughn Watson*          *Eddie Stern*
*Farrell Watson*              *Colonel Mitchell Wolfson*
*Mrs. Martin*                 *Stanley Stern*
*Sam Todd*                    *Marvin Reed*
*Heyward Morgan*              *Jack Mitchell*
*Willie Stembridge*          *Charlie Jones*
*Edna Eubanks*                *Roger Hill*
*Delane Eubanks*             *Wayne Lewellen*
*Mercer Eubanks*             *Phil Sherman*
*Homer Eubanks*             *Foster McKissick*
*Dick Huffman*               *Jack Jordan*
*Dave Garvin*                *Mac MacAfee*
*John Huff*                  *Bernard Myerson*

*When someone you love dies, you don't lose them all at once. You lose them in pieces over time, like how the mail stops coming.*
*– Jim Carrey (Narrator), Simon Birch*

# CONTENTS

# CAST

*Doneata Vaughn – Larry's wife*

*Larry Vaughn – as Himself*

*Steven Spielberg – Director*

*John Huff – VP / Head Film Buyer, ABC Southeastern Theatres*

*Mary Vaughn Watson – Larry's mother*

*Farrell Watson – Larry's stepbrother*

*Mrs. Martin – Landlord*

*Sam Todd – Manager, Plaza Theatre*

*Victor Young – Larry's closest childhood friend*

*Heyward Morgan – Entrepreneur and Visionary*

*Buddy Poole – Larry's brother*

*Walter Matthau – Actor*

*Frank Yablans – Producer; President of Paramount Pictures*

*David Eubanks (Vaughn) – Doneata's son*

*Dick Huffman – Vice President, ABC Southeastern Theatres*

*Walter Powell – Division Manager, New World Pictures*

*Eddie Stern – Vice President / Head Film Buyer, Wometco Theatres*

*Colonel Mitchell Wolfson – Cofounder and President, Wometco Enterprises*

*Stanley Stern – Senior Vice President, Wometco Enterprises*

*Marvin Reed – Director of Advertising, Wometco Theatres*

*Jack Mitchell – Vice President and General Manager, Wometco Theatres*

*Joseph E. Levine – Producer*

*Charlie Jones – Branch Manager, 20th Century Fox*
*& later Southern Division Manager for Distribution, Orion Pictures*

*Arthur Hertz – CEO, & later Chairman, Wometco Enterprises*

*Michael Brown – Executive VP, & later President, Wometco Enterprises*

*Mentora Mary Vaughn – Larry and Doneata's daughter*

*Wanda Glass – Doneata's Christian friend*

*Charles Glass – Treasurer of Eastern Airlines and Larry's Christian friend*

*Suzanne Pleshette – Actress*

*Pastor Carey – Preacher*

*Roger Hill – Florida Branch Manager, Warner Brothers Distribution*

*Barry Reardon – President, Warner Brothers Distribution*

*Larry D. Vaughn, Jr. – Larry and Doneata's son*

*Fred Mound – General Sales Manager, Universal Pictures Distribution*

*Burt Reynolds – Actor*

*Dolly Parton – Actress*

*Bob Heffner – Florida Branch Manager, Warner Brothers Distribution*

*Mitchell Goldman – General Sales Manager of Distribution, Embassy Pictures*

*Clint Eastwood – Actor*

*Bruce Snyder – President of Distribution, 20th Century Fox*

*Bryan Holliday – Orion Pictures executive*

*Wayne Lewellen – President of Distribution, Paramount Pictures*

*Bert Livingston – Branch Manager, & later Senior VP of Distribution and General Sales Manager West, 20th Century Fox*

*John Hersker – Branch Manager & later Executive VP of Distribution, Paramount Pictures*

*Phil Sherman – Assistant General Sales Manager Eastern Division, Universal Pictures Distribution*

*David Forbes – President of Distribution, MGM/UA*

*Foster McKissick – Entrepreneur and Visionary*

*Ulmer Eaddy – Executive VP, Litchfield Theatres*

*Jack Jordan – Director of Advertising and Marketing, Litchfield Theatres*

*Frank Jones – Film Buyer, Litchfield Theatres*

*Mac MacAfee – Atlanta Branch Manager, Paramount Pictures*

*Ira Meiselman – President, Eastern Federal Theatres*

*Douglas D. Richardson – Chairman, Litchfield Theatres*

*Stephen Colson – President, Litchfield Theatres*

# FOREWORD

IN THE MOVIE *SUNSET BOULEVARD*, screenwriter Joe Gillis, the character played by William Holden, laments that "audiences don't know somebody sits down and writes a picture . . . they think the actors make it up as they go along."

While less celebrated than actors, those who write the movies at least see their names listed in the opening credits. But there are thousands of other dedicated professionals who work in the film industry and yet are invisible to the general public.

The motion picture business is populated with cameramen and studio accountants, marketing executives and theatre operators, all of whom help to bring magic to the silver screen. From the electrician on a movie set to the teenager popping popcorn at the neighborhood multiplex, all are part of a process that ends in an audience being entertained.

*Hollywood's Chosen* is the story of a film buyer. For as long as there have been movies there have been film buyers, and yet hardly anyone outside the motion picture industry has heard of the job, much less actually knows somebody who does it. There are probably fewer than a hundred full-time film buyers in North America, and yet they are essential to the business: without them some 40,000 theatre screens would be—quite literally—blank.

For over twenty years, Larry Vaughn negotiated with the Hollywood studios to earn the right to play their films in the theatres he represented. His vocation was as much art as science, requiring the mind of a businessman and the heart of a gambler.

Today film buying still includes negotiating how many weeks a movie plays and how the box office receipts are divided between theatre operators and the studios. In other respects, however, the job has changed significantly.

National chains control most of the theatres in major markets, while in Larry's day, regional theatre companies held enormous leverage in the cities where they were based. Movie studios would even enlist their stars to take time from publicity tours to personally lobby local film buyers for playtime in the best theatres.

The advent of the modern multiplex theatre has also had an impact. Today's theatres have enough auditoriums to play virtually all of the major films that Hollywood releases at any given time. A variety of movies under one roof benefits the consumer, while also eliminating risk for the theatre operator. When you're playing all the movies, there's no chance of missing a hit.

In the 1970s and 1980s, the landscape was dotted with far fewer theatres, and most complexes had only a handful of screens, perhaps as few as two or three. Choosing which films to play was a tricky business with potentially hundreds of thousands of dollars at stake. Such choices could make or break a theatre's year, and while they may seem clear in retrospect, they were far from obvious at the time.

In the spring of 1977, it seemed easy to predict that of Twentieth Century Fox's two summer releases, *The Other Side of Midnight*, based on the best-selling novel, was by far the bigger film. Science fiction was considered a washed-up genre by most of Hollywood, so few paid much attention to Fox's other attraction, *Star Wars*.

What happened? *The Other Side of Midnight* fizzled at the box office, while *Star Wars* became the highest grossing film up to that time and a cultural phenomenon to boot. Screenwriter William Goldman's axiom that, in the film industry, "nobody knows anything" had been validated yet again.

I spent much of my career on the opposite side of the negotiating table from film buyers like Larry Vaughn. Then, as now, Larry displayed great integrity in his business dealings and his personal relationships. And when it came to the most important aspect of film buying, the ability to pick winners and losers, no one was better than Larry.

In 1987, I was the Florida branch manager for Paramount Pictures, and Larry was the film buyer for Miami-based Wometco Theatres. Paramount's summer films included *Beverly Hills Cop II*, the much anticipated sequel to what at the time was one of the highest grossing comedies ever made. And while Larry made sure to book *Cop* in many of his theatres, he elected to pass the film in his flagship location in North Miami in order to play Paramount's other release that summer, a big-screen adaptation of a 1950s television crime drama.

Larry had a hunch that the teaming of director Brian De Palma with Robert De Niro, Kevin Costner, and Sean Connery added up to what he called "an important film." Plus, there was a local angle: the real-life villain of the piece, Al Capone, had once maintained a home in nearby Miami Beach.

Larry bypassed the safe bet of *Beverly Hills Cop II* in order to book *The Untouchables*, and while his competitor did predictably healthy business with the Eddie Murphy comedy, Wometco scored big with what turned out to be the surprise hit of the summer.

Larry made countless such gambles in his career, and most of his bets were good ones. Film selection was a game of averages and every season presented fresh opportunities and risks. A good film buyer had to follow Eliot Ness's advice from *The Untouchables*: "Never stop fighting till the fight is done." For Larry, that fight was done when, for reasons of conscience, he left the job he loved and at which he excelled.

But as these pages make clear, Larry's passion for the movies and the movie business remains undimmed. In chronicling his career, Larry pulls back the curtain to provide a look at a largely undocumented aspect of the film industry. And in the process, he shares stories from his remarkable life that, were they to be filmed, would make one heck of a good movie.

So grab a bag of popcorn, find a comfortable seat, and get ready . . . the show is about to begin.

—**JOHN H. HERSKER**
President and CEO, Movie Tavern
Former Executive VP of Distribution, Paramount Pictures

# PROLOGUE

*If one advances confidently in the direction of one's dreams, and endeavors to live the life which one has imagined, one will meet with a success unexpected in common hours.*

– Henry David Thoreau

"THE BEST THING ABOUT DREAMS," Oprah Winfrey has said, "is that fleeting moment, when you are between asleep and awake, when you don't know the difference between reality and fantasy, when for just that one moment you feel with your entire soul that the dream is reality, and it really happened."

Oprah Winfrey's description of the dream world perfectly expresses my experience as a child. I had a recurring dream as a young boy, in which I dreamed of movies and the theatre. I dreamed about being Cary Grant or falling in love with Marilyn Monroe. I dreamed of popcorn and fizzy fountain Coke. I dreamed of movie stars and thrilling movie plots. My dreams were so real to me that some nights I could almost smell and taste the movie theatre popcorn.

One day, some years later, I found myself sitting behind a large desk in an office, working for a premier theatre company. My dreams had come true—I had become the vice president and head film buyer of a theatre circuit. I now traveled from coast to coast screening films, reading scripts in progress, and meeting with producers, directors, actors, and distribution heads of all the major and independent film studios. When at the office, I negotiated with the studios for top films or sat in my private screening room where I watched and critiqued reels of yet-to-be-released motion pictures. I was part of a golden era of Hollywood, where the ultimate fate of a movie was decided by bid or split, by personal relationships, or, if all else failed, by the luck of the draw.

As a film buyer, I found out firsthand what it means to be . . . one of Hollywood's chosen.

# THE LUCK OF THE DRAW

*You've got to ask yourself one question: "Do I feel lucky?" Well, do ya punk?*
– Clint Eastwood, *Dirty Harry*

DONEATA AND I ARRIVED AT the Park Terrace Theatre forty-five minutes before the feature began. I immediately spotted the row of seats reserved for us and other ABC home-office personnel in the special VIP section of the auditorium. I wanted to arrive at the theatre early to experience the excitement—yes, excitement—of watching over seven hundred moviegoers all but stampede into the auditorium. They, like me, wanted to be the first movie patrons in Charlotte, North Carolina, to see the sneak preview of what was rumored to be one of the highest-grossing movies ever made.

The director of the film was at that time relatively unknown outside the film community. Earlier in his career he had directed a very good, intense, and highly suspenseful made-for-television movie, *Duel*, starring Dennis Weaver. (Dennis Weaver played Chester in the TV series *Gunsmoke*.) The sheer terror of that movie, with its unseen villain and sweaty hero, still gives me the creeps!

After his success with *Duel*, the director was later asked to direct a Goldie Hawn film, *Sugarland Express*, which turned out to be a good film, though not a great one. However, this film we were about to see, *Jaws*, was rumored to be nothing short of sensational. *Jaws* was going to make its director, Steven Spielberg, a household name.

All the advance publicity from Universal Pictures was true: *Jaws* was two hours of edge-of-the-seat entertainment. About forty-five minutes into the film, the great white shark came roaring up out of the ocean for the first time, and when it did, it scared me half to death! I was thankful I didn't have a drink in my hand, because I *literally* almost flipped backwards out of my seat into the lap of the man sitting behind me. After the showing of *Jaws* was over, I raced to the back of the auditorium to listen to all the chatter as enthusiastic customers left the theatre, talking excitedly to each other about the movie and how they couldn't wait to see *Jaws* again. I knew I had just seen the biggest picture of the year, and quite possibly the biggest picture ever made.

*Jaws* had all the ingredients to make it number one: action, suspense, drama, and that music. The music was terrifying. *Boom, boom, boom*—the incessant rhythm of the tuba blasts grew as the great white shark swirled at warp speed to attack the dangling legs of its helpless victims. And just when you felt your heart couldn't take another *boom*, Spielberg gave the much-needed comic relief of Roy Scheider and his fear of the ocean and its creatures within.

Driving home from the theatre, I felt great because I knew it was because of me that *Jaws* played at the Park Terrace that day. All of a sudden, I chuckled. Then I started laughing uncontrollably.

Doneata looked at me and said, "Okay, let's have it. What's so funny?"

"Honey, I was thinking. If those seven hundred people at the theatre tonight had any idea about how *Jaws* ended up playing in the Park Terrace, and not in some other theatre in Charlotte, well, they would never, never in a hundred years believe how it happened."

Doneata nodded her head in agreement as she smiled rather sheepishly and said, "Larry Vaughn, you're one crazy film buyer in one crazy business, but I love you anyway."

My mind drifted back to a few weeks earlier. Several of us film buyers who represented all the theatre circuits in Charlotte were having a very important "split" meeting in John Huff's office. John Huff was the VP and head film buyer at ABC. We met together to discuss "splitting" the upcoming summer's movies among ourselves rather than bidding against each other for the right to play a particular movie. Negotiating among ourselves to decide who would play a given film was always much less expensive than bidding against each other for the right to play a film.

Well, this was a very interesting split meeting because every film buyer in the room desperately wanted *Jaws* to play in his company's theatre. We spent the better part of an hour trying to decide which circuit would play *Jaws* and what it would take to satisfy the other circuits that didn't get to play it. We went around and around and got absolutely nowhere. No one was willing to back off on this mega-film. Every buyer in the room that day wanted to play *Jaws* in his theatre—period! And if he didn't get it, it could very well mean a tough and extremely expensive bidding war.

After trying for the better part of the afternoon to put a round peg in a square hole, everyone became frustrated and tired. An uneasy silence fell over the room. I was the first to break the silence. "Mr. Huff, may I make a suggestion?" With his elbow resting on the arm of his chair and his chin resting in the palm of his hand, Huff nonchalantly bobbed his head up and down, as if to say, "Why not?"

I cleared my throat and began speaking. "Listen, men, you can't horse-trade when you have only one thoroughbred and a bunch of colts. I believe we all realize that's what we have here. We all know *Jaws* is at the very least the biggest picture of the year. Maybe it's the biggest picture ever made. And what's left in the pot after *Jaws*—a bunch of colts, or should I say, little movies. So, gentlemen, let's forget trying to horse-trade. We're a group of professional men who strive, sometimes under the most unusual circumstances, to make the best decision for our respective companies. In a situation like this, where we have one picture far superior to every other picture, I suggest an alternative for your consideration."

I paused a moment, then continued, "Gentlemen, shall we cut high card, and winner take all?"

That unexpected suggestion seemed to have every bit the effect of a slap in the face, or you might say a wake-up call, to those weary, tired

men in the room. I could tell each man was considering the proposal
that I had just made. Heads were turning and eyes were wandering
from man to man as each film buyer entertained the most unusual solution to the problem.

Huff broke the silence. "Well, why not? Does anyone have a better suggestion?"

One by one, each man cast his vote to cut high card for the right to
play *Jaws*.

Loosening his tie, Huff said, "I guess we need a deck of cards?"

One of the other guys quickly spoke up. "It has to be a new deck of
cards, never before opened."

Huff buzzed his secretary, "Mary, please have one of the girls go over
to the drugstore to pick up a deck of playing cards, pronto!"

While we were waiting on the cards, one of the men asked, "What are
the rules?"

Huff replied, "Rules? We're not going to play poker. We don't need any
rules. We'll have someone shuffle the cards. Then we'll each draw one.
Whoever draws the highest card wins. Everyone else loses. Of course,
we all know that an ace is the highest card in the deck and a deuce, or
two, is the lowest." He then looked over at me as if to say, "Rules? What
a dumb question!"

Huff's secretary brought the deck of cards into the room and handed
them to him. On her way out, she glanced my way. I noticed a rather
peculiar smile on her face, as if she wanted to ask, "What are you men
up to now?"

Huff asked, "Okay, who does the shuffling?"

One of the men, who was not noted for his card-playing abilities,
was picked to shuffle the cards. After shuffling the deck, he placed it on
the corner of Huff's desk. One by one, each man walked to the edge of
the desk to make a draw. One man would walk over and draw quickly.
Another would act very cautiously, as if there were a snake under the top
card. Each of us knew this was a million-dollar draw.

Huff and I were the last to take a card. Huff pushed his large leather
chair back from his desk, dropped his arms by his side, and very calmly

lifted his right arm and motioned for me to step forward. He lifted his eyebrows. I noticed a look of concern on his face.

He said, "Mr. Vaughn . . ."

I thought to myself, "What happened to 'Larry'?"

Huff continued, "Since this was your bright idea, I think it's only right for you to have the honor of drawing for ABC."

I smiled on the outside but was quite tense on the inside. As I reached for the deck, I said, "My pleasure." I picked a card and cupped it in the palm of my hand. Immediately, I raised my hand up to where only I could see the card. I studied it for a moment and then glanced toward Huff.

Acting somewhat irritated at me, he said, "Well, get on with it! Let's have a look at it!"

In a Frisbee-like manner, I tossed the card toward the center of the desk. I then watched each man's expression as he saw the ace glide to its resting place atop the large mahogany desk. Immediately, Huff released a huge sigh of frustration as the other men frowned, shook their heads in disbelief, and mumbled to themselves as they walked slowly back to their seats. Huff was the first to speak. "This business is bad for the heart."

Someone echoed right back, "You ain't got no heart."

Huff said, "Well, if and when there's a *Jaws II*, Larry will draw for ABC."

Driving home from the theatre, I heard Doneata's voice. "Larry . . . Larry, you're not listening to me."

"I'm sorry, honey," I mumbled. "I was just reminiscing about *Jaws* and the luck of the draw." We stopped for a red light. While we waited for the light to change, Doneata pointed across the dark, empty street.

"Honey, look at that old lady standing over there by the bus stop. She shouldn't be out here by herself so late at night. It's not safe for a woman to be out this time of night, especially in the downtown area."

I took a long look at the old, silver-haired lady. She looked tired standing there, waiting for the bus to come and take her home. I wondered if there would be anyone at home to meet her, or if home was just a dark, lonely, empty apartment. "Doneata, do you know who that old lady reminds me of?"

"I knew you were going to ask that question. Yes, darling, she reminds you of your mother."

As we continued our drive down Independence Boulevard, Doneata leaned over and put her head on my shoulder. Tired from a long day, she dozed off as I started to let my thoughts wander. That old lady standing at the bus stop brought back memories of years gone by. Many times I had seen my mother stand at the bus stop waiting for the bus to take her to work in the early hours of the morning. Then in the late hours of the evening, I watched as the bus dropped her off.

I thought to myself, "If people knew the story of my childhood and my young adult years, they would probably find my story just as unbelievable and shocking as, say, the idea that businessmen would cut high card to play *Jaws* in a Charlotte movie theatre!"

# THE LIE

*Mama always said life was like a box of chocolates. You never know what you're gonna get.*
– Tom Hanks, *Forrest Gump*

I WAS TOO YOUNG TO remember what happened that day. If the truth were known, I wasn't even in the room when my father died. Throughout my early years, however, I heard my mother, Mary, tell the story so many times that it seems like I was there—that I was very much a part of it all. But I was only twenty-three months old.

We were living in Cordele, Georgia. My father, Andrew Jackson Vaughn, named "Jackson" after Stonewall Jackson, the famous general of the great Confederate army, was a tall, attractive, thirty-eight-year-old man with a zest for life. Mother loved to show me pictures of him and tell me how dashing, stunning, and good-looking he was. She commented quite often on how he liked to dress: white, heavily starched shirts; pinstriped suits; wing-tipped black-and-brown leather shoes; wide, expensive ties coupled with a gold tie pin and chain. His attire complemented his rather long, jet-black hair, which was always parted perfectly down the middle.

But what my mother appreciated most about my father was his genuine love for us. Her voice still echoes in my mind today. She would say, "Oh Larry, if your father had only lived . . . he loved us so much. We would have never gone without. He wanted so much for you to become a doctor."

It was Thanksgiving Day, 1948. Dad, not wanting to break his daily breakfast routine, even if it was "Turkey Day," still had to have his Coca-Cola and Baby Ruth candy bar for breakfast. In honor of the holiday, my mother even served her knight in shining armor his indulgence in bed.

I was told the three of us had a wonderful Thanksgiving afternoon. Dad and Mom spent the better part of the sunny but rather chilly day in the backyard, playing with me.

My grandfather, the distinguished L.L. Blackman, a wealthy Georgia pecan farmer, basically disowned Mom when her mother died. I can recall seeing the old gentleman only once, and that was years later. I remember, even then, he wasn't very friendly. I don't know anything about my father's family. Mother never talked about them, and I never thought to ask.

After Mom and Dad finished off the last of the turkey and dressing, Dad suggested that the three of us take a nap before enjoying the apple pie. Mom wholeheartedly agreed. She took me to my room and put me down in my crib with some of my favorite toys while Dad started his evening ritual of clearing off the table. Mom returned to the kitchen just in time to stop Dad and usher him into the bedroom.

After resting a few minutes, Dad became very quiet and started feeling sick. At 8:00 p.m., Dad asked Mom to call our family physician, Dr. Wooten.

Being a small town, Cordele didn't have that many medical doctors. Our doctor, the good Dr. Wooten, was known by everyone and loved by all. It didn't take a lot of prodding for him to grab his little black bag and make a house call to any of his patients when the need arose, even if it was Thanksgiving night.

Dr. Wooten arrived at 8:30. As he walked into the bedroom, Dad sat up in bed, looked at the doctor, and said, "Dr. Wooten, it's my heart." At that moment, my father died from a massive heart attack.

My mother, Mary Blackman, had grown up enjoying the finer things in life. Being an only child does have its advantages, especially when you're the daughter of a rather wealthy, prominent businessman.

Mary was a popular young lady, especially with the boys. She was very attractive with her natural tan complexion, dark brown eyes, and warm, pleasant smile. She had a round face and long, beautiful gingerbread-brown hair.

In school, Mary was known more for being runner-up in the high school beauty pageant than for her academic achievements. She struggled with books and studying, and her father often said, "Mary, you must get a good education if you are going to succeed in this life. Nothing ever comes easy."

Mary would reply, "Dad, I just want to get married and be a loving wife and mother. You don't need a lot of education to be a homemaker." Neither of the two really understood the thinking of the other.

My mother always seemed very vague when talking about my grandmother. My grandfather made the longest-lasting impression in her life; he was the strong, firm, final authority in the home.

I don't remember how or when my grandmother died. Mom had very little to say about it, but she did tell me that my grandfather remarried a girl young enough to be his daughter. As a matter of fact, Mom said she went to high school with the girl!

After my grandfather married this young lady, he and Mom grew further apart. What really severed the relationship—that is, what relationship they had left—was when my Mom told him that she wanted to marry Jack Vaughn. My grandfather emphatically forbade the marriage. Mom never told me why, but my grandfather did not like Jack Vaughn. He told my mom that if she married Jack Vaughn, he would take her out of his will, and she would never again be welcome in his home.

That is exactly what happened. Mom loved Jack and was unhappy at home, so she went against the demands of her father and married Jack Vaughn, and she paid the price. My grandfather, true to his word, disowned her, took her out of his will, and, to my knowledge, only once did the two ever speak or even see each other again.

When my father died, the strangest thing happened—we left Cordele. Rather than stay in familiar surroundings, her hometown, where she had loved ones—folks she had known all her life—Mom left in the middle of the night with just me and our suitcase, telling no one where she was going.

# ERNEST WATSON

*I coulda had class. I coulda been a contender. I coulda been somebody,*
*instead of a bum, which is what I am.*
– Marlon Brando, *On the Waterfront*

MY PERSONAL MEMORIES BEGIN AROUND the age of six. I remember that Mother and I moved to Athens, Georgia. Mother no longer looked like the high school beauty queen I remembered seeing in her old photographs. Prematurely gray and rather portly, she had changed into a tired, forty-five-year-old widow, who worked many long, hard hours standing on her feet in a downtown clothing store, trying to make enough money to support us.

I remember very well those early days in Athens. Mother and I shared a room on the second floor of a boarding house, and it was that same year that I started school.

That's when *he* came. His name was Ernest Watson. I don't remember how or where he met my mother, but they started dating and married shortly thereafter. He had two grown children—a son, Farrell, who lived at home, and a daughter, Regina, who was married and lived in another city. I don't know what happened to Ernest Watson's first wife.

Mother changed her last name to his, but my name, however, stayed the same. Mother wanted me to keep the name Vaughn in memory of my father, and so did I.

Ernest Watson was nothing like Jack Vaughn. Ernest was a hard man, a rugged trucker, and he smoked Camel cigarettes one after the other—over a carton a week. I was always a little afraid of him. His language was as rough as he was, and he always had bad breath from his liquor. When he told me to do something, I did it immediately.

Ernest's son, Farrell, was nothing like his father. Tall, slim, red-headed, freckle-faced, the seventeen-year-old Georgia boy was very polite and had good manners. From day one, Farrell was nice to me, and, even though he was much older than I, we enjoyed being with each other. I really felt as if I had gotten a big brother out of this new relationship.

Mother's marriage to Ernest ended shortly thereafter. I came home one day and found Ernest in our kitchen in the arms of our next-door neighbor's wife. He threatened me severely, telling me that, if I knew what was good for me, I would not say a word to my mother about what I had seen that afternoon. I loved my mother very much, and I didn't like seeing Ernest kiss and hug our neighbor's wife. I knew Ernest would get mad, but I decided that as soon as Mother came home, I would tell her about what I saw Ernest doing that afternoon.

Mother went straight into the kitchen to question Ernest. In anger he called me into the kitchen, he denied everything, and, in one swift blow, slapped me. The blow threw me across the room, and I ended up on the floor on my side, leaning against the wall. Blood started to flow from my swollen lip and bruised nose. I was afraid to move. Surprisingly, my fear was not of Ernest—it was of my mother.

I saw a side of my mother that I had never seen before. She looked over at me, not saying a word. She just stood there a few seconds and then slowly looked away. Calmly, she walked over to the kitchen counter, picked up a very long, very thick cutting knife, and turned and looked at Ernest. This big, rugged man was frozen in his tracks. Mother said nothing as she walked towards him that night, but her eyes said it all.

She put the knife firmly under Ernest's chin, and I kept waiting for the blood to flow. She told him, "If you ever touch my son again, I will kill you."

I think Ernest and I both knew that was no bluff. Mom gently laid the knife down, walked over to me, helped me up, and we left the room. It took her only a few minutes to pack our bags and call a cab. Then we were gone.

Farrell took the news hard. He wanted the marriage to work, for all the obvious reasons. He knew that in their brief time together, Mother had been good for his father. He promised to keep in touch and visit often.

After looking at several boarding house rooms, small efficiency apartments, and even one place that looked like a skinny barn, Mom, against my plea not to do it, rented the ugly house that looked like a barn. I couldn't believe it. I was truly embarrassed and even cried. I didn't want to live in a barn. It had rotten wood everywhere, windows with large holes in the screens, and a roof that needed fresh patches on the old patches. Mother assured me that everything would be okay once we moved in and got the place cleaned up.

Next, Mother needed to find a full-time job. Mother found employment downtown in a clothing store as a saleslady in the women's wear department. I liked her working downtown, because every Friday after school I got to take the bus downtown and have dinner with her at my favorite restaurant, the Varsity. Then I would go to a movie at the Palace Theatre while she worked until 9:00 p.m.

Saturdays were even better. While Mom was at work, I would go to the theatre and watch the kids' show. I would watch either a Roy Rogers or Gene Autry western, or maybe the latest Tarzan movie. Then at noon, I would meet Mom for lunch at the Varsity.

The Varsity was a fast-food restaurant before fast-food restaurants were popular. Located right across the street from the University of Georgia, it had what I thought were surely the best hamburgers and hot dogs in the world.

After lunch, Mother would go back to work, and while waiting for Mother to get off work, I would go to another theatre and watch their Saturday double feature, two movies for the price of one. At 5:00 I would meet Mom for dinner, and then we would go to the evening movie at the third and last movie theatre in town. That was what we did every weekend.

As expected, Farrell and his sweetheart, Kathy, were married. They rented a small home in town, and it wasn't too long before they were blessed with a beautiful baby girl. Because of his busy schedule with work and his new family, I didn't get to see much of Farrell, but I enjoyed those times when he would drop by to take me out for a quick burger. His friendship was the only thing good that came out of Mom's marriage to Ernest Watson.

One day while at school, my teacher asked me some questions about my home life. She wanted to know if I walked to and from school every day by myself and how I got to school when it rained or when it was very cold outside. She asked who was at home when I returned from school every day. She even asked about my meals, like what kind of food I ate. Plus she wanted to know who stayed home with me when I was absent because of sickness. She asked a lot of questions. I was glad that I knew the answers to all those questions and answered every one that she asked.

I told her that I always walked to school. That's the only way to get there when you don't have a car. After school I stayed home by myself from 3:00 until 6:00 when Mother finished her work. The food part was easy. We ate sandwiches during the week and burgers on the weekend. As for being sick, I told my teacher I was old enough to stay by myself when I was sick.

What I thought would please Mother disturbed her greatly. She got very upset with me for volunteering to answer those questions the teacher asked me. I knew I had done wrong because she was so upset with me. I told Mother I was sorry and said that I would never, ever say anything to my teacher again, but nothing seemed to help. Mother was worried, and I didn't know why.

Shortly thereafter, Mother said that we were moving away.

I asked her, "Where are we moving?"

She said that she did not want anyone to know and that she would tell me when we got there. I asked her how we were going to get there, and she said we would go on the Greyhound bus and that anything we couldn't carry with us would stay in Athens. I started crying. I didn't want to leave; I liked the barn, my school, and my friends.

Everything happened so quickly, it was like one big blur. One day we were there, and the next day we were gone.

# FOUR

# GREENVILLE

*Maybe things work out in ways we can't always understand.*
– Joan Allen, in *Bonneville*

I WAS QUIET ON THE bus. Mother told me how much she loved me and that I was her whole life. She said that she worried every single day of her life, afraid that she would lose me. She reassured me that she would never, ever marry again, so no man would ever have the opportunity to hit me or to hurt her again.

Then she said, "If only your father hadn't died . . . he loved us so much. We would have never gone without. He wanted so much for you to be a doctor." I felt sorry for Mother, so I kissed her and then hugged her. I told her that I was glad we were moving, and I promised her that I would never, ever leave her.

We got off the bus in Greenville, South Carolina. Mother had a taxi take us downtown to a very nice hotel, the Ottaray, which was the nicest hotel I had ever seen. I wondered if selling all our household goods had made it possible for us to stay in such a nice hotel.

We checked into the most beautiful room. There was a big wooden bed with the fluffiest mattress and pillows that I had ever seen. The room

41

even smelled good. But the best thing of all was our bathroom. We had our own private bathroom, which even had a tub.

Mom said, "I take claim to the tub first, but you may pick which side of the bed you want to sleep on."

I thought, "That's fair. I want the side that faces the window."

Our big, wide window with its frilly drapes overlooked Main Street. I could look across the street and see a movie theatre and all sorts of nice stores.

We had dinner downstairs in the hotel restaurant. It was a grand experience. The people were all so quiet, the waiters so polite, and the food was delicious! At dinner, Mother told me about her new job at Shirby Vogue, Greenville's very exclusive ladies hat and fur store.

I said, "Mom, you mean we are going to stay here forever? And we can live here in this hotel?"

She smiled, "You would be spoiled rotten in no time if we stayed here. Tomorrow we will start looking for a permanent place to live."

I will never forget those wonderful days in the Ottaray Hotel. Mom worked during the day and went through apartment rental ads in the evening. It was fun to be in a new town, staying in a nice hotel, eating out, and best of all, going to the movies in the evenings.

After a couple of days, Mother found a small duplex for us to rent, over in the Sans Souci section of Greenville. Located in a nice, established neighborhood with lots of kids to play with, the house was much nicer than anything we had ever lived in before.

Shirby Vogue must have been a well-paying company, because Mom kept spending money. It was fun to watch her get so excited over decorating our new little home. I remember Mom, smiling and sitting at the kitchen table in our cozy home, sipping her coffee. I thought she looked so beautiful when she smiled. She laughed as she told me that she would have enjoyed our time at the Ottaray Hotel *even more* if she had known that Shirby Vogue was going to pay our entire hotel expense. She said, "Oh Larry, you should have seen the look on my face when the hotel clerk told me our bill was paid in full." In those days she was so happy.

After we had been in Greenville only a few months, Mother came home from work one afternoon extremely upset. She took me into the kitchen, sat me down, and told me, in tears, that Farrell's wife, Kathy, had called her at work to tell her that Farrell had been in a bad automobile accident.

I asked her if Farrell would be okay.

She said, "I don't know. We must go and see him right away."

It seemed to take forever, but finally the big Greyhound rolled into the terminal at Athens. Mother and I went straight to the hospital, where we were taken to the intensive care waiting room. As soon as Kathy saw Mom, she started crying. Immediately, Mother went over to Kathy, put her arms around her, and held her. Then Mother cried with her.

Standing there, I realized that Farrell might die. Kathy's eyes told the whole story. They were so swollen that I wondered how she could even see. Could it really be this bad?

After they regained their composure, Kathy proceeded to tell Mother everything that had been happening between her and Farrell. With tears in her eyes, she explained that Farrell had been admitted into the hospital (before having the car accident) to be treated for pneumonia. While in the hospital recovering, Farrell had confessed that he was having an affair with another woman. He had told Kathy that he was going to break off the relationship with the other woman and get his life and marriage back together. Kathy loved Farrell, and she told him she was willing to forgive him for his unfaithfulness.

Unbeknownst to Kathy, Farrell then slipped out of the hospital one night to meet with the woman.

Farrell and the woman had gone for a drive in her car; he was behind the wheel. Apparently Farrell was driving too fast in the rain when he rounded a curve, swerved over the yellow line onto the other side of the road, and hit, head on, another car full of college girls, students at the University of Georgia.

Four women died that night: the woman with Farrell, and all three of the college girls in the other car. (Kathy told Mother that she thought

Farrell had been meeting with the other woman to tell her of his decision to stay with his family.)

Farrell himself was still in a coma. The doctor asked Mother and me to go in and talk to Farrell, hoping that if Farrell heard our voices, he might come out of it.

At thirteen years old, I wasn't ready to see what I saw when I went into that hospital room. If the doctor hadn't been there, I would never have known that the swollen, blue, broken, and bruised individual lying there on that bed was the Farrell I had come to know and love. I walked over to him, careful not to interrupt the many tubes that were helping him stay alive. I looked at his terribly swollen head, and I wondered why the doctor failed to mention anything about having to sew Farrell's chin back onto his face.

I did exactly what the doctor asked me to do. I leaned over right next to Farrell's left ear and talked gently to him. I told him that I wanted him to get well, that Kathy and their daughter needed him, and that everything would be okay. I said that I missed seeing him, that I loved him, and that he would always be my big brother. Then I left the room.

I never saw Farrell again. He died a few days later. It's probably just as well. The doctors said that if he had lived, he most likely would have had severe brain damage. And legally, he was responsible for the deaths of four people. As for Kathy, I don't know what happened to her or her daughter. After the funeral they moved, and we never heard from them again.

The bus ride back to Greenville reminded me of that earlier bus ride Mother and I had taken from Athens to Greenville. Like the trip before, there was a lot of thinking, but very little talking.

I knew what was on Mother's mind, and I really didn't want to ask. But I asked her anyway. "Are you okay, Mom? Are you feeling all right?"

She replied, "Yes, I'm fine. I was just thinking about you and me. I must take good care of myself, so no one will ever have reason to take you away from me." Her next statement I could recite by heart. "If only your father hadn't died . . . he loved us so much. We would have never gone without. He wanted so much for you to be a doctor." Without trying to, I think Mother was teaching me how to worry.

It was that same year that Mother lost her job at Shirby Vogue. I don't know what happened. She told me we would have to make arrangements to move to a less expensive place to live. I really hated to hear her say that, because I enjoyed our home and the children I played with in the neighborhood.

Mother went to work at Greene's 5 & 10 Cent Store on Main Street. It was sad to see her go from a well-paying job to a minimum-wage job. I believe she made less than a dollar an hour.

We moved across town to a large boarding house at 5 Cateechee Avenue, owned by a retired, sweet old widow named Mrs. Martin. Our apartment had only one bedroom and a kitchen so small that the refrigerator was on the back porch.

Being fourteen now, I wanted my own bedroom. I told Mother I would take the back porch and make it into a bedroom, but she worried about the weather. Without insulation, she felt it would be too cold in the winter for me to sleep out on the porch. However, she agreed to give the porch a try.

Then I thought I would press my luck and ask Mother for a set of bunk beds. She liked the idea, because I would have a place for friends to occasionally stay over.

Our first year in the house was a lonely one. Mother seemed to work all the time. She had to ride the city bus to and from work, which caused her to be away from home several extra hours a week.

Mother decided not to notify the proper authorities at the school board of our move from Sans Souci to the Augusta Road area. By using our old address, I was able to continue my ninth grade education at Sans Souci Junior High.

I either rode my bicycle to school or took the city bus. The distance must have been ten miles or better. I was home every day by 3:30 p.m. After homework I usually spent my free time playing in the yard, but occasionally, I would go next door to Mrs. Martin's apartment. She asked me if I knew how to play canasta. I told her no, but I would love for her to teach me. I believe that was exactly what she wanted to hear.

Since she worked Friday nights and Saturdays, the weekends were always tough for Mother. While she was gone, I spent my time watching television, playing canasta with Mrs. Martin, and going to the neighborhood movie theatre.

Sunday was Mother's one and only day off, and we both enjoyed that special day of rest. Mother would cook her one meal of the week—country-style steak, mashed potatoes, brown gravy, fried okra, crowder peas, and corn bread—and we always concluded the special day with watching *Bonanza*, the best western on TV.

In August of 1960, I enrolled as a sophomore at Greenville Senior High School. That year began a turning point in my life, and, unfortunately, in many ways in the wrong direction.

That same month, Mother was fired from Greene's 5 & 10. I'm not sure exactly what happened, but I think she may have given a sandwich to a friend of hers without charging for it. We had no cash, no savings, and we had bills to be paid. I remember Mother went over to speak with Mrs. Martin about our fifty-dollar monthly rent payment that was due. Between her tears, Mother told Mrs. Martin that we were completely out of money and had no means to pay the rent. Mrs. Martin graciously gave Mother an extension on the rent due and even lent her enough money for us to buy groceries.

I hated to see my mother get so upset. I was afraid she might have a heart attack. The sad thing was that even if she got the job she applied for at Rose's 5 & 10 Cent Store, I knew she wouldn't make enough money for us to live on, let alone to get us out of debt. It was time for me to get a job and go to work.

I went to work for Latham Brokerage Company, where I stocked grocery shelves three days a week. At fifteen years of age, I was making as much money an hour, $1.10, as my mother was making at age fifty-four. Because of my work permit, I was able to get out of school early every day. I told my school counselor that I loved my job, but I still needed to work more hours.

One afternoon my counselor called me and asked me if I would be interested in working on the weekends in a movie theatre. I couldn't believe what that lady had just asked me. I said very emphatically, "Yes! Yes! Yes! I would love to."

She said, "It only pays fifty cents an hour."

I said, "Great! I'll take it!"

She said, "Don't you want to know which theatre you'll be working in?"

I told her, "It doesn't matter. I've always wanted to work in a movie theatre. I love the movies!"

At five o'clock on Friday afternoon, I hit the shower and did the best I could to make my six-foot two-inch, 135-pound body look presentable. I wanted so much to impress the theatre's management and staff that I probably went overboard on the hair spray and the cologne. It didn't take long to decide what to wear that night; I owned only one sports coat and one tie.

It was a wonderful night at the movies. The theatre was playing a Jackie Gleason film, *Papa's Delicate Condition*. I spent the whole evening learning how to usher, sweep, mop, clean a commode, tear a ticket, greet someone, thank someone, make popcorn, butter popcorn, serve a Coke, and say "Good night" and "Thank you very much for coming."

I made only two dollars for the night's work, but if the truth were known, I would have gladly *paid* two dollars to enjoy the experience of actually working in a movie theatre.

That night when I got home, I couldn't stop talking. After a while Mother said, "Larry, we must go to bed." I was so wound up, however, that I knew that I wouldn't be able to sleep. I spent the better part of the night tossing and turning, counting the hours until I could go to work at the Plaza again.

My love for the movie theatre grew more intense. I was miserable working at Latham's, even though I made twice as much an hour there as I did at the theatre.

Our financial problems were still severe at home. My small salary from the theatre—even adding in my larger salary from Latham's—didn't produce enough money to give Mother the financial support she needed. But then something good happened: I got a morning newspaper route.

Delivering the *Greenville News* gave me an additional twenty dollars a week in income, and the only thing the paper route affected was my sleep. I had to get up every morning at 5:00 a.m. in order to have all the papers delivered by the 7:00 a.m. deadline. I was thankful Mother was finally out from under all the financial pressure she had experienced for such a long time. Happy days were here again . . . or so it seemed.

# VICTOR

*Money won is twice as sweet as money earned.*
— Paul Newman, *The Color of Money*

THE SOUND OF THE BASKETBALL hitting the gym floor seemed miles away, even though I was standing right beside the basketball court. The loud chatter of my classmates as they scurried in front of me didn't have any effect on my trance. I am sure others around me noticed my lack of interest, or maybe no one paid me enough attention to care. P.E. class was never my thing. I did only what was required of me in order to get a passing grade.

As I slowly came out of my trance, I noticed another young man standing a few feet away from me. He looked like an all-right guy, somebody I might enjoy talking with. I walked over to him and introduced myself. "Hi, I'm Larry, Larry Vaughn. What's your name?"

He answered, "My name is Victor, Victor Young."

We talked a while, and it didn't take long at all for us to become friends. Victor and I were a lot alike. I don't mean in looks. Where I was tall and all skin and bones, Victor had a medium build. I had a narrow face and big ears. Victor had a round face and small ears. He thought he was good looking—I always told him he looked okay at best—but the girls saw something in him that I didn't. They always gave him all the attention.

When I met Victor, he had only two shirts to his name. He lived in a small wooden house in an older neighborhood with his mother, father, and younger sister. From the way they lived, you would never have guessed that his father had a good job with the post office. Victor and I often wondered what his father did with all his money.

Victor's mother was a dear lady, but in the years that I knew her, she always struggled with mental problems. Before I knew the Young family, Mrs. Young had spent some ten years in the state mental hospital.

Even though Victor had a family, he was very much a loner—even more than me. His home seemed to have no rules: Victor could come and go as his heart desired, and many times he would spend the night over at my house. I always had to remind him to call home and let his family know where he was staying. At age sixteen, he might as well have been out of his parents' house, living on his own.

One day during those early days of our friendship, Victor asked me, "Have you ever played a pinball machine?"

I replied, "No." I didn't even know what a pinball machine was!

He went on, "Well, there are pinball machines, and then there are *pinball machines*," vocally emphasizing the latter one. He went on to ask, "You mean you have never even played a pinball machine for fun? Do you like to play pool?"

I answered, "I don't know. I've never played pool."

Then he asked me, "Would you like to go to a place where they have real pinball machines and pool tables?"

I replied, "Yeah, I guess so."

That afternoon Victor introduced me to a place that changed my life—the Brown Derby, a pool hall located downtown.

If you walked by the Derby, you couldn't see inside the building because of its dark, smoked-glass windows and closed blinds. When I walked into the Derby for the first time, my eyes had to adjust, the lighting was so dim. Victor pointed to the area that had the pinball machines and showed me the pool tables.

Gus, a young Greek man, managed the Derby. Gus guaranteed that if you drank enough beer, it would most certainly take your mind off of whatever ailed you.

The air was thick and cloudy—cigarette smoke was everywhere. I looked over the place and thought, "How could a person possibly eat food in all this cigarette smoke?"

Victor immediately walked over to one of the pinball machines. He said that this was no ordinary pinball machine. "You play this baby to win money." He put a nickel in, and while he played, he explained how to play the game.

Victor didn't win that first game, so he started a new game. But this time he asked Gus for a $2.00 roll of nickels and proceeded to put all forty nickels, one behind the other, into the machine before he played the first ball. I asked him why he put all the nickels in the machine at one time on one game when it took only one nickel to play.

He said, "I'm building my odds."

Victor explained further. "There are pinball machines that take only dimes, while others take only quarters. On a quarter machine you can feed it ten or twenty dollars' worth of quarters in a single game, but if you're hot, you might win $150 or better." He looked at me. "Wanna try?"

I said, "Win $150! That's a month's pay!" I spent the afternoon and several dollars getting familiar with the art of playing pinball. I had just been introduced to a brand new world, and I loved it! I asked Victor, "Where do you get your money? You don't work, do you?"

His reply was, "What money? I'm broke, man." He went on to tell me how his dad periodically gave him a few dollars to spend.

"Would you like to have a part-time job at the Plaza?" I asked. "It only pays fifty cents an hour, though."

"Sure, why not? They have some cute girls working there."

I assured Victor that I would talk with Mr. Todd about a position for him. I also told Victor he should try to get a morning paper route, so Victor applied to the *Greenville News* and within a few weeks got a route near mine. Mr. Todd also hired him to work on Friday and Saturday nights during the busy times at the Plaza.

Victor and I walked to Greenville High School together every day. One day, he asked me, "Larry, have you ever skipped school?"

"No, it's never crossed my mind."

He said, "Let's do it sometime. We can go downtown to the Brown Derby and play the machines." After further discussion, we decided to skip school that very day, and for many days thereafter, as I was introduced to a way of making fast money while enjoying the thrill of the game.

I loved going to the Brown Derby. There I learned how to play pool, but with me, however, pool always ranked second to playing the pinball machines.

During this time, I started smoking. Victor smoked Winston cigarettes and suggested that I might like to try one. I didn't think much of the first few cigarettes that I smoked. After inhaling the cigarette, I felt sick to my stomach and dizzy. That sick sensation soon passed, though, after smoking several more cigarettes. Within a month I was a full-fledged cigarette smoker, smoking anywhere from half a pack to a pack a day.

At first, Mother objected to my smoking cigarettes, but I reminded her that even she smoked on occasion. I promised her I wouldn't take advantage of the situation; I would smoke only a few cigarettes a day. She was pleased that if I was going to smoke, at least I discussed it with her, and I did not smoke behind her back. From that day on, though, I never let my mother know how many cigarettes I really smoked in a given day.

I talked to Mr. Todd about the possibility of me working additional days each week. In the back of my mind, I wanted to get enough hours in at the theatre so that I could quit my job at the Brokerage Company. I knew I would have to work twice as long at the Plaza to make what I was making at Latham's, but I loved the Plaza so much, I didn't care how long I had to work. I just wanted to be at the Plaza. Mr. Todd liked my spirit, and especially my willingness to work anytime and do anything, so he told me that he would work with me and see to it that I got additional work in the future.

The remainder of my sophomore year at Greenville High went by quickly. For the first time in my life, though, I barely passed! Where the year before at Sans Souci I had made the B honor roll, this year I was earning D's instead of B's.

I also wasn't spending nearly the amount of time at home that I had the year before. Instead of playing canasta with Mrs. Martin, I gave her excuses about why I didn't have the time to spend with her. I always felt bad about abandoning Mrs. Martin—she was such a nice old lady—but once you play a game for money, it's no longer satisfying to play a game for fun. Mother was well aware that I spent a lot of time at the Brown Derby, but she knew I was with Victor. She thought Victor was such a nice boy. As a matter of fact, Victor stayed at my house more that year than he stayed at his own home.

I couldn't keep my poor grades or skipping school hidden from Mother. She got really upset with me about the school calling her at work. Some days she would just give in to me and let me stay home "sick," knowing in her heart that I wasn't sick and that as soon as she left for work, I would be back out on the street.

That same year, Mr. Todd gave me the additional hours I needed to work. I quit my job at Latham Brokerage and concentrated on my morning paper route, my wonderful job at the Plaza Theatre, and—of course—the Brown Derby.

In August of 1962, at the age of sixteen, I started the eleventh grade at Greenville High. I wasn't excited at all about the upcoming school year. I felt I didn't need an education. I only needed money, and lots of it!

Victor and I had spent the past summer living and working together and doing the same daily routine. We worked mostly nights at the Plaza, from 6 p.m. until 11 p.m. After work we would go out to the Waffle House and have some bacon and eggs before ending up over at my place. We usually got to bed around 1:00 a.m. We then dragged our weary bones out of bed at 5:00 a.m., just in time to help each other get the papers delivered by 7:00 a.m. Then we went back to my place and slept from 7:30 until noon. We spent the afternoons at the Brown Derby, where Victor shot pool with some of the locals while I played the pinball machines. At the Brown Derby, we lost the few dollars we were getting up so early to earn.

I saw very little of my mother during those days. She worked all day, rode the bus home, ate a sandwich, and watched TV until Johnny Carson said it was time to say good night.

I saved nothing. I spent my money as quickly as I made it, sometimes even before I made it. I had established a line of credit at the Derby. Gus knew that the Derby was my home away from home, and with my thirst for gambling, I was a safe loan as long as he didn't allow me to accumulate too much debt.

Every Friday I gave Mother the cash she needed to meet our financial commitments, but sometimes I had to borrow from Gus to pay Mother. Other times, when I was already too much in debt to Gus, I took my collections from my paper route customers and gave that money to Mother, falling behind on paying my paper bill. Robbing Peter to pay Paul became a way of life to me.

SIX

# THE BREAK

*I like the smell of film. I just like knowing film is going through the camera.*
– Steven Spielberg

MR. TODD TOOK A PERSONAL interest in me. A middle-aged man in his early fifties, Mr. Todd was rarely seen without a cigarette hanging out the corner of his mouth. He had a pencil-thin mustache and always wore a brown hat with a wide rim around it.

Mr. Todd asked me one day, "Larry, how would you like for Alvin to train you to operate the projectors?"

I replied, "Mr. Todd, are you serious?" He went on to tell me that Jim, the relief projectionist, had given notice, and I could have the job if I was willing to train for it. I couldn't believe what Mr. Todd had just said, but I managed to say, "Yes sir, I would love to become a projectionist."

He went on, saying, "Okay, first you must spend four weeks upstairs in the booth, learning the fundamentals. You will also have to prepare to go before the Board of Electrical Examiners and pass the test so you can obtain your Class D electrician's license. After that, you're in business at $3.50 an hour."

I thought, "I'll be bringing in seventy dollars just for two days work. Yes sirree, happy days are here again!" Mom and I celebrated the wonderful news by going out for dinner.

A projectionist must always be careful performing his job, because, when he makes a mistake, the entire audience knows about it. For this reason, Mr. Todd had installed a buzzer downstairs at the head of the aisle leading into the auditorium. The buzzer would notify the employee on duty to alert the projectionist of any problems on the screen: one buzz meant to raise the volume on the sound, two buzzes to lower the volume, three buzzes to check the focus on the screen.

When I didn't work downstairs as an usher, I trained upstairs in the booth. I took notes, listened to all of Alvin's instructions, and studied daily for the electrical exam, which I had to pass before I could be allowed in the booth alone.

Mr. Todd cautioned me: "Larry, it's all for naught if you can't pass the exam. You must have a license to operate these projectors."

I assured him, "Mr. Todd, it will be a piece of cake. Don't worry about a thing." He liked my confidence. Now I had to deliver.

During those weeks in training, I spent very little time at the Brown Derby. Sure, Victor and I would skip a day of school every now and then to go to the Derby to spend some money and have a little fun, but for the most part my mind and body were consumed with the Plaza.

In six weeks, I had the projection booth down to a fine art. Alvin might as well have been on vacation. I could do it all: check in a feature film (check the reels to make sure they are in sequence and the film is in good condition), build the show (splicing the previews onto the cartoon and the short feature that played before the film), clean the projectors, thread the projectors, splice a film, curtain lights up, curtain lights down, light the lamp house, change the carbons, sweep the floor, make the changeover. You name it—if it concerned the projection booth, I could do it! The only thing left was the exam.

I went downtown to the county courthouse and took the Class D Electrician's Exam, and I had a skip in my step as I left with an electrician's Class D card and license in my back pocket.

I decided to celebrate my new position by buying myself a motorcycle. I went over to the Harley-Davidson store and bought, on credit, a brand-new Harley. It wasn't one of those big ones like you see on the street today. It was rather small, but it more than met my needs. Mother had the usual motherly concern about my owning a motorcycle—that I might wreck the thing and break my neck.

I barely passed the eleventh grade. Academically, I was going no-where. I remember one of my teachers commenting before class one day, "Students, has anyone noticed who is with us today? Mr. Vaughn is back. Everyone be sure and speak to him before he leaves. Who knows when we'll see him again!" The class got a good chuckle out of her snide remark, but her point was well taken. I seldom made it to school two days in a row.

During that summer, I started venturing out to other places besides the Brown Derby to have some fun. Now that I had a motorcycle, I didn't have to depend on my feet or the bus to take me where I wanted to go. I found a hamburger joint that went by the name of Cudd's Drive-In. Cudd's stayed open until 2:00 a.m. It wasn't Cudd's greasy burgers that got my attention, but his new twenty-five-cent pinball machine.

It was a good thing that I was making more than fifty cents an hour, because it was nothing for me to drop fifty to seventy-five dollars[1] into the quarter pinball machine in one sitting. But many nights I would win back fifty, a hundred, or even more.

I was starting to gamble so much that it didn't even bother me whether I won or lost. I was there for the thrill of the game. I knew that if I won tonight, so what? I would give it all back tomorrow, and vice versa.

I quit my morning paper route. It was all but impossible to stay up half the night, sleep a couple of hours, then get up and deliver those papers.

Victor quit his paper route shortly after I did. He landed a good job working after school stocking grocery shelves. He continued to work at the Plaza on the weekends.

I entered what was supposed to be my last year of high school. I was a seventeen-year-old senior with only ten months of school left. I had no idea about what I was going to do after high school. I knew that on my

---

1    About $400 to $600 in 2014 dollars.

eighteenth birthday I would have to register with the local draft board. If I didn't go straight into college, I knew that Uncle Sam would like very much for me to have an all-expense-paid trip to Vietnam, courtesy of the United States Army.

Mother lost her job at Rose's 5 & 10. I don't know the specifics about why she was let go. At least this time, we didn't have to worry about losing our apartment or how we would be able to put food on the table.

Mother wasn't out of work long at all. She found a position with another discount department store. The downside was that she was back having to take the bus to work.

My focus most of my senior year was on my work and my gambling. I went through the motions of going to school, but I put zero energy into my studies. That year I became very street-smart and learned there are many ways to make a fast buck. You don't have to restrict your pleasure to just pinball machines and pool tables—not when you have basketball games, football games, and other sports games being played year-round and on a daily basis.

That year I failed the twelfth grade. You can only fool around so long and not have to pay the price. I most certainly pushed my teachers beyond the limit. The school principal told me, "I hope you are proud of yourself. You managed to make an F in every single subject. You may return next year to repeat the twelfth grade, if you so desire." That year Victor graduated, and I didn't.

SEVEN

# THE FEVER

*I live for myself and I answer to nobody.*
– Steve McQueen

VICTOR AND I DIDN'T SPEND much time together the next year. We had been so close for three years that when people saw one of us, they saw the other, but now we were starting to veer apart.

Ahead of me I had another year of school, my work at the theatre, and my love for gambling. Victor was working full-time at the brokerage company, where he stocked shelves in grocery stores, spending only a couple of nights a week at the theatre. And after he bought his car, he wanted to spend his free time dating.

When Victor and I did go out together, we would usually get into a heated argument over my gambling. He would agree to go to the Derby, but he wanted to shoot pool for only an hour or so and then leave. He got upset with me because I would start playing a pinball machine and refuse to leave until the Derby closed.

After the Derby closed, Victor wanted to cruise the town, or maybe go to the Waffle House. That was not what I wanted to do. I wanted to go to Cudd's and play the pinball machines.

Late one evening, Victor dropped by the Plaza and said to me, "After the theatre closes, Larry, let's go out for some bacon and eggs."

From the moment the waitress brought the coffee, it was quite obvious Victor was there to talk more than he was to eat. Without interrupting him, I let him speak his mind. He said, "Larry, I have concerns about where I see you going in life. You're like the brother that I never had, and it bothers me watching what is happening to you. I know I'm responsible for introducing you to a lot of things that I probably shouldn't have, but what I don't understand is why it is that you have to go to the extreme in every single thing that you do."

He continued, "You do absolutely nothing in moderation. You can't even smoke in moderation. You smoke at least twice as many cigarettes in a day as I do.

"Frankly speaking, Larry, I think you're obsessed with yourself. It always has to be Larry's way or no way at all. All you want to do is gamble and work at a job that is eventually going to take you nowhere. So, you got lucky and started making some money running the projectors. Is that really what you want to do with the next twenty years of your life—sit upstairs in some dark booth by yourself ten long hours a day, five days a week, watching the same old movies over and over again? And where can you go from the booth? I'll tell you where—nowhere. You can forget about becoming a theatre manager anytime soon. Mr. Todd is going to be around for a long time. Face it, Larry, your obsession with the Plaza and gambling is a dead-end street."

I lit another cigarette before giving Victor a reply. "You have got to feel much better, now that you have that off your chest." We both chuckled. Then I leaned over, put both my elbows on the table, and looked at Victor, staring straight into his eyes. I said, "Let me tell you a fact, old friend. There is a difference between you and me. I know exactly what I want out of this life, and I'm going after it, full speed ahead. I am going to be a successful gambler. Money and guts are the only two tools I must have to be successful in my quest to become a professional gambler. The guts I already have. Now I need the money. In your opinion, I'm in a dead-end job. I couldn't disagree with you more. I love the theatre business, and

I plan on staying in the theatre business, even if the only job available is mopping floors for the rest of my life."

"Now as to the difference between you and me, let me explain to you how I think we differ. Victor, you want to count the cost in something before you are willing to do it. I don't. You're very conservative with your money and in your decision-making. I'm not. I want to live wide open, and let the chips fall where they may. If I can't gamble beyond my means, then there is no satisfaction in my gambling. My adrenaline will only start pumping after I have crossed that imaginary line of danger. And, as for smoking, I might just start smoking two packs of cigarettes a day if I so desire. Who cares? I don't."

Victor lit a cigarette, inhaled a deep breath, blew out his air of frustration, and said, "You're crazy." We both laughed and decided it was time to go to bed. We realized that night that we were still good friends, but we were both very much aware that Larry Vaughn had no intention of changing his bad habits for Victor, or for anyone else.

A few days later, I almost killed myself while taking a joy ride on my motorcycle. I was riding on one of the busiest streets in Greenville, when all of a sudden my front wheel hit a deep hole in the highway. My motorcycle flipped over in midair with me on it. In actuality, I ended up underneath the motorcycle. I just about scraped all the skin off of my backside trying to get the cycle to lie down and stop dragging me down the highway. In a desperate attempt to avoid hitting me, cars were slamming on their brakes, skidding and sliding all over the highway.

When the dust settled, I staggered to my feet. I was rather embarrassed to be standing there with my pants in many small pieces scattered down the highway forty yards behind me. With no broken bones, but bruised all over, I decided to sell that motorcycle as soon as possible and buy a car.

I bought a 1957 Plymouth for $125 and got my license on the first try. It was good for Mother and me to finally have our first car together. Even though she didn't drive, it helped her greatly that year for me to be able to take her to and from work when my schedule permitted.

In May of 1964, after four long years, I finally graduated from Greenville Senior High School. My biggest immediate concern was my eligibility for the draft. I knew I must continue my education, or I most certainly would be heading for Vietnam.

Mr. Todd was also concerned about my military status. He asked, "Would you like to go into the military, Larry?"

I replied, "Mr. Todd, I really think I would enjoy being in the service. No, I'm not nuts about going to Vietnam, but a two-year break in the routine might be good for me. Victor wants me to join the Marines with him. My biggest concern right now is leaving my mother. When I was young, she worried herself sick about someone being able to take me away from her. Now that I'm of age, she doesn't worry about losing me anymore, but she worries about everything else. She has worried so much that I think she has given *me* an ulcer. I think my being in the military would be very hard on my mother."

Mr. Todd said, "I understand all that, but what do you intend to do about the draft?"

I answered, "I have a plan. I am going over to Greenville Tech and take a course in something, anything that will give me a deferment for a year. Then, during that year while in school, I will try to get into the Army Reserves or the National Guard."

Mr. Todd commented, "If that comes about and you get your deferment, there is a job opportunity for you in Clemson working two days a week running the projectors in our company's other theatre, the Clemson Theatre. Larry, working the projection booth two days a week in two theatres will give you a very good paycheck."

# THE ARMY WAY

*I wouldn't dream of working on something that didn't make my gut rumble and my heart want to explode.*
– Kate Winslet

I ASKED THE YOUNG MAN sitting at the Greenville Tech information desk a question. "Can you tell me which one-year course commands the best pay upon completion?"

Without any hesitation the young man said, "Yes, welding."

I repeated, "Welding?"

He replied, "That's right. Certified welders do very well."

The welding class consisted of working with blueprints, math, and fire—lots of fire. Our instructor demanded that we all stay very busy and attentive while being taught the many facets of welding. All the men in the class were looking forward to getting their certification and starting out making top dollar as welders with construction companies. All, that is, except yours truly. The only thing I was looking forward to was getting into the Reserves and getting away from welding. I hated everything about welding!

Victor joined the Marines. He went to Parris Island, South Carolina, for his basic training and then to Camp Lejeune, North Carolina, for advanced training. Shortly thereafter, he went to Vietnam and stayed in Vietnam for his twelve-month tour of duty. He wasn't awarded the Bronze Star, but he did receive the Purple Heart when some enemy shrapnel caught him in his hip.

While attending Greenville Tech, I was fortunate enough to join the National Guard, as the unit I joined, from Williamston, South Carolina, needed an individual with both projection and welding skills. What's ironic is that I was never called upon to use either my welding or projection ability. After my advanced training, the powers that be had me operating a switchboard in the command headquarters.

I graduated from Greenville Tech certified in both arc and gas welding. On graduation day, I was offered several well-paying jobs from both local and national companies. Immediately, I turned them all down and walked over to the trash can. I then proceeded to throw my diploma and welding certification papers into the trash before leaving the grounds. I promised myself, "Outside of orders given by my superiors in the National Guard, I will never, ever, strike another arc or weld two pieces of metal together again."

That year went by quickly, because I was going to Greenville Tech, working in Clemson two days a week, spending another two days a week in the projection booth at the Plaza, and the remainder of the time working downstairs at the Plaza. I also had to spend one weekend each month at the National Guard Reserve Center.

With my active schedule, I still found time to work in an occasional evening on the pinball machines. Playing the machines didn't seem to mean as much to me as it had a year earlier, however. Maybe it's because I had started spending a lot of time and money betting on college and professional football and basketball games.

I would not attempt to guess how many sports bets I have made down through the years. During those long hours in the projection booth, I used to study teams so much that I knew everything about the coaches and the players.

I sold my old Plymouth and bought a late model, two-seater, MG sports car. It was a beautiful car: metallic green, black leather interior, five-speed transmission, with chrome wire wheels. And it was a convertible. Mother thought it was a bit much, but she seemed to have fun riding around town in the MG, especially with the top down.

I received orders in August of 1965 that I was to report within thirty days to Fort Jackson, South Carolina, for my six months of basic training. A month's notice didn't give me much time to tie up all the loose ends at home. Mother was my only genuine concern. She was having a hard time with my going away for that length of time.

I assured her, "Mother, you know I will find a way to come home as often as I can."

While I was away on active duty, both Mr. Todd and Mr. Mosley, the manager at the Clemson theatre, hired part-time projectionists to take over my duties at their theatres. Both men assured me that when I returned home, my job would be waiting for me.

Boot camp was most certainly a new experience for me. When I arrived at Fort Jackson, I was out of shape, both physically and mentally. I was used to being the independent one: the man who answers to no one, the guy who does what he wants, when he wants, where he wants, and only if he wants. That attitude lasted all of about five minutes.

The first thing they did was completely shave my head, and from there it got worse. I was up every day at 5:00 a.m. for exercises—jumping jacks, push-ups, all sorts of physical workouts. It seemed like all we did every day was exercise, march, run, wait in line to eat, do hand-to-hand combat, and listen to the drill instructor tell us how disgusting we were.

Before joining the Guard, I had been to the doctor several times with severe pain in my stomach. After drinking the hospital's barium cocktail and having my stomach X-rayed, I was diagnosed with a stomach ulcer. In boot camp my stomach seemed to hurt all the time.

Every night after dinner, I took two cartons of milk from the mess hall to my barracks with me. I cracked open the window that was located directly across from my bunk and placed the two cartons of milk in the bottom of the window frame. During the night when my stomach started hurting, I got up and drank some of the milk to relieve the pain, and then I tried to go back to sleep. I usually had to do this several times a night.

My barracks upstairs had twenty bunk beds—a total of forty men on the floor. Of the forty men, I think only two were from South Carolina: John Miller, another reservist from Anderson, and me. It seemed like everybody else was from New York or New Jersey.

When you're living with forty men, twenty-four hours a day, seven days a week, you really get to know one another. You learn what each man likes or dislikes—what makes him tick. During our free time, the men would do a variety of things; some would read and write letters to their loved ones, while others would use that time for getting a little extra sleep. There were always those guys who wanted to play a little basketball or touch football.

Then, there was a poker game. It doesn't take a Rhodes Scholar to guess which group I ended up in. The poker game was where I spent all my free time.

My first game was not one I would soon forget. I dropped by the latrine to see how the weekend card game was going—the action looked great. I decided I would wait around until a seat came open, and then I would play a while. Around two in the morning a player called it quits. I replaced him at his seat.

The first hand that I was dealt was a very expensive hand for me to play out. I put every dollar I possessed—I'm talking about my whole month's paycheck—and I still didn't have enough cash to play the hand out!

I told the other players, "Look, fellows, I'm all in. All my cash is on the table, but I want to play this hand out. Last night I bought this watch at the PX. It's brand new. Will you let me put the watch in the pot? It should more than cover my bet."

Each man examined the watch. Then they agreed to let me substitute the watch in lieu of the remaining cash needed. The hand I was holding was strong enough to win nine out of ten times. Unfortunately, this was that tenth time. I lost the hand.

I got up from the game and went to my bunk. I lay there thinking, "I have the rest of the weekend with no money, no place to go, and I don't even have a watch to tell me what time it is. And how am I going to make it for another month without even cigarette money." That was the longest single month of my life. I borrowed a few bucks from one of the guys: just enough cash to keep me in cigarettes and toothpaste until payday.

When payday finally came, I paid my debts from the weeks before and from there I went straight to the monthly poker game. That night, I fared much better than I had the month before. No, I didn't win back the paycheck that I had lost, but I did win enough money to buy me another watch with a few bucks left over.

I was full-fledged gambler, and I made no bones about it. Anybody who played with me knew that when it came to a bet, there wasn't a conservative bone in my body. I won more money by bluffing with losing cards, causing the winning player to fold his hand, than I did by winning the hand with good cards. The only part of basic training that I truly enjoyed was those late-night poker games in the latrine. We had to play cards in the latrine because it was the only room in the building that had lights on throughout the night.

One day, Mother received a phone call from Jane Dodd. Jane introduced herself as the older sister of one of the cashiers at the Plaza. Jane, a single girl who lived alone, was a recent graduate of Greenville Tech. Jane asked my mother, "Mrs. Watson, would you like for me to drive you to Fort Jackson one Sunday afternoon to visit your son, Larry?" Mother accepted Jane's most generous offer, and the two of them came and spent several hours with me one Sunday afternoon.

*Larry's mother with him at Fort Jackson*

Everybody who knew Jane Dodd liked her. She was a quiet girl, known for her warm, sincere personality.

It was great to finally have contact with the outside world. I could tell that visiting me was very good for Mother. The three of us spent the entire afternoon talking and picnicking. As they prepared to leave for Greenville, I told Jane how much I appreciated her taking the time out of her weekend to drive my mother to Fort Jackson to see me.

Jane said, "I didn't come here just for your mother. I also wanted to see you."

I finally completed the required six months of basic training at Fort Jackson. I was surprised, upon opening my orders, to find that I was to report to Fort Bragg, North Carolina, and not Fort Stewart, Georgia, for my advanced training. With me being a National Guardsman and Fort Bragg being the home of the 82nd Airborne Division, my first few days at Fort Bragg were intense.

When I first walked into the barracks, I received a lot of flak from the men. I guess I did look a bit out of place. I will not repeat the humiliating names I was called. At six foot three inches and weighing in at a mere 135-pounds in my regular army uniform, surrounded by paratroopers, well, I was a sight to behold. It was obvious the men were insulted that I would be assigned to an airborne unit, and they demanded an explanation as to why I, a National Guardsman, would be assigned to their unit. I wished more than anything that I had an answer.

Prior to their being assigned to the 82nd Airborne Division, many of the men had already served in Vietnam as a part of the famous 101st Airborne Division (better known as the "Screaming Eagles"). They wore their pants bloused in their boots, and they looked and acted like they had stepped right out of a Hollywood war movie.

I knew I had to do something to get on their good side. I hated not being accepted by the men. So, instead of arm wrestling, I decided to whip out my playing cards and show the men some tricks. I could make magic with a deck of cards. And it worked. I lured them in with my card tricks, but ultimately it was my style of gambling that really won them over. I owned my seat at the high-stakes card table proudly. I spent all my free time playing cards in the barracks with those physically fit men of steel known as high-rolling, card-loving paratroopers. Mission accomplished. Well, almost . . .

Being a paratrooper unit, the training was certainly much more physical than the training at Fort Jackson. This time, though, I thought I was in good enough condition to meet their strenuous physical requirements.

But then came my first run at Fort Bragg. The wake-up call started our day very early in the morning, around 4:30 a.m. The sergeant had all of us outside doing calisthenics before the sun even came up. After a strong physical workout, we went on a five-mile run.

I got about three miles into the run and had to stop. I was exhausted. Trying to run that far in combat boots was too much for me. I used the liner of my helmet as a chair and sat down on it beside the road. Soldiers kept running by looking down at me as I just sat there. I knew I could only go on if I could muster up a second wind. Sitting there, I began to wonder why no one else had fallen out of the run besides me.

One of the sergeants came running up to me just as I was about to stand up and said, "What's wrong, soldier?"

I said, "Nothing, Sarge. I'll double-time and catch up with my platoon." I finally caught up with my platoon and fell in at the back of the formation. At the end of the run, the sergeant said nothing to me about my falling out of the run. I thought, "Whew, I'm not in trouble."

Later that evening I went to my bunk. I thought, "No staying up late tonight. I'm going to put my weary, tired bones to rest at 8:00 p.m."

It was about that time that the sergeant stopped by to see me. He said, "Private Vaughn, you did something today that paratroopers don't do. You fell out of formation during an exercise, and because of that unacceptable act, you will report to KP in exactly six hours. Your duty of KP will be from 00:30 until 23:00 tomorrow night, unless the cook wants to keep you longer. If you don't perform on KP any better than you did on your exercise today, I'll have you back on KP this weekend and every weekend as long as you're fortunate enough to be in this man's Army. Do you read me?"

I quickly replied, "Yes sir, I'll report to the mess hall at 00:30 as instructed, sir."

I thought it best that I not remind the sergeant that I wasn't a paratrooper, just a National Guardsman who had the misfortune of being stationed with a bunch of overzealous paratroopers.

I made sure the mess sergeant was pleased with my twenty-two-and-a-half hours of KP duty. It was the longest day of my life. I knew then why none of the other soldiers had fallen out of formation during the five-mile run the day before. I promised myself, "I might die during a run, but I will never, ever fall out of a run again."

During my three months at Fort Bragg, I made several weekend trips home. I started dating Jane Dodd and enjoyed being with her. She was career-minded and had a good job working as a computer programmer, and Mother thought the world of her. She and Jane had become the best of friends. They spent a lot of time together while I was away at camp. Mother kept telling me, "She's the one, Larry. I think you ought to marry that girl. She would be very good for you."

NINE

# CHANGES

*The only kind of love worth having is the kind that goes on living and laughing and fighting and loving.*
– Spencer Tracy, *A Guy Named Joe*

IT WAS WONDERFUL TO BE home. It felt great to have my active duty behind me. Now I could concentrate on my future, get back to work, spend some time with Jane, and start making some important decisions.

Mr. Todd called me. "Larry, have you heard the news? Mr. Heyward Morgan is building a new theatre right here in Greenville, and I am going to be the manager of it. Larry, it's not going to be just another theatre, but a show place. Mr. Morgan said it is going to be the most luxurious theatre in the entire southeastern United States. He's named it the Astro."

I congratulated Mr. Todd on his well-earned promotion. Then he informed me that Mr. Morgan wanted to talk with me about taking the position of manager at the Plaza. I couldn't believe what I heard. "Are you serious? He is offering me the manager's job at the Plaza?"

Mr. Todd said, "That's right. You're first on his list."

Outside of saying an occasional hello to Mr. Morgan when he and his family would come to a movie at the Plaza, I had never really talked to the man. I knew Mr. Morgan only from things Mr. Todd had told me about him. He came from a very wealthy family. He was married to a very pretty lady, and they resided in one of the exclusive country club neighborhoods. Mr. Morgan divided his time between his two bowling centers, one in Greenville and the other one in Asheville, and his two theatres in Greenville and Clemson. Mr. Todd said Mr. Morgan's true love was the theatre business.

I went to his office and met with him. Mr. Morgan looked to be in his early-to-mid fifties and had a very slim build. He reminded me of the actor and singer Bing Crosby. I wondered if he was hard of hearing, because throughout our conversation he seemed to talk quite loudly. It surprised me that a man of his stature was even knowledgeable about the small stuff: marquee letters, threading a projector, and even how many squirts of butter go into a cup of buttered popcorn.

Mr. Morgan told me, "Larry, I've had my eye on you for a long time. Sam Todd has kept me abreast of your progress at the Plaza. He tells me you are willing to do anything when it comes to that theatre. Well, my question to you is, can you manage the Plaza and manage it well?"

Before I had a chance to answer his question, he went on to say, "The key to being a good theatre manager is to never ask or expect more out of your employees than you yourself are willing to give. Listen to your employees, train them well, teach them to love their work, and most important of all, you must know and love your job. Larry, you must be dedicated to the company if you are going to work for me."

It was impossible for me to hide my feelings. I responded with excitement in my voice. "Mr. Morgan, this is exactly what I have always wanted, my own theatre. I'll do my very best to make you proud of me. Thank you so very much for this opportunity."

After that day Mr. Morgan and I became very close. I spent a lot of time at his office each week working with him on newspaper and radio advertisements. Mr. Morgan had a remarkable imagination. He spent several weeks teaching me all the different facets of advertising. At the close of a meeting, he often gave me a brief idea about how he would like to see a film advertised. I would leave with that idea, think about it, build on it, and meet with him later for further discussion.

While working for Mr. Morgan, I began to take an interest in my personal style and started shopping at expensive men's stores. I even bought a beautiful pair of red patent-leather shoes that had a gold "V" on the heels. Women seemed to notice my clothes—especially my shoes.

Mr. Morgan commented to me one day that the Plaza needed a makeover. He was concerned the lobby was starting to show some wear. He asked me, "Would you be willing to spruce up the Plaza?"

"Sure," I replied. He assured me he would provide the necessary funds, and I was at liberty to put my golden touch on the place. I was excited to show Mr. Morgan my design skills.

I went shopping and found some beautiful red velvet wallpaper, which had a gold-embossed design that complimented the soft red velvet material. I put the wallpaper everywhere throughout the lobby of the theatre. I was thrilled when I found some large, bright red, cigarette urns. The whole place was transformed, and I was so proud. It even matched my shoes. I couldn't wait for Mr. Morgan to see it.

One evening, Joe Hiller, a respected architect who had designed Heyward's theatres, came to our theatre to see a movie. I stood up straight when I saw him and walked toward him with an air of confidence. "Good evening, Mr. Hiller. It's good to see you."

Mr. Hiller looked around the entrance as he replied, "Larry, did you do this?"

I knew what he meant by *this*: he meant my masterpiece. It was obvious he was taken aback by the transformation. "Yes sir, I did!" I said proudly.

"This place," he continued to look around as he spoke, "looks like a Chinese whorehouse!"

I couldn't believe my ears! I thought the place looked great—first class all the way. As Mr. Hiller turned and abruptly walked into the auditorium to watch his movie, I thought to myself, "I wonder how he knows what a Chinese whorehouse looks like?"

The next week Mr. Morgan called me and informed me that the Plaza would be closed for a few days as he had had a change of heart and wanted to have the lobby remodeled by an interior designer. This time, he didn't ask me for my input on the remodel. I learned a valuable lesson from the experience: theatre manager I may be, but designer I am not.

Amazingly, after a few months, Mr. Morgan began to implement many of my thoughts and suggestions for marketing films. One afternoon he remarked, "Larry, you have a great creative ability, and I intend to make use of it. In the future, you will be responsible for all three of our theatres' newspaper and radio advertising." He went on to say, "Along with that responsibility comes a lot of hard work, and a good raise."

Mr. Morgan commented that, at twenty-one, I was the youngest theatre and advertising manager in all of South Carolina. I couldn't believe my good fortune. I made good money working in an industry that I loved.

I wanted to share my good news with Mother and Jane, so that night the three of us went out to dinner. I told them about my meeting with Mr. Morgan, trying to remember it word for word, as I wanted to leave nothing out. Then I looked directly at Mother and said, "To celebrate my good fortune, Mother, I am going to buy you your own home."

Mom said, "Oh no, you're not! You're going to save your money for your own home."

Jane and I laughed at Mother, knowing that she wanted her own home more than anything in the world.

I replied, "Mother, I've already picked out the house for you. Do you remember that cute little white house three houses down from us that's for sale?"

She replied, "Why, yes. Of course, I do."

I said, "Well, it's yours, if you want it."

Mother and I met the realtor at the house. Right away I started getting upset with Mother when the three of us were walking through the house. Mother was so excited she couldn't stop talking. She told the realtor, "Oh, I can do this here, that there, and won't this look good if I do such and such."

*Larry bought his first home at the age of twenty-one.*

I pulled Mother off to the side and warned her, "If you don't stop making such a fuss over this place, I'm going to have to pay top dollar to buy it for you."

Mother gave me that little cheesy smile of hers and nodded her head in agreement. She said, "I'm sorry. I'll be good."

I said, "You're always good—just be quiet."

For as old as it was, the house was in good condition. It needed a coat of paint on the inside, but the outside looked just fine. That evening I put a contract on that cute little house. I gave Mother a hug and a kiss and said, "Congratulations, you now have your retirement home." Six weeks later the loan was approved. Mother was about to become a full-fledged home owner, and I was now in debt for thirty years.

Mother wanted to move in immediately and fix up the house as we went along. I told her, if she would only wait three weeks, I would have some of the kids from the theatre come over and paint the inside of the house while I was away at Fort Stewart for my two weeks of summer camp. I promised Mother, "We'll move in the week after I return home from camp."

I left for my annual two weeks of summer camp at Fort Stewart on a Saturday morning at the end of June. It was exhausting trying to get everything done that had to be done before the army convoy left that day.

It was only when I was actually driving down the highway that I finally felt that all the bases had been covered.

I lit a cigarette, inhaled a deep breath, and held it; then I exhaled the smoke. I relaxed a moment and then thought, "I have two weeks free. It's poker time."

The worst part about going to Fort Stewart in the middle of the summer is the mosquitoes. The mosquitoes were so big that they looked like some of the Army's helicopters. Insect repellent was a must if you planned on coming home alive. Our company always had the misfortune of staying miles deep in the woods, right in the middle of mosquito city, and near absolutely nothing else. That year was no different.

I finished my shift on the switchboard at noon on Wednesday. Most of the men had taken a jump-start on the Fourth of July and had already started the celebration. When I got back to my bunk, the poker game was well underway. There was still one seat open, and that seat was mine.

Except for a quick trip to the latrine, I never left my seat from 1:00 p.m. Wednesday afternoon until 3:00 p.m. Thursday afternoon. When you're playing in a high-stakes game, that's the way you play. You do not leave the table. The beer and coffee flow freely, and you can eat a sandwich for energy. But you never leave the game.

Then I heard someone yelling, "Vaughn, PFC Vaughn. Has anyone seen Vaughn?"

One of the guys watching us yelled back, "Moneybags is over here."

The sergeant came over to the game and said, "Vaughn, the captain wants to see you pronto in the command tent."

I was up around seven hundred dollars, and I thought, "Just my luck. I'm on a roll, and he has to call me." I played out the hand and then assured the guys that I would be back shortly.

While taking the brief walk over to the command tent, I tried to figure out why the captain would want to see me, as I was scheduled to be off duty for another twenty-four hours. I looked a mess. I was unshaven, in desperate need of a bath, and my uniform was completely wrinkled, since I had been wearing it for two days. I decided the captain's calling me couldn't be good news. I must have done or said something wrong the last time I was on duty.

I walked into the headquarters tent and saw Captain Conner standing at the far end of the tent talking to one of his lieutenants. He looked over at me, said something to the lieutenant, and immediately started walking toward me. I snapped to attention and said, "Sir, PFC Vaughn reporting as ordered."

Captain Conner looked directly into my eyes. Then he dropped his eyelids, tilted his head forward toward me, and said very quietly, "At ease, Vaughn. Please sit down."

My heart was starting to beat fast, and I didn't even know why. I knew bad news was about to come. Captain Conner went on to say, "Private Vaughn, I received a call from headquarters. They were notified by the Red Cross that your mother is in critical condition in Greenville General Hospital. The only other pertinent information I have is that the doctors suspect she has had some form of hemorrhage in her brain. I have cut you special orders. You are to return home immediately."

I ran back to the barracks and took a fast—a very fast—shower. I put on my civilian clothes, grabbed a pack of cigarettes, and without telling anyone any specifics, I left. I averaged over ninety miles an hour, trying to get home that day. With the excessive speed I was driving on those old country roads, it's a miracle I didn't kill myself, or someone else.

Up until that day I had never had a religious bone in my body. The only time I remember even going to church was to see an attractive young girl who worked at the Plaza. At age seventeen, I had a terrible crush on her. Her name was Frankie Taylor. One Sunday morning I got up, put on my suit, and went to her church. I stood at the back of the church until she and her family came in and were seated. I then proceeded to sit down in the row directly behind her, where I foolishly looked at the back of her head for the better part of an hour or so. That just about summed up my experience in church.

Those hours I spent alone in my car, I was trying desperately to take away the long distance, shorten the amount of driving time, and get to the hospital as quickly as possible, knowing inside that every second counted. "I must get there before it's too late." I thought, "I must pray. I will pray, right now. God, please, don't let Mother die, not now. She has so much to live for: her new home, and me. Please, God, don't let her die."

I pulled up to the front door of the hospital at 7:30 p.m. I left my car half-parked, keys in the ignition at the entrance. I ran to the information desk and asked for directions to Mary Watson's room. The receptionist directed me to the intensive care unit.

As I opened the door of her room, the reality of death encompassed me. It was hard to see Mother lying there in that dreary, miserable hospital room. She was very pale—almost gray—and in a deep coma. I leaned over, kissed her cheek, and whispered to her, "Mother, it's Larry. I'm here. You must wake up. I love you, Mother, so very much. I need you. Please don't leave me now." I squeezed her hand and waited.

We had a total of fifteen minutes together before Mother died. Even though she never came out of the coma, I always felt like she hung on to life for those few extra minutes until I could get there to see her and to be with her one more time. The death certificate stated that my mother died of a cerebral hemorrhage to the brain at 7:45 p.m. on Thursday evening, July 4, 1968, at the age of sixty-one years.

Disturbing thoughts clouded my mind. My mother was the only family I had left in the world. Being twenty-one years of age suddenly didn't feel so old anymore—and I was too young to be burying my mother. Plus, my mother's dream of having her own home had never become a reality.

Victor had completed his tour of duty in Vietnam and was stationed at Camp Lejeune, North Carolina. Victor arrived back in Greenville on Friday evening for the funeral, which had been scheduled for late Saturday afternoon.

It was Jane who found Mother the day she became ill. Jane had dropped by the house to make her routine check on Mom, just to see how she was doing. When there was no reply to her knock on the door, Jane went on in, as she had done many times before. She found Mother unconscious, lying on the kitchen floor. Jane called an ambulance and stayed at the hospital with Mother until I arrived.

The service was held at Jones Funeral Home. I purchased a very expensive silver casket with all the trimmings, and Jane found Mother a beautiful new dress to be buried in. A preacher from one of the local Baptist churches that Mother had occasionally visited spoke at the service. There were more people at the service than I thought would be there: Mrs. Martin, Mr. Todd and his family, many of my employees, Mother's store manager, Mr. Williams, plus several ladies with whom Mother had worked with down through the years.

"Mother would have been pleased with the arrangements," I thought. "Yes, everything was done that could be done. Mother would have been pleased."

After the funeral, Victor got angry with some of the things the minister had said during the service. Victor said, "Larry, the way that preacher was talking, he insinuated several times that your mother wasn't a Christian. I think I'll go straighten that man out."

I told Victor, "Knock it off. I heard the man. The service was fine. It's over. Leave it alone!"

On Sunday we all went our separate ways. Victor had to report back to Camp Lejeune. Jane was needed desperately at her office. And I had to report to Fort Stewart. Because of Mother's death, the Guard offered to let me stay home and make up the remainder of my lost active duty time later in the year with another reserve unit. I thought it best to return to Fort Stewart and put the remainder of summer camp behind me.

Everything looked so different that Sunday afternoon, driving back down the highway to Fort Stewart. How could everything have changed so quickly? The hospital, Mother's death, the decisions, the funeral—all of it happened in only three days. Now here I was back on that same highway, the highway that just days earlier was taking me home, to bring me together with my mother. Now, though, it was nothing but an empty highway, a terribly lonely, empty space in the middle of nowhere . . . very much like me. I pulled my car off to the side of the road and just sat there, crying.

After a while I regained my composure and started the engine to continue my journey to Fort Stewart. I lit a cigarette as I thought, "I must shake this depression and live with the facts. Mother is dead, and I will never see her again. That's a fact. Even though there is so much I wish I could change, undo, and say to Mother, I can't. It's too late. That's a fact. At least I bought her a home. She was happy with the possibility of retiring in her own place, and that's a fact. And the fact that concerns me the most right now is that I miss her and that at twenty-one years of age. I am all alone."

When I walked into the tent, the expressions on the men's faces said it all. I knew then that they had been told the news of my mother's death. While I was unpacking, each man came over and offered his condolences. I thanked them individually for their kind words. Then I walked over to the poker game that I had left that Thursday afternoon. It was still being played. There was one empty seat at the table, so I sat down, laid $500 on the table, and asked, "How high are stakes this late in the game?" I played throughout the night until 6:30 Monday morning, not really caring whether I won or lost. I ended up $1,600 ahead.[2]

---

2    About $11,000 in 2014 dollars.

# TEN

# THE METAL BOX

*Love means never having to say you're sorry.*
 – Ali MacGraw, *Love Story*

"HELLO, MRS. MARTIN?"

"Oh, Larry, I am so glad you called. Can you come over and see me? I have something very important to talk with you about."

I knocked on Mrs. Martin's door at 10 a.m. sharp. Mrs. Martin, still in her granny housecoat and floppy bedroom shoes, greeted me with a warm, gentle hug and kiss. She told me to make myself at home in the living room. She said, "I will be back in a jiffy. The coffee has almost finished perking, and I've made some blueberry muffins."

That Sunday morning I sat in Mrs. Martin's living room thinking about the years gone by, of the hours upon hours that dear old lady and I had entertained one another in that very room playing canasta. I thought of how this sweet woman had met such a financial need, not once, but twice in Mother's life. It was hard to believe that it was exactly one week to the day since my mother had been buried.

Mrs. Martin returned shortly as promised. We each ate a muffin and drank some coffee, and then she excused herself from the room and returned a moment later with a small, black metal box. I had never seen the box before.

Mrs. Martin sat down beside me and placed the black box on her lap and started gently tapping the top of the box with her fingers as she spoke. She said, "Larry, this box was entrusted to me many years ago by your mother to give to you, only in the event of her death." Mrs. Martin then handed me the box.

I asked her, "Do you know what's in here?"

She replied, "Sort of." Immediately, she stood up and said, "Larry, this box might be something you want to go through on your own. I'm going to get dressed. You're welcome to stay here in the living room, or you might want to go through the box in the privacy of your own home."

I felt like she wanted me to leave. I thanked her for being such a wonderful friend to my mother and me. Then I went next door, sat down at the kitchen table, and gently laid the box on the table. I lit a cigarette and stared at the metal box. I waited a few minutes before unlocking the box, trying to anticipate what might be inside. My mind drew a complete blank. I took the key, placed it in the keyhole, and opened the box.

Lying on top of the pile of papers was an envelope addressed to me in Mother's handwriting with the instruction, "To be opened first." Beneath the envelope were several old, faded documents, an insurance policy, and a very old, faded letter from a lawyer. I opened Mother's envelope. Tears lightly stung my eyes. It seemed as if she entered the room, because her fragrance lingered on her favorite stationery. I stared for a moment at her meticulous handwriting. I noticed that my hands were shaking, as I proceeded to carefully read her letter.

*My Dearest Larry,*

*While I was alive, I could never bring myself to tell you what you are about to find out. I hope you won't be too upset with me. Larry, Jack and I adopted you when you were eight months old. Your mother by birth died when you were six months old. You have a brother, Buddy, who is ten months older than you are. Your father didn't want the responsibility of raising you or your brother after your mother died, so he adopted each of you into separate homes.*

*Your brother has known from an early age that he was adopted. Three years ago your brother hired a private investigator to try to find you. The investigator came to our home, fortunately for me, while you were at work. After hearing my plea, your brother agreed to honor my request and remain silent until after my death. I know what I did was probably wrong. If so, please forgive me for not wanting to share you with anyone.*

*Your name at birth was Larry David Stembridge. Your father's name is Harold Stembridge. Not long after your mother's death, Harold re-*

*Harold and Willie Stembridge*

*married. He now has a wife, three daughters, and a son. They live in Montgomery, Alabama. Buddy has spent several summers with your father and his family. Buddy has wonderful parents, the Pooles. They live in Fort Valley, Georgia.*

*Buddy is the only member of your family that has ever tried to contact you. Your father has never expressed any interest in wanting to see you. Your father's address and phone number are on the attached sheet of paper. You will note I have also included your brother's address and phone number.*

*Larry, you were my whole life, and I wanted nothing to separate us from each other. I was afraid that if you knew you had a brother and other family members, you might want to establish a relationship with them and not continue to live with me. Please forgive me for my selfishness.*

*I worried about losing you because Jack died before the adoption papers were ever finalized. What followed after Jack's death was a lot of litigation and court hearings. It was much harder back then for a single woman to adopt a child than it is today. In fear of losing you, I kept moving from town to town and from job to job. Down through the years I made a lot of mistakes. I do hope even through this deep, dark secret, you will know just how much I loved you.*

*In the box is a Metropolitan Life insurance policy in the amount of $5,000. That should more than cover my funeral expenses.*

*Larry, I wish things had been different. If only your father hadn't died. He loved us so much. We would have never gone without. He wanted so much for you to be a doctor. We would have had a wonderful life.*

*I will love you always,*

*Your Loving Mother*

I reread the letter several times before putting it down. I would have given anything if Mother could have been there at that moment, for just a moment, for me to tell her how much I loved and appreciated what she had done for me.

I always thought Mother went through all her suffering and poverty because of my father's untimely death. But no, she moved frequently and worked long hours in order to keep her adopted child, and she was willing to give, not only the best years, but the remaining years of her life for me. I thought, "Mother, I wish you could see what I had engraved on your gravestone: 'Mary B. Watson, a wonderful Mother.'"

After a few minutes I carefully placed all the papers back in the metal box, closed the lid, and locked it. Then I took a shower and shaved, dressed, and went to the theatre.

Later that evening, when I came home from work, I put on some coffee and opened a fresh pack of cigarettes. I waited on the coffee to perk before making the call.

My heart skipped a beat when I heard, "Hello?"

"Harold? Harold Stembridge? . . . How are you?"

"Just fine, thank you. How are you?"

"Oh, I'm doing okay. It's been a while since I've seen you, and I just wanted to check in to see how you've been."

There was a pause on the line. Then Harold said, "Your voice sounds familiar, but I can't remember the name."

"Oh, I'm sorry, it has been a while. It's Larry, Larry Vaughn."

"Who?"

"Larry, Larry David Vaughn, formerly Larry David Stembridge. You remember me, don't you? I'm your son!"

There was a moment of total silence. Then Harold very emphatically said, "Oh, that Larry Vaughn, of course. Larry, how have you been?"

"Just fine, thank you for asking."

"Larry, it has been so long."

"Yes sir, over twenty years to be exact."

"Well, what has been going on with you? Where do you live?"

I tried to put twenty years into a fifteen-minute telephone conversation. I could tell my father was totally blind-sided. He fumbled through his words, and I sensed a feeling of embarrassment in his voice.

Feeling sorry for him, I told him I understood completely about why he had to put my brother and me up for adoption after my mother's death. Those words seemed to make him feel better. At the close of the conversation, he invited me to come and spend some time with him, his wife, and the stepbrother and stepsisters that I had never met. That was the last conversation I had with my father for several years. Years later, I finally had the opportunity to meet my father at my uncle's funeral in Cordele, Georgia.

I then dialed another number. A lady answered the phone. "Hello?"

"Is this Mrs. Poole?"

"Yes, it is."

"Mrs. Poole, my name is Larry David Vaughn. I am your brother-in-law."

I then heard a loud scream over the phone. Many more screams followed. Her screaming caused me to drop the receiver, but I could still hear

*In the metal box Larry found this photograph of himself and his older brother, Buddy.*

her screaming as the receiver lay there on the floor. Tears filled my eyes as I picked up the receiver and asked, "Mrs. Poole, are you okay?"

She didn't reply to my question. I could hear her crying, "Buddy, Buddy, come quickly! It's Larry, your brother, on the phone." She then said, "Oh, Larry, I can't believe this is happening." Then she whispered, "Here comes Buddy."

His very first words were, "Hello, little brother, it's good to hear from you."

We talked for the better part of an hour. It was a wonderful time of sharing with each other things that had happened in each of our lives since our separation twenty years earlier. Buddy and I promised each other that we would get together in the very near future.

A couple of days later I moved out of the apartment and into the house. I enjoyed having my own home, but I didn't enjoy coming home to an empty house every night.

The following weekend my brother Buddy, his wife Ann, and their young daughter Pam came to visit me. I invited Jane to come over and meet them, and we spent the entire day together just talking and getting to know one another.

Buddy was only ten months older than me, but he acted like he was years my senior. Our resemblance was amazing. Buddy and I talked about our common interests. We found out that we both pulled for the same professional football team, the Oakland Raiders. Buddy also enjoyed gambling; not to the extreme I did, but he liked to make a good wager on a game every now and then. Buddy, like me, was a hard worker. He had been the backbone of his father's small grocery business.

Late that Sunday afternoon the Poole family loaded their car, said their good-byes, and headed back to Georgia. I was glad to have met my brother and his family. I wanted to be sure to maintain our relationship with one another in the years ahead.

The $5,000 insurance check came in from Metropolitan Life. Financially, I was in good shape. I had already paid off all the funeral

*Buddy Poole, Harold Stembridge (their father by birth), and Larry*

expenses with part of the $1,600 I had won playing poker at summer camp. I decided, "What better time than now to buy a new car?"

I bought a brand-new, 1968 Jaguar XKE, 2+2 Coupe. I paid $7,500[3] for the car. It was fire engine red with a black leather interior and a chrome high-performance engine. When I pulled up to a red light, heads always turned in awe at the beauty of that splendid machine. Sitting at the red light, smiling at my admirers, I thought, "This car cost almost as much as my house!"

About six weeks after my mother's death, Jane and I married. The wedding took place in the living room of her parents' small country home. If she had only been patient, Jane could have most certainly done better than to marry me. She knew going in what kind of a man I was, and I told her I would always be dedicated to two things—my theatre and my love of gambling. But she, like me, did not like living alone and was willing to take her chances. Our honeymoon was scheduled to be a week in Florida. I cut the honeymoon short by several days, however, as I wanted to return to Greenville to play in a two-day poker game. Our marriage had few expectations on either side. We each, more or less, had our own life to live. Therefore, after a period of time, our marriage ended in divorce.

3    Equivalent in 2014 dollars to $51,000

# ELEVEN

# INTRODUCTION TO HOLLYWOOD

*There's no business like show business.*
– lyrics by Irving Berlin, *Annie Get Your Gun*

"SAM TODD HAS HAD A heart attack," Mr. Morgan explained. My immediate concern was obvious. "Stop worrying! I just left Phoebe at the hospital. Sam is going to be okay, but he won't be able to return to work for some time. Larry, I want you to manage the Astro."

What was a bad break for Mr. Todd turned into a golden opportunity for me. He was transferred back to the Plaza, where things were slower, and I ended up as manager of one of the best-grossing theatres in the entire Southeast. I now had a strong weekly salary and a good expense account.

The Astro didn't play all the top films in town, so I would take the low budget films as a challenge and would use all sorts of stunts to get a full house. And most of the time, they worked!

For instance, there was a horror film scheduled to play in my theatre. I was concerned that the film would not generate much business on its own, so I decided to make several phone calls. I called Jones Funeral Home, Belks department store, and Greenville General Hospital. A month before the movie opened, when moviegoers came into my theatre to watch their film of choice, they had to walk past an open casket that had a veil draped over it. The fact that there was a real casket sitting there in the lobby unnerved people: many wouldn't go near the casket, however, they remembered it was there. In addition, there was an IV pole with a bottle and tubing beside the casket; the tubing extended from the bottle into the casket. Brave patrons were curious to see what was under the sheer veil and were surprised to see what looked like a person lying inside the casket. The manikin I borrowed from Belks worked perfectly. I even put a very dim light in the casket, which cast an eerie shadow on the manikin. Many spooked patrons were sure to come back to see the 1969 film, *The Oblong Box*, and the Astro ended up with the best gross in South Carolina on that film. I never passed Belks' storefront again without giving a nod of thanks to the manikin that helped to make a horror of a film appealing.

Mr. Morgan and I met again one afternoon. He said, "Larry, I want to take you to Charlotte, introduce you to some of the film exchanges, and show you what really goes on in the film business." Mr. Morgan gave me the agenda: "When we arrive in Charlotte, I want you to take $200 and go to the liquor store. Be sure to buy a bottle of everything on this list. Oh, and don't forget to pick up four decks of playing cards." He paused and then smiled, "I hear you like to gamble almost as much as I do. Is that true?"

I answered him very emphatically, "Yes, sir. I just can't afford to gamble at the level that you are known to."

Mr. Todd had told me many stories about Mr. Morgan's love of gambling and how Mr. Morgan frequently went to Las Vegas just to gamble. Mr. Morgan even rubbed shoulders with Howard Hughes.

When Mr. Todd mentioned the name Howard Hughes, I asked, "You mean *the* Howard Hughes, the richest man in the world?"

Mr. Todd nodded and went on to say, "That's right. I've been in Mr. Morgan's office and seen personal stationery on his desk from Howard Hughes." To say the least, at twenty-two years old, I was very impressed with Mr. Heyward Morgan.

Once in the Charlotte hotel room, we set up the portable bar and card table. Mr. Morgan had invited several film executives to drop by our room to meet me, have a cocktail or two, and play poker.

Little did I know that the men I met that afternoon would play such an important role in my life in the years to come. I met the branch managers from several film companies: Warner Brothers, 20th Century Fox, Columbia Pictures, Paramount Pictures, MGM, the Walt Disney Company, and more. I found out quickly that when Heyward Morgan is in town, it is not business as usual. It's party time!

The card playing and drinking started in the afternoon and went right through the night until the next morning. I don't even remember if I won or lost. I wanted so much to be accepted by everyone in the room that I couldn't really concentrate on the thrill of the game. The next morning we all went out for breakfast and Rolaids.

On the drive back to Greenville, Mr. Morgan said, "Larry, for a first timer, you handled yourself very well with the boys in Charlotte. They like you. I can tell. Larry, you have the opportunity to go a long way in this business. Just be sure to stick close to me."

When he said that, I thought to myself, "Glue. That's how close I plan on sticking to you, like glue."

There were many, many more trips that I took with Mr. Morgan. We went everywhere together: New York, Hollywood, Las Vegas, Dallas, and Atlanta. He showed me the entertainment industry from a first-class seat. We made a great one-two punch. I had the creative advertising abilities, and he had the film-buying expertise.

One afternoon Mr. Morgan called me into his office. "Here," he said, "read this." It was an invitation to Paramount Pictures' screening of Eric Segal's *Love Story*, to be held in Beverly Hills, California.

Mr. Morgan said, "Let's you and me go out to the studio, see the film, meet with some of the studio brass, and then drop by Vegas for a couple of days on the way home."

"Sounds great, I'm looking forward to it!" Then I smiled and said, "Especially the Vegas part."

He laughed, then said, "Take cash, and lots of it."

On the flight out, Mr. Morgan said, "Larry, you will be making many trips in the future, and sometimes you will go on your own. I want you always to travel first class. If we can't afford to send you first class, then you just stay at home. Also, when you take film people out, you are representing me. You are always to take them to the very best restaurants and buy them only the very best liquor. See to it that the film executives always have an evening to remember, and don't you ever be concerned about my questioning your expense account, because I won't. I have complete trust and confidence in you and in your ability to represent Star Enterprises. I just want to be absolutely sure you know the rules I expect you to play by."

Mr. Morgan ordered two scotch and waters. I changed mine to a scotch and milk as I was still nursing my ulcer. Then he emphatically said, "Enough of the shoptalk. Let's play some gin rummy."

He was an excellent gin rummy player. I wasn't. But I was a good student, and he was a good teacher.

We had reservations in the Beverly Wilshire hotel, which is considered by most people to be the hotel of choice in Beverly Hills. The Beverly Wilshire is where many of the rich and famous stay. After checking in, Mr. Morgan said, "We must go to the Brown Derby for lunch. It's one of the very best restaurants in all of California." When he said "the Brown Derby," I immediately thought of Lucille Ball's encounter with William Holden in one of my favorite episodes of *I Love Lucy*.

To top off that grand day, that evening Mr. Morgan and I went to the movie screening. When I walked into the theatre, I felt like someone had just dropped me into a fantasy world. Celebrities were everywhere. I whispered to Mr. Morgan, "There are the stars of *Love Story*: Ali McGraw and Ryan O'Neal. And there is Robert Evans, who is married to Miss McGraw." I noticed that Mr. Evans and I had something in common: we were both skinny and had long dark hair.

Mr. Morgan added, "Robert is also head of production at the studio. I will introduce him to you later."

Mr. Morgan seemed to enjoy my being star-struck. He commented, "Larry, you had best get used to the Hollywood crowd." He winked at me as he commented, "These folks are no different than you and me. They put their pants on one leg at a time." Smiling, he said, "Tonight is just the beginning."

After the screening, we had a VIP invitation from Paramount Pictures to attend a private cocktail party with the cast and director of *Love Story*, along with other studio VIPs.

Mr. Morgan knew no stranger, and he was gracious to introduce me to so many familiar faces that I had seen so many times on the silver screen. The most memorable part of the evening for me was the long conversation we had with the famous actor, Jack Lemmon. I listened as Mr. Lemmon and Mr. Morgan discussed what was right and what was wrong with the entertainment industry. Each man had his own thoughts and arguments, but what was obvious was the mutual respect they had for one another. That evening I realized how intelligent Heyward Morgan was, and how he was respected by even the Hollywood elite.

We spent the majority of the following day visiting the distribution arm at Paramount Studios. We had lunch with William Shatner and Leonard Nimoy at the Paramount commissary. Mr. Shatner and Mr. Nimoy were taking a lunch break from filming their weekly *Star Trek* television series. Walter Matthau stopped by our table while on lunch break from filming the film version of the Neil Simon play, *Plaza Suite*.

A comical moment happened during lunch while Mr. Morgan (who always spoke extremely loudly) was speaking. Mr. Nimoy interrupted Mr. Morgan, cupped his Vulcan ear in his hand, and then leaned in toward Mr. Morgan and bellowed, "What? What did you say? My Vulcan ear makes it hard for me to hear." I laughed out loud, as I couldn't help but think, "Now, that's got to be a first: asking Heyward Morgan to speak louder!"

Our lunch was a most enjoyable one, especially for me. I had been a fan of Walter Matthau's for years. He didn't know it at the time, but he, Heyward Morgan, and I had something very special in common: we all loved to gamble. It was no secret that Mr. Matthau was known to be a high roller, especially when it came to the horse track. The short time that I got to spend with him was one of the highlights of my trip.

After lunch, Mr. Morgan and I walked across the studio lot to the sound stage where *Plaza Suite* was being filmed. That was my first experience in watching a movie being made. The scene was as one might expect: the cast were in a large room that was decorated to look like a hotel suite, except this room only had three walls. Outside the room were the director, camera man, and the other technicians whose job it was to capture the moment on film. This was truly one of those "Lights! Camera! Action!" moments.

Mr. Matthau played a triple role in *Plaza Suite*. It was a good movie, but not a great movie. The memory of being there on the set and being able to chat with the lead actor, however, made for a very special memory.

When we boarded the plane for the short flight from Los Angeles to Las Vegas, Mr. Morgan quipped, "Well, now that the work's over, we can go to Vegas and have some real fun."

I thought, "Work? This has been the best week of my life." I was exhausted, not from work, but from trying to keep up with Heyward Morgan. He had only one speed—and that was wide-open!

A chauffeured limousine was awaiting our arrival at the airport. I noticed that Mr. Morgan never gave instructions to the chauffeur about where to take us. We got into the limo and were whisked away to the hotel without any further ado.

The hotel casino was the first casino I had ever been in. Mr. Morgan explained to me how a casino works. Then he said, "I'm going to the craps table. Do you want a piece of the action?"

I said, "Sure, I'm in for ten percent."

I went over to the blackjack table. I stayed about an hour and lost over $200. I walked over to see how Mr. Morgan was doing. I was impressed at the way the man gambled. I saw him lose $5,000 in less than five minutes. And I noticed that when he needed chips, he didn't take cash out of his wallet. He had an open line of credit.

I hesitated to ask, but I did anyway. "How are we doing?"

"Well, let's see. You're in for ten percent, right?"

"Yes, sir."

"Right now, I'm down $8,000, which means you're down $800."

I took a walk as I didn't want to distract him from what he was doing, even though at the time all he was doing was losing.

When we walked into our suite that evening, I was flat broke. I thought to myself, "Great! I have two more days here and not a nickel to my name."

Mr. Morgan interrupted my depression when he said, "Larry, I'm going to take you to one of the best restaurants in all of Las Vegas tonight. We're going to have a dinner fit for a king."

And we did. I don't remember what I ate, but a better meal I have never had. When it came time to pay the very expensive dinner bill, the waiter informed Mr. Morgan that there was no charge for the dinner and drinks, as everything was compliments of the casino boss. Mr. Morgan thanked the waiter, and then proceeded to tip him fifty dollars for his services.

When we got back to the suite, Mr. Morgan said, "Larry, I've got to get some sleep before I can go back to the casino. I know we took a beating on the tables today. Don't worry! We'll come back strong tomorrow. If you want to go back downstairs and play some more tonight, my wallet is on the dresser in the other bedroom. Take whatever cash you need. There's plenty there, but don't wake me up when you come in."

My mind was willing, but my body wasn't. I was exhausted and went straight to sleep.

We stayed in Las Vegas two more wonderful days. It was a financial roller coaster. I was up, and then I was down. During those two days my adrenaline got a complete workout. After all was said and done, I left with only $275 of the $2,000[4] that I had taken on the trip with me, but I had a wonderful trip with no regrets.

Both Mr. Morgan and I received an unexpected financial windfall from that trip to Beverly Hills.

While driving around Beverly Hills, I noticed something I had never seen before. There was a large highway billboard with a stunning advertisement of the movie *Tora! Tora! Tora! Tora* was a war movie based on the Japanese attack at Pearl Harbor. The billboard with Japanese planes diving toward a destroyer made for a most remarkable sight. The fire, smoke, and debris from other torpedoed ships really caught my attention.

4    Equivalent in 2014 dollars: I left with less than $1,700 of the $12,000 I had taken to Vegas with me.

When I returned to Greenville, I asked Mr. Morgan about booking *Tora* to play in the Astro, which he did. Since *Tora* had a fall opening date, I had several months to prepare my advertising campaign.

The first thing I did was rent a billboard, but this was not just any billboard. This billboard was located directly across the street from one of the best-grossing new theatres in Greenville, to make sure all those movie lovers would see the ad for *my* movie. This street also happened to be one of the busiest streets in town. Then, a month before our opening of *Tora*, I had the same display as the one I had seen in Beverly Hills plastered on my billboard, and I used the billboard advertisement as the springboard to launch my marketing blitz of the Greenville area for the Astro Theatre's engagement of *Tora! Tora! Tora!*

The Monday morning after our Friday opening, I received an unexpected phone call from Charlie Jones, the 20th Century Fox branch manager. Mr. Jones asked me, "Would you take a moment and give me a breakdown of your Friday, Saturday, and Sunday gross receipts on *Tora*? I think the numbers I have are all wrong."

After I gave him the figures he enthusiastically stated, "This is unbelievable. The Astro has the number one gross in the entire South on *Tora*—you even outgrossed Atlanta!"

When Mr. Morgan heard that we had the top gross in the South, he was beside himself with pride. He immediately gave me a raise in salary for a job well done.

During my years with Mr. Morgan, we made several trips to LA for meetings and studio screenings. I was thrilled when Mr. Morgan told me to mark my calendar to be in LA for an invitation-only showing of Mario Puzo's *The Godfather*. As I reflect back, however, my first trip to LA was far and away my most memorable. As a young man from South Carolina, I was mesmerized to be in a screening room, sitting two rows behind Ali McGraw and Ryan O'Neal, watching them watch their movie, *Love Story*, which happened to be the most anticipated motion picture of 1970. And then, to be one of the chosen few to be invited to the private party after the screening was almost too much for me to comprehend.

# TWELVE

# THE SALE

*To play it safe is not to play.*
                                                    – Robert Altman

I WALKED INTO MR. MORGAN'S office and, without looking up, he said in a mild manner, "Close the door and please sit down." He stood up, slowly walked around his desk, and sat down on the sofa directly across from me. "Larry, I don't know how to tell you this. I guess I just have to say it. I have sold the theatres to Martin Theatres."

I sat there in shock, and my body went numb. After a few moments he continued, "Larry, you know how much I love this business, but Martin offered me a price that I cannot turn down." He continued, "Martin Theatres owns and operates several hundred theatres throughout the southeastern United States. They are headquartered in Columbus, Georgia. They will be an excellent company for you to work for. They know all about your marketing and management abilities, and they have assured me that they want you to be an important part of their management team."

I said, "Mr. Morgan, this is one of the saddest days of my life. I'm sure everything that you have just said is true, but without you, this business won't be the same for me. I want to thank you for putting in a kind word for me at Martin. You have taught me a lot about the theatre business. Many men have spent their entire lives in this industry and haven't had the experiences I have had, and that is all because of you."

Sixty days later, I was newly employed by Martin Theatres as manager of their flagship theatre, the Astro, in Greenville, South Carolina. That year, 1971, I entered a promotion on a Paramount Pictures teen film, *Friends*, and was awarded Martin Theatres' top honor, Showman of the Year. This was an annual award given to the manager who put together the most successful advertising campaign on a movie. I was pleased to have been awarded a plaque and check for $500 during my first year with the company.

Frank Brady, President of Martin Theatres, felt that my marketing abilities would best be used in Columbus, so he requested that I relocate there and take over the newly created position of assistant to the vice president in charge of marketing. After spending two days at the home office, I turned down the promotion. Reason being, I enjoyed my weekend card games in Greenville and did not want to give them up.

After I declined the Columbus advertising position, Mr. Kurtz, the Executive Vice President of the company, made a trip to Greenville with another proposal for me. He offered the position of area director for all of North and South Carolina.

Mr. Kurtz explained, "Larry, now you can have your cake and eat it too. I understand that you don't want to leave Greenville. Well, with this position you won't have to. What do you think?"

I told him I liked the idea and asked him to let me think about it over the weekend.

The very next night Mr. Morgan, my former boss, called me at my office from his hotel room in Vegas.

"Larry, what's going on between you and Martin?"

I filled him in the best I could.

He said, "Larry, listen to me. Don't make any commitments to them before I get home. You're coming back to work for me. Don't ask any more questions. You're gonna love it. I'll call you when I get home. Let's talk this Saturday."

I met him at his office late that Saturday night, and he laid his new project out on the table. "Larry, the name of the company will be Ideas, Inc. We'll sell campaigns to all the major studios on their yet-to-be-released feature films."

I interrupted him. "Mr. Morgan, how are we going to get past their marketing people? They have huge marketing departments with state-of-the-art equipment and very qualified people who make big bucks to do just that—sell their films. Why should they pay twice?"

"Larry, trust me! I can open the doors of opportunity. I can go straight past their advertising departments to the heads of the studios, and you can work with their marketing team to put the idea or campaign that will make the picture work. Well, what do you say? Do you want to take a gamble, or not?"

I thought a moment. Then I slowly answered, "Mr. Morgan, Martin has been very good to me. In less than a year I received the top award in their company. In addition, they have offered me two big promotions. They have gone out of their way to make me feel welcome. I have heard it from both Brady and Kurtz that they have big plans for me."

I stopped talking, as I could tell my words were starting to depress Heyward Morgan. There was a moment of silence. I thought back to how he had taken a personal interest in me and given me the opportunity to meet many of Hollywood's elite.

"Mr. Morgan, you have always treated me like a son. I'll do anything you ask me to do, even if I have my doubts about whether or not it will work. I'll give Martin my notice Monday."

We planned a trip to California to introduce the studios to Ideas, Inc. Everyone seemed impressed with our work, but expressed concern about how their marketing departments would fit in with a so-called "joint marketing venture." That had been my greatest concern all along.

On that trip I learned, once again, that one should never underestimate Heyward Morgan. One evening we were down at the hotel lounge around midnight. I was worn out from a long day of tooting my own horn to the Hollywood elite. I told Mr. Morgan, "I've had it. I'm going to bed." He said good night and that he would be up later.

I went to my room, got in bed, and was half asleep when Mr. Morgan started banging on the door. "Larry, Larry, you in there?" In undershorts and T-shirt I stumbled to the door. I opened the door to find him standing there with another man. They walked into my room.

Mr. Morgan said, "Larry, do you know who this is?"

I looked at the man, extended my hand, and said, "No, sir."

The man introduced himself. "Hello, Larry, I am Frank Yablans."

I said, "Mr. Yablans, would you excuse me while I put some clothes on? I had just turned in for the night."

Mr. Morgan spoke up. "Phooey with clothes, Larry, I told Frank all about your work. Where is your briefcase?"

Frank Yablans was not only one of the most respected producers in Hollywood, he was one of the most respected producers in the entire world. His movies were household names around the world. Besides being a celebrated producer and director, he was currently the President of Paramount Pictures. And there I was, undressed, hair messed up, sitting on the side of my wrinkled bed telling Frank Yablans how great I was.

He listened, asked questions, and made several positive comments about my campaigns. Then he said, "Fellows, I'm sold! Your work is very good, but you have to sell my marketing guys. Here, write this name and number down. Call Jackson's secretary tomorrow and make an appointment to see him. Be sure to tell her I told you to call."

We chatted a few more minutes before Mr. Yablans said good night and left the room. After Mr. Yablans had gone, I looked at Mr. Morgan and said, "Boss, if you ever pull a stunt like that on me again, I'll shoot you!"

He laughed and said, "At least you could have put some clothes on."

I slammed the door as he whisked out of the room. Needless to say, I was so wound up from the last hour's events that I slept very little that night.

The next day we went over to the studio, met with Mr. Jackson, showed him our work, and left. I told Mr. Morgan, "That guy would hire us to work in his department for him, but he will never use our independent service."

Mr. Morgan said nothing, but his silence told me he agreed with what I had just said.

# DONEATA

*You had me at hello.*
*– Renée Zellweger, Jerry Maguire*

ONCE WE RETURNED FROM CALIFORNIA, there was little to no work to do at the office. Mr. Morgan dropped by my office, "Larry, I know you're used to having several irons in the fire at one time, and now, all of a sudden, you find yourself with not much to do. I don't want this down time to become an issue for you. If you don't have anything to do at the office, don't come in here just to be seen. Take the day off. Take the week off. Go play golf. When things pick up, I'll get my work out of you then."

I took his advice. I started playing golf four to five days a week. I dropped by the office every morning to check the mail—what mail I had. Then I headed for the golf course.

In the evenings I went downtown to a private club called the Amvets and gambled the night away. They had a small private room there where I spent many long hours. Most of the time an employee was posted at the door to admit only those individuals with a clearance to enter. There were two tables in the room: a poker table and a blackjack table. I spent the majority of my time at the blackjack table. Blackjack can have up to seven players sit at the table. There were many nights, when the other seats were empty, where I would play all seven hands by myself.

My weekends were typically spent playing in private card games in homes, with men who enjoyed playing for much higher stakes.

Victor had completed his tour of duty with the Marine Corps. He was now living at home, waiting on August to roll around so he could start his freshman year at the University of South Carolina. Victor decided that since Uncle Sam was willing to foot the bill, he might as well get a college education. One day, Victor called me.

"Hi, Larry. What are you up to?"

"I'm up to absolutely no good, as usual. But some things never change."

"Larry, when was the last time we went out together and had some fun?"

"I don't know. It's been a while."

"Larry, do you remember Kathy Simpson?"

"Kathy Simpson? Sure, a blonde. You used to date her."

"That's right," Victor explained. "I saw Kathy last week. We talked about going out this weekend. Then Kathy suggested double-dating. Kathy has a friend named Doneata Eubanks who she would like to bring along. Kathy said that Doneata is a real sweet girl, and pretty too. She asked me if I knew of anyone I could bring along to be Doneata's date. Well, your name popped into my mind, so I thought I would give you a ring and see if you're available."

"Victor, count me in."

I really enjoyed the time I spent with Doneata that night, and I was amazed to find out that she had grown up living only two streets from my home. As a matter of fact, I had been their morning paper boy. On warm mornings, when delivering my papers, I used to lie down in the gully beside their front yard and take a break. Doneata commented about how many times she used to walk past my house on her way to do grocery shopping for her mother. In all my years of living on Cateechee Avenue, though, I never remembered seeing her.

During the dinner, Doneata showed me a photo of her two-year-old son, David. He was a real cute kid. She went on to tell me, "I've been divorced for over a year. My husband abandoned my son and me shortly after he was born."

I thought, "Foolish man!" I already wanted to get to know Doneata better. At the close of the evening, I asked Doneata if it would be possible for me to see her again. I told her that I really enjoyed the time we spent together and that I would like to meet her son.

She was noncommittal. Doneata said, "I have a very busy schedule right now, but maybe sometime in the future we can have dinner again."

That was not what I wanted to hear her say. I thought to myself, "I'm going to have to work overtime on this girl."

After several calls and much persistence on my part, Doneata finally agreed to go out to dinner with me. We spent the entire evening talking. I asked her to tell me about her family.

She took a deep breath and said, "Well, my parents had four children, and I am the oldest. My father is a rather quiet, simple man. He has spent his whole life standing on his feet, working twelve-hour days in one of the mills here in Greenville. My mother, on the other hand, has been the politician and entrepreneur of the family. She knows governors, lawyers, and senators. You might say that she has traveled in some most unusual circles."

I asked, "How did she come to know the political elite?"

Doneata replied, "Through her various business dealings. At one time she owned a lot of property in Greenville and the surrounding area."

I asked, "What happened?"

She continued, "Mother was involved in a very bad car accident which left her in and out of the hospital for years. She has had so many operations on her poor back that it looks like a road map. Consequently, she wasn't able to maintain control of her business investments."

"Tell me about your brothers and your sister."

Doneata said, "The three of them live at home along with my parents, my child, and me."

"Sounds like a full house," I commented.

She agreed, "It is. Delane is twenty and very intelligent. He stays busy running errands for Mother and doing odd jobs. He's also in college. My sister, Mentora, and my younger brother, Homer, are both students at Greenville High School. Mentora is a wonderful sister. I love her dearly, and Homer is a very special brother. He has a good heart."

Then Doneata said, "That's all you're going to get out of me. Now, if you don't mind, I have a couple of questions for you."

I smiled and said, "Shoot."

She continued, "Kathy has told me some most remarkable stories about you. What I would like to know is, are they true?"

I smiled and asked, "During this interrogation, will I be allowed to plead the Fifth Amendment?"

Doneata said, "Absolutely not."

I sat back and said, "All right. Fire away."

"Larry, are you as big a gambler as Kathy says you are?"

"Yes."

"Have you spent the majority of your life in the movie business?"

"Yes."

"Is the company you're now working for, Ideas, Inc., a legitimate company, or is it a front for some sort of gambling syndicate?"

I did a double take to see if she was serious. I believed she was very serious. I responded, "What! Of course Ideas, Inc. is a legitimate company. Why would you ask such a question?"

"Because Kathy told me that Victor told her all you do during the day is gamble on the golf course. Then at night you live on the gambling tables in private clubs."

I replied, "With a friend like Victor, who needs an enemy? Doneata, it's not really as bad as it sounds."

She said, "Good, I have the time. Please straighten me out with the facts."

I thought a moment. Then I said, "Well, the gambling, golf, and night club activities are all true, but as far as my work, I am very good at what I do."

She said, "Again, exactly what is it that you do?"

I said, "I think. I'm an idea man. I come up with creative ways to sell motion pictures to the public. It's my job to give the public a desire to see a certain film."

Doneata surmised, "Larry, I have been trying to find something that you and I have in common, but there is nothing there."

I replied, "What are you talking about? I think we have a lot in common."

"Listen, Larry. You're a gambler. My family has never had a deck of playing cards in our home. You were brought up in the theatre business. Did you know that I have been to a movie theatre only once in my entire life, and I was there for all of fifteen minutes before I left? And as for gambling, I have never so much as bet a penny on anything."

I quickly stated, "Doneata, all of this is wonderful news!"

She asked, "How do you figure?"

I replied confidently, "Haven't you ever heard that opposites attract? It's absolutely wonderful that we have nothing in common. We must have been made for each other!"

Doneata did not look convinced. "Larry, Kathy also warned me that Victor told her you're nuts! I believe Victor is right on that account too."

I took Doneata home feeling like I had lost ground instead of gained ground in our relationship. I decided I'd best come up with another strategy before it was too late and I had lost her—even though I didn't yet have her.

I decided to send Doneata flowers—I mean lots of flowers—trying to win her over. Then, after sending dozens of roses, roses of all colors, for several weeks with no response, I decided to make the call. Doneata answered the phone, "Hello?"

"Hi, Doneata, Larry here. Did you get my flowers?"

She replied, "Which ones? It looks like a florist shop over here."

I explained, "My flowers are the ones with the smiley face on the card."

She said, "They all have a smiley face on the card! And by the way, my mother is very upset with you. She has instructed the family not to accept any more flowers with a smiley face on the card."

Then she hung up the phone. "I'm calling her back," I told myself. But the line was busy. For over one hour I kept calling, but all I got was a busy signal. I finally dialed the operator and asked if she would mind checking the line. The operator came back shortly to inform me that the receiver was off the hook at their home. I knew I had to do something about this situation.

I went to my old friend, Scott Bolton, and asked him if he would do something rather strange for me without asking any questions. Scott thought the world of me. He said, "Sure, Larry, as long as you'll come visit me if I land in jail."

I said, "Scott, it's nothing like that; I promise." I went on to say, "Here's what I need you to do. Go to this address and knock on the door. Tell whoever comes to the door that you are from the telephone company and their phone has been reported off the hook. Then tell them they must put the phone back on the hook immediately, as you are having problems in the neighborhood with other phones, and this phone being off the hook might be what's causing the other problems."

Scott said, "Do you want me to steal a phone truck to make it look real?"

I replied, "Don't be silly! Just do as instructed and make it look believable."

It worked. As soon as Scott left their house, the phone was back on the hook, and I had Doneata back on the line. I wouldn't let her hang up until she promised to go out to dinner with me the following Friday night.

The following Friday I picked up Doneata at her house and drove her to Atlanta, Georgia, for dinner in a restaurant located high above the city. It was that night that I told her that I loved her and that one day she and I would be married—because I was going to come up with an idea, a way, to make her learn to love me.

FOURTEEN

# STARTING OVER

*Even if you're on the right track, you'll get run over if you just sit there.*
– Will Rogers

I PUT MY FINGERS THROUGH my windblown hair and cleared my throat as I walked into Mr. Morgan's office.

"Come in, Larry. Lib said you need to talk with me. Do you want to shut the door?"

"Yes, thank you, sir." I knew what I was about to say was going to upset him terribly. But, I said it anyway. "Mr. Morgan, I think it best that I come right to the point. I can't help but be troubled about the future of Ideas, Inc. I think it's high time we fold the company." I shrugged my shoulders as I added, "Plus, I think it's best for me to move on to something else."

He shot right back at me, "Larry, we have already had this conversation once, haven't we? I told you that it doesn't bother me that we're slow right now and that it shouldn't bother you."

I interrupted him, "But that's just the point, Mr. Morgan. It is bothering me that I don't have anything to do! I feel like I'm stealing from you, dropping by every Friday and picking up a paycheck for work that hasn't been done."

He looked at me as if I were stupid. Shaking his head he turned and walked away from me. I could tell by his body language that he was upset with me.

He walked to his desk and sat down. Without looking up he said, "Larry, I really don't know what I am going to do with you." He then just sat there deep in thought. After what seemed like forever, he finally spoke. "Well, Larry, you might be right. When we started Ideas, Inc., I thought we could find a way around the studios' advertising and marketing departments." He frowned. "But it's like running into a brick wall trying to get past those guys." He paused, "Larry, what about bowling? I could easily make a place for you in the bowling business."

"Mr. Morgan, nothing personal, but I don't like bowling. I want to go back into the theatre business."

"Would you like for me to make a call to Martin Theatres, and see what I can do to get you back with them?"

"No, sir, after the way I treated Kurtz, I know he doesn't want to hire me back. Would you, if you were him?"

Mr. Morgan sighed, and then he reminded me, "Larry, don't forget that I am still one of the major stockholders in Martin Theatres."

"Yes, I understand that. However, I have no intention of asking Martin to take me back."

He closed his eyes as if he were in deep thought. Then he asked, "Larry, have you ever met Dick Huffman?"

"No, sir. Of course I know all about Dick Huffman, but I've never had the pleasure of meeting him."

"Well, maybe I should give Dick a call."

Dick Huffman was Vice President of ABC Southeastern Theatres, located in Charlotte, North Carolina. ABC not only owned the famous television network, but at that time ABC operated one of the largest theatre circuits in the United States. I had heard many good things about Mr. Huffman, not just from local industry people, but from several senior executives in California when I was out on the West Coast on business.

The following week, Mr. Morgan arranged a meeting for me with Mr. Huffman.

Dick Huffman was in his late fifties or early sixties. He looked a lot like former President Ronald Reagan did during his White House years. I was admiring his view of downtown Charlotte when he interrupted my thoughts. "Larry, do you like barbecue?"

"Yes sir, very much." He smiled a very warm, personable smile and said, "Good, I know just where I want to take you."

We had a delicious barbecue dinner, with all the trimmings. While eating, we discussed the movie industry, its strengths, its weaknesses, and the concerns we saw in the days ahead. I enjoyed listening to his thoughts and comments.

He finally got around to the purpose of my visit. "Larry, Heyward tells me you're unhappy with the advertising company and would like to get back into the theatre business."

"Mr. Huffman, it's not that I'm unhappy. I just don't see a future for the company. Mr. Morgan is very busy with his bowling centers and other activities. Rather than waste another year of my life, I say it's time for me to go back to work."

"Larry, I heard through the grapevine that you turned down a good position with Brady and Kurtz to go back to work for Heyward."

"Yes, sir. I had mixed emotions at the time, but I guess it was easier to say no to Martin than it was to Heyward Morgan."

Mr. Huffman smiled and nodded his head as if to say he knew exactly what I was talking about. He thought a moment and then said, "Larry, you most certainly have an impressive résumé. For being only twenty-five years old, you've worn a lot of different hats in the theatre business. I believe you have a thorough knowledge of every department except film buying. Is that correct?"

"That's correct. During the nine years I worked for Mr. Morgan, he personally did all the film buying for his company. And of course, Martin has its own film department."

Mr. Huffman commented, "I'm glad Heyward was opposition to us in only one town. He was a heck of a film buyer. I heard that ABC never even had a chance to play *Patton* in Greenville. Rumor has it that Heyward won

*Patton* playing gin rummy with one the Fox boys. Actually, the scuttlebutt has it that he was playing with Charlie Jones, here in Charlotte."

I smiled but made no comment.

"Larry, I would like very much to have you come aboard our team, but unfortunately, with your qualifications, I have nowhere to put you. Every department here in Charlotte is covered with very good men." He sighed and then continued, "Unfortunately, for you and me, I don't have a position available at this time where your talents could be utilized to the fullest."

I thought to myself, "Okay, Larry, how badly do you want to get back into the theatre business?"

I collected my thoughts and said, "Mr. Huffman, what about me managing a theatre? Would there be an opening for a manager?"

His reply was quick. "Larry, we don't pay our managers a salary anywhere near what you are accustomed to making. If you managed any one of our theatres, you would be looking at a fifty percent or more pay cut."

I asked, "Do you have a management position open?"

He thought a moment, "Larry, are you absolutely sure you want to go back to managing a theatre, especially a theatre with a very small grossing potential?"

"Mr. Huffman, may I ask in which city this theatre is located?"

He paused a moment, then he said, "Would you be willing to relocate to Raleigh, North Carolina? We have a single-screen theatre, the Cardinal."

I thought about his question. Starting over at age twenty-five was not so bad. I replied, "Mr. Huffman, I would love to manage the Cardinal. When can I start work?"

Driving back to Greenville, I had mixed emotions about whether or not I had done the right thing taking the theatre manager's job in Raleigh. I could have always contacted one of the major studios about employment, and switched from exhibition to distribution. However, that would most likely have meant a move to California, where the cost of living was sky-high, and everything else I cared about was so far away. I thought, "No, this is only a small detour in my climb to the top in the wonderful world of the motion picture industry."

I met with Mr. Morgan and gave him the gist of my meeting with Dick Huffman.

He said, "Larry, you've made the right move. You'll go straight to the top at ABC. You won't be in Raleigh any time at all. Remember my words—you'll go straight to the top."

I thanked him for his vote of confidence and gave him my two-week notice, which was just a formality since there was absolutely no work for me to do those last two weeks.

I had dinner with Doneata that night. We talked much more than we ate. I told her, "I am about to go through a rebuilding program, sort of like a boxer does when he loses a fight. I am starting back where I was five years ago. My salary is going to be less than half of the salary that I have been making with Mr. Morgan. Well, Doneata, what do you think?"

"Larry, my concern is not with your work, but with your gambling. Your gambling scares me to death. The way you gamble, it really doesn't matter if you make $200 or $2,000 a week. Money is simply a tool that enables you to be able to do what you really love, and that is to gamble. Until you deal with that issue, it doesn't matter where you work, how much you work, or how much you make."

I quickly replied as I reached across the table and held her hand, "Doneata, I love you very much, but I am what I am. I don't want to lose you, though, so I am going to make a serious effort to work on my bad habits. Will you and your son come to Raleigh with me?"

Dave Garvin was the district manager for Raleigh and the surrounding areas. He was a very tall, thin middle-aged man. He looked a lot like the actor Jimmy Stewart, except Mr. Garvin always wore wire-rimmed glasses. He had the reputation of being the mastermind of the company's Friday and Saturday night late show business. I was told going in, "You can get on Garvin's good side very easily—just do good business on your late shows."

My first experience with Mr. Garvin was in a meeting with all the managers in his district. There must have been twenty men in the meeting.

I had been with the company only a month. Mr. Garvin gave us a pep talk. "You men need to concentrate more on these late shows. It's extra income for you. We need to put some new life into them. Now let's hear some new, fresh ideas." Then he looked directly at me and said, "Mr. Vaughn, I hear you're supposed to be such a hotshot when it comes to advertising. Well, what thoughts do you have for us?"

Without putting any serious thought into what I was about to say, I replied, "Mr. Garvin, I have noticed the theatres play double-feature late shows: comedies, westerns, rock-n-roll films, war movies, action films, etc. Well, what would you think about maybe playing two opposite types of films together, like maybe *Love Story* and *Night of the Living Dead?*"

Mr. Garvin straightened his body, leaned his head forward, squinted his eyes, and looking straight at me, he opened his mouth, dropped his jaw, and stared at me for what seemed like forever. Finally he said, "Mister, we have work to do here. We don't have time to listen to foolishness. If you can't say anything intelligent, then keep your mouth shut until you can think of something intelligent to say."

That was it! I was so embarrassed I was speechless. During a break in the meeting, one of the other managers said to me, "Garvin can be quite crude at times. You just have to overlook him."

I thought to myself, "Mr. Garvin will eat his words before this month is over."

After the meeting I went straight to my office. I called Joe Johnson, my movie booker in Charlotte. "Can you get me a print of *Love Story* and *Night of the Living Dead* for a late show in four weeks?"

Joe answered, "Sure. There are plenty of prints around. But Larry, you need to be aware that both those films have already played numerous times in the Raleigh area. Last time they played at the Cardinal, they didn't do any business. Are you sure you want to play them again?"

I replied, "Yes, please book them for me to play the first weekend of next month."

"Okay, Larry, which one do you want to play first?"

I responded, "Joe, you have misunderstood me. I want to play them as a double feature, together."

"Larry, you're going to do what?"

"You heard right. I'm playing them as a double feature."

That night I worked up the campaign. The radio spot went like this:

> [*Background piano music—theme song to Love Story*] *"Ladies and gentlemen, this Friday and Saturday night, the Cardinal is proud to present, for the first time ever on the same program, Ali McGraw and Ryan O'Neal in Eric Segal's classic, Love Story. And on the same program—"* [*piano music abruptly stops and suddenly you hear an absolutely terrible, long scream*] *"the greatest horror movie ever made, Night of the Living Dead."* [*more scary sound effects*] *"That's right ladies and gentlemen, both Love Story* [*piano music*] *and Night of the Living Dead* [*screaming*] *together, for the first time on the same program. Be sure to be at the Cardinal this Friday and Saturday night. It's the place where love ends* [*piano music*], *and horror begins* [*a terrible scream*]*."*

When the spot played on the radio, the disc jockeys went crazy. One DJ commented, "Well, it's quite obvious that the Cardinal has two different managers, and one doesn't have the foggiest idea what the other one is doing."

My *Love Story* and *Night of the Living Dead* combo was a huge success. My two nights' gross was head and shoulders above any other late show gross in the entire company.

Monday morning I received the call I had been waiting for since Saturday night.

"Larry, congratulations on the wonderful success of your late shows this past weekend."

"Thank you, Mr. Garvin."

"Larry, I owe you an apology for what I said to you in the manager's meeting. It's just that—well, I could never imagine such a combo working. Please forgive me for what I said. I shall not take your suggestions so lightly in the future."

I accepted Mr. Garvin's apology, and after that day he and I became very good friends.

Word spread that Mr. Huffman had developed serious health problems and would be stepping down from the controls of the Charlotte office. Harvey Garland, President of ABC Theatres, had made a decision to replace Mr. Huffman with John Huff, another vice president out of the Atlanta, Georgia, office. Huff had the reputation of being a hard-nosed businessman, a hard worker, a man who had worked his way up through the ranks. He was diversified in his capabilities. He knew all facets of theatre operations including film buying; plus, he had worked his way through night school to obtain his law degree.

Mr. Garvin called me at the office one Monday morning, with instructions for me to be in Charlotte the following Wednesday for a meeting with Mr. Huff. Only a year earlier I had been in the Charlotte office and had met with Dick Huffman about the possibility of a position with ABC.

The office appeared just as I remembered it from the last time I was there. The only notable difference was my new boss sitting behind the desk. Mr. Huff walked around his desk, extended his hand, and said, "Larry Vaughn, I've been looking forward to meeting you." He motioned to a chair, "Please sit down."

He was a much younger man than Dick Huffman. He had a medium build and a dark complexion with slick, black hair. I noted how round his dark brown eyes were. I could tell from the aroma of his cologne that it was expensive. He carried himself very well in a suit, which was tailored and made of fine material. He wasn't at all what you would call handsome, but he did have an interesting face. I thought, "I wonder if he has ever played any cards?"

After a few minutes of socializing, he asked the question, "Larry, do you know why I had you come in to see me today?"

"No sir, I don't."

"Larry, I have a folder here given to me by Dave Garvin outlining the work that you have done during the short time that you have been in Raleigh. You do more business on your weekend late shows than many of our theatres do in seven days. I want you out of Raleigh and in that office right there." He pointed to the office outside of his. "I want you here in Charlotte within two weeks."

I thought about what Mr. Morgan had said to me a year earlier, "You'll go straight to the top at ABC, Larry. It will be a good move for you."

I thought a moment. Then I said, "Mr. Huff, I assume I am being brought to the Charlotte office for a support position in the advertising and marketing department—a position where I may be able to utilize my creative abilities throughout ABC."

He leaned back in his chair, looked at me, and frowned as if I had said something wrong. Then he remarked, "Advertising? Larry, I'm not bringing you to the Charlotte office to draw ads. Heck, no! I'm going to make a film buyer out of you."

# FIFTEEN

# THE MAKING OF A FILM BUYER

*They say marriages are made in Heaven. But so is thunder and lightning.*
— Clint Eastwood

ON THURSDAY NIGHT, THE FOURTEENTH of November, 1974, Doneata and I were married. It was a simple wedding in the Reverend O. Edmonds's parsonage, located beside his small country church some twenty miles outside Charlotte.

I remember it was wet both outside and inside the car that night. It was pouring down rain outside, and Doneata was sniffling and crying terribly inside the car.

I asked her, "What's wrong with you? Do you want to marry me or not?"

Her whole body shook with emotion. She replied, "I think so."

"What do you mean you think so? I told you a long time ago that I love you and that we were made for each other. Remember, we're opposites! Haven't I been good lately? It's been so long since I placed a bet on a football game that I have forgotten how."

She looked over at me with a look of disbelief, took her hanky, wiped her eyes, and said sarcastically, "Sure you have."

I looked at my watch and said, "Doneata, we will be there any minute now. I don't want to get married with you crying throughout the wedding. I am going to be the best thing that ever happened to you and David. I know I'm absolutely crazy on the outside, but inside I have a wonderful heart with your name written right across the middle of it. There are some things I can't promise you, but this I can—I will always love you with all my heart. Because of my love for you, I will always work very hard at being a good husband to you and a good father to David."

Doneata started trying to do something about her terribly smeared makeup. Her mascara had blackened her cheeks, and her lipstick was smeared. She momentarily gave up on the makeup and dropped her arms beside her. She sniffed, blew her nose, and looked over at me with red, teary eyes. She exhaled slowly, trying to control her emotions, and then took a deep breath. "Larry, I love you so very much. It's just that you scare me sometimes. All I have ever wanted out of life is just a normal home, with a husband who would love me and be a good father to my children. I know that you love David and me very much. Well, that's not the problem."

She looked down, wiped her nose with her hanky, and stared out the window into the rain. I knew she was trying to choose the words that matched her feelings. Finally, she said, "The problem is that, well, you're crazy. I'm caught in a trap. I'm afraid to marry you, but I can't live without you. I do hope we're doing the right thing."

"Doneata, trust me. We're doing the right thing."

She was quiet for a moment. Then she looked over at me and gave me the cutest smile, and I knew then that she was going to be okay.

While Doneata was busy getting herself together, I thought to myself, "Larry, she really has second thoughts. You'd best behave yourself."

True to his word, Mr. Huff gave me the office next to his. It was a little smaller than his, but what I liked best about the office was the view of the downtown Charlotte area. In 1974, Charlotte was a key exchange center for both exhibition (the theatre circuits) and distribution (the film companies.)

All the major film companies had branch offices in Charlotte. I already knew most of the branch managers from my Heyward Morgan days.

On Monday morning, I walked into my new office to find two large books placed right in the center of my desk. One book was labeled *North Carolina*, the other, *South Carolina*. They were my booking books. Little did I know that during the months ahead those two books would become very good friends of mine, as I would be living and working out of them not five, but six to seven days a week.

Mr. Huff walked into my office and helped himself to a pack of M&M's sitting on my desk. He sat down across from my desk and waited for me to finish my phone call.

"Larry, do you have any idea how many men would give their right arm to be offered a position in the film buying department? This is a golden opportunity for you to learn film buying under my direction. One of the most important and, I might add, best-paid employees in the company is the film buyer. You might have the most beautiful theatre in Charlotte, but if you can't get the movies in your theatre that the public wants to see, what does it matter how nice your theatre is? The people won't be there. The public doesn't know ABC Theatres from CDE Theatres. They just want to go to the theatre that is playing the movie they want to see. The engine that drives this business is the picture. You must have the picture the public wants to see before you can sell a drink, a candy bar (he held up my pack of M&M's), or a box of popcorn."

He went on to say, "Film buying is in a world all its own. A film buyer has to be able to communicate with a variety of individuals. You will work daily with people who are as different from one another as night is from day. There are times that you will have to push, or you'll get run over. But a good film buyer knows when to push and when to back off. You cannot be afraid to take chances, or you won't last a month working in the film department.

"Film buying is very much like gambling, except you're gambling with someone else's money." When he said that, little did he know, he struck a nerve with me.

He went on, "It's nothing to bid a guarantee of $35,000 to $40,000[5] on a picture and lose that picture to the opposition theatre. You then say, 'Well, maybe I should have put up more money to get the picture.' However, what if the picture you lost for $40,000 opens in the other guy's theatre and only ends up grossing $20,000? See, you won by not playing the picture, and the other guy lost when he got the picture he wanted because he had to pay too much money for it."

I interrupted Mr. Huff and asked, "Does that happen often?"

"Unfortunately, too often. Film buying is a very expensive guessing game. No one is an expert when it comes to figuring out what the public wants to see."

I commented, "I guess the film companies are the ones that make all the money."

"Not so! They spend a fortune before the picture ever opens. Sure, they pick up what we call 'blood money' in these towns where we have heavy bidding, but the film company needs the picture to work across the board—I mean everywhere—for them to see a profit."

I asked, "How many towns do we bid in?"

"Not that many across the South: mostly just in the Carolinas. By the way, Larry, in this office we have three other film buyers: Dan Gattis, Tony Rhead, and Joe Johnson. You are the fourth, and of course, I am the head film buyer. All your bids will go by my desk before being submitted to the film companies."

"My bids? So I will be responsible for some bid towns."

"Larry, you will be responsible for the majority of our bid towns. I am giving you the Carolinas."

"Mr. Huff, with all due respect, why would you give the new guy on the block the Charlotte territory?"

"Several reasons. You aren't afraid to take chances. You proved that by going to Raleigh. And you know how to sell a picture. Subsequently, I think you will be good at guessing just how well a picture will do in a given market. Plus, you worked all those years for Heyward Morgan. Heyward was one of the best film buyers around. You could not have worked as closely with Heyward as you did and not have picked up some of his ways."

He looked at his watch. "Well, it's lunchtime. I gotta run. Larry, I want you to learn film buying from personal experience. These are your theatres. If you have a question, ask. Someone around here will be able to answer the question for you. As of right now, however, the film buying for these theatres is your responsibility."

That first week in the office was like a whirlwind. Mr. Huff wanted me to be everywhere at once. I knew as much about the actual process of film buying as Huff knew about building a bomb, but that's the way he taught me. It was all trial and error with a lot, I mean a *lot*, of questions thrown in between. What helped me get through that first Monday were the many calls I received from the various branch managers, welcoming me into the mad world of film buying.

Within a short period of time, Mr. Huff and I were working very well together. He spent a lot of time with me, teaching me the art of film buying. It was obvious he was a lawyer, as he was always questioning me about how I came up with figures for this or reasons for that. It didn't take long at all for us to build up a mutual respect. He even gave me a nickname, "Superbooker."

During those first few months at ABC, I learned why Heyward Morgan had never introduced me to film buying. Film buying is where the action is. John Huff was right. The engine that drives the business is the picture, and the excitement comes from trying to get the picture, especially the picture that everybody else wants. And since the bidding process was so much like gambling, I was able to enjoy my two favorite activities, films and betting, and still keep my promise to Doneata. She didn't seem to mind that I would cut high card at the office to book a film, and I was able to enjoy the thrill of risking everything—using someone else's money!

The next year went by very quickly. Huff kept me running at the office; I averaged a good ten hours a day. Prior to John Huff's arrival in Charlotte, ABC didn't have a reputation as a big spender when it came to bidding for films. However, John Huff was a lot like me when it came to spending money. He went after all the so-called important movies. He made a lot of costly mistakes, but ABC became a very tough circuit for the opposition to go up against when it came to buying film for their theatres. Working beside John Huff was a great film-buying experience for me.

On a cold, windy afternoon in November of 1975, I received a call at the office from Doneata.

"Hi, honey. What are you doing?"

"You only get one guess," I replied.

"Trying to make Huff-n-Puff happy?" (Huff-n-Puff was a private nickname that Doneata and I had given to Mr. Huff.)

"Bingo, you're right on target, sweetheart. How is your day going?"

"Great! I just wanted to call you and tell you that I have a babysitter for tonight. You and I are going out to dinner, so don't work late tonight. Tell Huff-n-Puff that tonight you've got better things to do."

"Okay, I'll be home by 6:30. Bye for now. Love you!"

Doneata made reservations at a little Italian restaurant that we both enjoyed going to on special occasions. The menu was a bit pricey, but the atmosphere and food were wonderful. The waiter seated us in a private booth, not too far from the warmth of the fireplace.

After the waiter took away our empty plates and returned with two hot cups of coffee, Doneata whispered, "I have something special for you."

I said, "Honey, forget the coffee, let's go home."

She smiled, "Not so fast."

"Well, I can't wait. What do you have for me?" I replied.

She took her finger and put it right in my face. Then she curled it, motioning for me to come closer to her. I leaned over; we were almost nose to nose, and she said, "You can't have our baby until the end of August."

That was the most wonderful moment of my life—Doneata and I were going to have a baby. I wondered if we were having a girl or boy. I was so glad she told me about our baby after dinner, though. If she had told me earlier, I would have been too excited to eat.

# MIAMI

*A job is not just a job. It's who you are.*
<br>– Jude Law, *Repo Men*

IT WAS A BRISK AFTERNOON in February of 1976 when Walter Powell from New World Pictures dropped by my office to chat. Walter was an older man who had been in the film industry most of his life. He was a guy who knew who's who and what's what on film row. In his lifetime he had worked for several of the major studios. I liked talking to Walter, as he always had an interesting story to tell.

Walter stepped inside my office and closed the door. I thought that was strange, as he had never closed my door before.

Walter asked, "Larry, do you know the name Eddie Stern?"

"Eddie Stern? No, I don't believe I do."

"How about Wometco Enterprises? Does that ring a bell?"

"Why sure. They own WLOS-TV in Asheville. They're big in the vending machine business, especially in the South. I believe Wometco is also a big distributor for Coca-Cola. Wometco has the best-grossing theatres in Florida; they are opposition to ABC in South Florida."

Walter added, "Wometco also owns and operates all the theatres in the state of Alaska, as well as the number one track of theatres in Puerto Rico. They operate theatres in Freeport and Nassau in the Grand Bahamas. Wometco owns the number one television station in Miami, as well as the Miami Seaquarium."

I commented, "I'm impressed with your knowledge of Wometco, but what does any of this mean to me?"

"Larry, this morning I had a phone conversation with Eddie Stern. Eddie is the Vice President and Head Film Buyer for Wometco. Eddie's been at Wometco forever, some thirty years or better. Eddie is in the big leagues. The only game he knows how to play is hardball. On any given weekend, any one of Wometco's theatres in Miami will out-gross all of your theatres in the Carolinas—combined."

I interrupted him. "Are you exaggerating a little bit?"

"Well, maybe a little. But I've seen one Wometco theatre take in $125,000[6] just on a weekend."

I laughed, "Well, maybe you aren't exaggerating that much."

"Larry, Eddie is looking for a man to bring into his department. He asked me if I knew of anyone I could recommend. The first person who came to my mind was you."

"Walter, I appreciate you thinking of me. Tell me about Eddie Stern."

"Well, there's only one Eddie Stern. He's probably in his early sixties. He has the reputation of being a jet-setter. He and his wife, Jerry, travel all over the world. Some of the branch managers don't think too much of Eddie, because he is known to leapfrog over them and deal directly with the presidents at the studios. He is well educated, a very polished man. He has done a great job for Wometco the past thirty years or so that he has been there. He also has the reputation of being a very hard man to work for. Well, what do you think? Do you want me to set up a meeting with Eddie Stern?"

"Yes, I would like that very much." Then I smiled as I added, "By the way, don't they have dog racing in Miami?"

---

6    Equivalent to $521,000 in 2014.

That evening, I told Doneata about my conversation with Walter Powell. We looked at each other, and I said, "Miami is not that far away."

Doneata smiled and said, "I go where you go."

"You got that right, honey, but I don't know, even if he offers me the job, that we should go."

She replied, "We'll see. At least we don't have to make that decision right now."

Doneata and David took me to the airport Sunday morning.

"Larry, now you promise me that you won't make a decision today. I know how you are, and I want us to talk before you give him a firm answer."

"Honey, don't worry. I promise. I'll leave him on the hook—if he offers me a hook."

Doneata parked our Pontiac Grand Prix at the airport's passenger drop-off curb. I got out of the car and looked in the back seat at David, who was sound asleep. I reached over and gave him a peck on the cheek. Then I gave Doneata a kiss, a hug, a pat on the tummy, and told her that I loved her.

The seatbelt sign came on as the jet made its descent toward Miami. I had never been to Miami before, so I really didn't know what to expect as far as the people or the lay of the land. Some five minutes before we landed, I noticed how densely populated the area below us was.

The flight was on time. I left the plane and walked through the doorway into the waiting area and heard a man say, "Larry, good morning—Eddie Stern."

"Good morning, Mr. Stern."

"Larry, let's go this way. I got lucky and found a parking space out front."

We got into his Cadillac and made the fifteen-minute drive from the airport to Wometco's downtown headquarters. Mr. Stern did all the talking. He was telling me all about the city, the people, and how Miami had changed during his thirty years of living there.

While he was talking I thought to myself, "Cary Grant! That's who this guy reminds me of. Mr. Stern is very handsome, he has lots of class, and he carries himself like he is a somebody. How old did Walter say he is—in his sixties? He sure doesn't look, talk, or act like it."

We got out of the car, and Mr. Stern began explaining the company to me. "Larry, Wometco owns this entire block of buildings. That big pink building on your right is our television station. In that building is also the corporate headquarters. That's where Colonel Wolfson, our Founder and CEO, has his offices. You see that door going into the back of the building? That's my screening room. And that building down on the corner is the Wometco film lab. This building that we're going into is all offices, and the theatre division occupies the entire second floor."

"Mr. Stern, I have a question."

"Well, I'll answer it only if you promise to stop calling me Mr. Stern. Call me Eddie."

"Eddie, why are all these buildings painted pink?"

"Larry, everything Wometco owns is painted pink. That's Mrs. Wolfson's favorite color."

"Are all the theatres painted pink?"

"Larry, if Wometco owns it—it's pink."

He then gave me a look as if to say, "What are you gonna do?"

We got off the elevator on the second floor. Eddie continued the tour.

"This is Stanley Stern's office. No relation to me, just the same last name. Stanley is the Senior Vice President of the entertainment division. On your left is our art department. The next office on your left is Marvin Reed's, our Director of Advertising and Marketing. This office on your right is Jack Mitchell's, who is our Vice President and General Manager. Marvin and theatre operations answer to Jack.

"Now, let's look at the film buying department." Eddie stood up straight. He had an air of pride, as if he were a proud father introducing me to his newborn child. He said, "Larry, humility is not one of my strong suits. For me, being a Jew means something. While I'm by no means a practicing Jew, I do like the idea of being one of God's chosen." Eddie laughed and said, "I feel the same way about being a film buyer. It's a special profession.

*Larry and Goldie Hawn in Miami*

We are part of a small select group that makes Hollywood happen. Larry, don't take this calling lightly."

I smiled, "You mean I'm one of Hollywood's chosen."

Eddie looked pleased. "Yes, Larry, you've got it. You've got the vision." Eddie smiled, "I knew I was going to like you; we think alike."

We walked into a set of offices. Eddie said, "If you come aboard, this will be your secretary's desk. Her name is Betty Woodall. Betty has been with the company a long time. She is in her early fifties, kind of set in her ways, but a good secretary. If you come with us, this will be your office— nice desk, very comfortable chair, but sorry, Larry, no window."

Next, Eddie went into his secretary's office.

"This is Frieda's desk. She has been here forever and a day. I'm not sure who bosses whom when it comes to Frieda. She tries to run everything, even me."

The phone started ringing, and Eddie said, "That's my private line."

He opened the door leading into his office and made a dash across the room. I walked to the doorway to take a peek into his office. Eddie had the largest office and largest desk that I had ever seen. His desktop was beautiful, made of mahogany. He also had three black leather chairs, two large sofas, a television set, and a refrigerator. I stood in awe looking at the many photographs of Eddie with movie stars. Eddie asked me to come into the room and sit down. He put his hand over the phone and said, "I must take this call. It's Joseph E. Levine."

I looked around the room trying to figure where I should sit and chose one of the sofas. I saw an ashtray and held up a cigarette for Eddie's approval before lighting. He nodded okay, so I lit up and sat there thinking, "Here I am in Miami, waiting on this guy to get off the phone, and who's he talking to? Joseph E. Levine! Now, let me see. What all has Joseph E. Levine done outside of making Dustin Hoffman a star by giving him the lead in his film *The Graduate*? He also made—"

Eddie put the receiver back into its cradle. "I'm sorry, Larry, that was an old friend of mine, Joe Levine. When my wife, Jerry, and I married a few years ago, we went to England on our honeymoon. Joe gave us his Rolls Royce and chauffeur to use while we were there. He is such a nice guy, and talented too."

We chatted a few minutes. After he asked about my family, he went on to say, "Larry, I am looking for a good, qualified assistant—a man who can help me run this department. My needs are twofold. One, this man must be able to work alongside me and do things exactly as I want them done, and two, during my absence this man must be able to take charge of the department and make decisions as needed. I'm no spring chicken. Jerry and I are planning to do a lot of traveling in the years ahead, but I'm not planning on retiring anytime soon. The Colonel is in his sixties and going strong. As long as he's here, I plan to be here. Outside of the Colonel, I am the final authority in the film department. I don't discuss my business with the other guys. Film operates autonomously from the other departments within the company.

"Now, Larry, I have checked you out thoroughly, and I might add that you're the man I want for the job. I have never been one to quibble over money. So let's just say that if you come to work for me, I'll double your present salary."

I thought to myself, "Larry, don't let him know that your blood is try-ing to pop out of your veins. Don't let him know that you want to jump up and shout, 'Whoopee!'"

I cleared my throat and said, "Eddie, I like what I've seen of Wometco so far. May I have some time to think about your most generous proposal?"

"Absolutely! Go back to Charlotte and talk it over with Doneata, and call me Tuesday night."

I thought to myself, "No! Don't make me wait until Tuesday to say 'yes, yes, yes!' I could call you ten minutes after the plane touches down in Charlotte today."

But I didn't say it. Instead, I replied very casually, "Tuesday evening will be just fine, Eddie. Now let's go have some lunch."

I told Doneata the whole story. I tried not to leave out one single word. When I finished she said, so sadly, "Tuesday night, honey. Why didn't you tell him 'yes' today?"

Before I could react she said, "You know I'm just teasing. Oh, Larry, this is all so exciting!"

We both agreed that this was the opportunity of a lifetime. My life was about to change in a big way.

On Tuesday night I took a deep breath, picked up the phone, and di-aled Eddie's number.

After a few moments of small talk, I said, "Eddie, Doneata and I talked, and if you still want me, I'm yours."

"Larry, that's exactly what I was hoping to hear. Fly back and forth as often as you need during this time of transition, and keep all your receipts. Let me know what the charges are for breaking your apartment lease. Remember, the company will take care of your moving expenses. I must run, Larry. One of my favorite shows is coming on TV."

I told him good night, and that was the end of the much-antici-pated conversation.

The next morning, I broke the news to Mr. Huff.

"Good morning, Mr. Huff."

"Good morning, Superbooker! What's up?"

"Well, Mr. Huff, I guess there's no other way to say it than just to say it." He looked up from his papers. "Mr. Huff, I am going to be leaving the company. I am prepared to give you a four-week notice—that is, if you want me to stay on that long."

Mr. Huff asked, "May I ask where you are going?"

"I have taken a position in the film department at Wometco Enterprises."

"Eddie Stern? You're leaving me to go to work for Eddie Stern? You won't last three months!"

"Mr. Huff, that remains to be seen."

"Have you checked Eddie out? He needs a revolving door in his office. That's how fast Eddie Stern goes through assistants."

"Mr. Huff, I have already accepted the job."

"Larry, you should have talked with me first. I think you're making a big mistake. Besides all that, I don't think you're ready for the Miami market. They play hardball down there."

"So I've been told."

"I guess he will pay you twice what you're making here."

I thought to myself, "Bingo! You're right on the money." But I made no comment.

"Larry, is it a done deal?"

"Yes, sir. It's a done deal."

# WOMETCO

*The greatest single human gift is the ability to chase down our dreams.*
– William Hurt, *Artificial Intelligence*

IT WAS A LONG FOUR weeks at the office. Mr. Huff kept me extremely busy, as he wanted all loose ends tied up before my scheduled departure. I was on a countdown to my last day at ABC and my first day at Wometco.

Eddie went out of his way to help us find the right apartment. We found one we liked at Kingston Square, which was a mile from the Dadeland Mall. Across the street from the mall, Wometco had their flagship theatre, the Dadeland Twin. It was the best-grossing theatre in Florida.

Eddie and Jerry were very gracious hosts: they would invite us to their Coral Gables condo for cocktails, and they took us to some of Miami's finest restaurants. We enjoyed each other's company. It was especially good for Doneata to spend some time with Jerry. They hit it off right from the start.

When we returned to Charlotte, Doneata had her hands full trying to get everything packed while keeping her strength up, as the birth of our baby was only a few months away. It was good to see the Mayflower moving van pull out of our driveway heading south toward Miami.

On my first Monday at Wometco, I felt like a school kid getting ready for his first day at school. I awoke early with butterflies in my stomach. I wanted everything to be perfect. I put on my freshly starched and pressed shirt, and I retied my tie twice. I was tempted to pinch myself when I arrived in my assigned parking space at Wometco Enterprises.

I arrived early and was surprised to find Eddie already at work. I walked into his office and said, "Good morning, Eddie."

He looked up from his papers and gave me a warm greeting. Then he said, "Come on, I want you to meet Stanley."

Stanley was sitting at his desk reading the *Miami Herald*. When Stanley stood up, I noticed he had an impressive appearance, for being in his early sixties. He was tall and handsome, and was like Eddie in his expensive style of dress.

Eddie spoke, "Stanley, I want to introduce you to Larry Vaughn."

"Hello, Larry, I am certainly glad you're here. Our booking department has been running on empty for over a month now. Maybe you can get us some movies. We sure need the business."

We all laughed. Then Eddie said, "Stanley, you'd best be kind, or I'll start telling Larry some secrets on you." Eddie gave me the short version of how Stanley started with Wometco some forty years ago as an usher, and how Stanley had worked himself up through the ranks into the office of senior vice president in charge of the entire entertainment division.

As we left his office, Stanley said, "Larry, one day I am going to get into film buying. Then maybe I can have a big office like Eddie's."

Eddie replied, "Larry, I get the office, but guess who gets the money?" We left on that note.

Next we went to Jack Mitchell's office. Jack, too, was reading the *Herald*. Eddie commented, "Don't you guys ever do anything around here but read the *Herald*?"

Jack looked up and smiled, "Good morning, Mr. Stern. I was just reading through the society section to see how your and Jerry's weekend went."

Eddie pointed his finger at Jack as if to say, "Behave."

"Jack, I would like to introduce you to my new assistant, Larry Vaughn."

Jack got up from behind his desk and gave me a very sincere, warm welcome. Eddie gave me a brief work history on Jack. "Larry, Jack has been in and out of the theatre business. He spent several years in the hotel business, and since joining Wometco he has done an exceptionally good job for the company. He has been with us for about ten years. The Colonel and Stanley think a lot of Jack. He's a good general manager. Oops, we'd best go, Larry." Eddie pointed toward Jack's head. "Look! Jack's head is starting to swell!"

We all laughed. Then Eddie and I went next door.

Marvin Reed broke the chain when we walked into his office. Marvin was drinking a cup of coffee, but he wasn't reading the paper. Eddie introduced me to Marvin.

Marvin shook my hand and said, "Hi, Larry, I've heard all about you. Welcome to South Florida. Now maybe Mr. Stern here will stop being so grumpy. You know, Larry, Eddie's had to work these last couple of months, and Eddie's not used to having to work."

Eddie said, "Come on! Can't anybody around here say anything good about me?"

Marvin started laughing. I could tell Marvin had ribbed Eddie before. Marvin reminded me of my deceased stepbrother Farrell, except Marvin was a much older man than Farrell had been when he died. Marvin looked to be in his late forties or early fifties. He had red hair and freckles, with a fair complexion.

I asked him, "Marvin, are you by any chance from Georgia?"

"I most certainly am. Did my Southern accent give me away?"

"Yeah, I guess that's what it is. You remind me of someone I used to know who happened to be from Georgia."

I knew right away that I was going to like Marvin Reed. We chatted for a few moments, and then Eddie and I left.

When we returned to our offices, Eddie introduced me to my secretary, Betty Woodall. Betty was exactly as Eddie had described her. I thought, "I bet Betty could tell me some interesting stories. In her many years at her desk, she has watched all of Eddie's assistants come and go."

"Now, I want to introduce you to *the* Colonel Wolfson."

While walking across the parking lot to Colonel Wolfson's office, Eddie stopped me and introduced me to two other men. "Larry, I would like for you to meet Arthur Hertz and Michael Brown. Arthur is the Chief Financial Officer for the company, and Michael is one of Wometco's Senior Vice Presidents."

We talked briefly before Eddie and I continued on our way. "Larry, those two guys are the money men. They are the very best when it comes to moving money. Art has had the Colonel's ear for many years. He has been instrumental in making Wometco as diversified and prosperous a company as it is today."

The Colonel's secretary, Sarah, another senior employee who had worked for Wometco for more than forty years, sent us in to meet with the Colonel. Eddie introduced me as his new assistant.

Colonel Wolfson said, "Larry, Eddie has told me all about you. Please sit down." The Colonel spent several minutes asking me about my background and the various companies that I had worked for. He asked several questions about my family. He wanted to know where we were living in Miami and if I thought my family would be happy living in South Florida. He then went on to say that Wometco, even though it had several thousand employees, was one big family, and that his door would always be open to me for any need that I might have, be it business or personal. I thought that was a very kind and unusual statement for him to make, considering that he really didn't know me and that this was my first day at work.

The Colonel then asked Eddie, "How were the numbers over the weekend?"

As the two of them started talking business, I had the opportunity to look around the old gentleman's office. The walls were all beautifully polished wood. There were pictures throughout the room with the Colonel and famous people, from US presidents to movie stars. This old gentleman had most certainly made the rounds. At the far end of his office, mounted in the ceiling, were four television monitors. Each monitor was tuned in to one of the three major television networks, and the fourth monitor was a continuous update about how the stock market was faring.

Indeed, it was a very impressive office, with several sculptures, paintings, and plaques of appreciation and recognition scattered throughout.

I looked over at the Colonel. He had to be at least in his late sixties. He seemed to be a most gracious man. Even though his eyes looked tired, his mind seemed to be very sharp as he talked with Eddie about the weekend's receipts. I thought to myself, "Everyone who works for the Colonel stays with him forever. The average age of an employee around here must be the late fifties. If you can get in here, you're in forever—unless you're Eddie Stern's assistant. That's where I've been told the revolving door is always in use."

When we left the Colonel's office, Eddie stopped me in the parking lot and said, "Larry, you heard what the Colonel said about his door always being open to you, for either business or personal needs. Well, he meant just that. Colonel Wolfson wants his employees to be happy. If you ever have any needs, he wants to be aware of them. That's the way the Colonel is."

I thought to myself, "I can't wait to tell Doneata about this most remarkable day."

That evening I went home exhausted from the stress of my new environment. During dinner, I brought Doneata up to date with all the people I had met during the day.

She asked, "Larry, do you really think you're going to like working for Eddie Stern?"

"Honey, I'm going to love it. These are good people. I can tell."

# TWO YEARS

*Tough times don't last; tough people do.*
*– Gregory Peck*

OUR FIRST FEW WEEKS IN Miami were wonderful. Doneata felt like she was on vacation. Every afternoon she took five-year-old David to the pool, and he swam and played while Doneata socialized with our neighbors. Mel and Sally Rosen lived directly across the hall from us. Mel was a medical student at the University of Miami.

I was having a great time both at work and at home. Things couldn't have been better at the office. I enjoyed learning to buy film in a top ten market from a man who had spent his whole life doing it. Eddie Stern was one smooth operator with a style all his own. I thought to myself, "After working for Heyward Morgan, Dick Huffman, John Huff, and now Eddie Stern, I have no excuses. I should be a master craftsman when it comes to the film business."

Eddie wanted me to travel first thing, to meet with all the film distributors, reintroducing myself as Larry Vaughn of Wometco Enterprises. I spent my second week with Wometco doing just that, wining and dining the film distributors, telling them how pleased I was to be a part of the Wometco team.

Every day, someone different in the office invited me to lunch. The two men I most enjoyed working with were Jack Mitchell and Marvin Reed. I knew the three of us were going to become the best of friends.

One Saturday, Doneata asked, "Larry, would you mind if David and I visit that church on the corner tomorrow morning?"

"Why would you want to do something like that?"

"Oh, I'm not sure. I just think I would like to visit it, that's all."

"Doneata, if you want to visit it, that's fine, and it's okay to take David with you. But don't ask me to go. And don't go bringing any of those strange Christians around our home."

She agreed, and I secretly hoped her interest in church would fizzle out soon.

One lazy Saturday afternoon, David and I decided to take an afternoon swim in the pool. It wasn't five minutes before David got out of the pool complaining about his arm hurting. Then he started crying. It was obvious he was in a lot of pain. I took him home to have Doneata look at his arm.

Doneata checked David's arm. She said, "Let's see if Mel Rosen is home." Doneata stepped across the hall and tapped on the Rosen's door.

Mel answered the door. After examining David, he asked, "Have you noticed this lump on David's shoulder?"

Doneata replied, "Mel, I don't think the lump was there an hour ago."

"Well, I think you need to take David to the emergency room and have a pediatrician look at his arm."

Dr. Flicker, the pediatrician on call at the hospital, ordered an X-ray of David's shoulder and arm. Doneata told Dr. Flicker how pale David had looked the last few weeks.

Dr. Flicker asked us to sit down. He said, "Mr. and Mrs. Vaughn, I think it extremely important that we admit your son. I don't want to alarm you, but I think something is going on in David's body. I want to keep him right here where I can watch him until I get the results from his blood work back."

I asked Dr. Flicker, "What are you looking for? What concerns do you have?"

"Mr. Vaughn, until I see his blood work there's no reason to get into any specific areas of concern. We'll watch him tonight, get our test results tomorrow afternoon, and talk when we have additional information."

At seven-thirty Sunday evening, Dr. Flicker took Doneata and me into a small corner room at the hospital. Dr. Flicker seemed troubled. I thought to myself, "I hope he is just having a bad day and his looks are no reflection of the report he received on my son's condition."

Dr. Flicker greeted us and asked Doneata how she was holding up, being so close to her due date. Then he went right into his report. "Mr. and Mrs. Vaughn, I have all the test results back." He was quiet for a moment. He then glanced away and sighed as he gave us his findings. "I am so sorry to have to be the one to tell you that your son has leukemia."

Doneata looked directly at me. She started crying, and I started shaking. I pleaded, "Dr. Flicker, are you absolutely sure?"

"I'm sorry. There is absolutely no doubt. It's leukemia. We need to make arrangements to transfer David to Jackson Memorial Hospital first thing in the morning. I'll be back in a few minutes, and we'll talk more in detail." Dr. Flicker then left the room.

Doneata and I both cried. I put my arms around her, and we just held each other.

"Leukemia, why does it have to be leukemia?" Doneata sobbed. We were both very emotional, and I appreciated Dr. Flicker's giving us that time to be alone together. Our paradise, our new life, our dreams—all those things had suddenly become unimportant, now that our son had been diagnosed with leukemia, a deadly killer.

That evening I called Eddie and gave him the news. He couldn't believe it. "Larry, are you absolutely sure it's leukemia?"

"Yes, sir. They did a bone marrow test on Sunday afternoon. It's leukemia: acute lymphatic leukemia."

"Larry, don't worry about the office. Call me when you have the boy in his room at Jackson Memorial. And if you need anything, I mean anything, I want and expect to be your first call."

"Thank you, Eddie. I really appreciate your concern."

On Monday afternoon, Doneata and I met with David's two doctors, Dr. Flicker and Dr. Paul. Little did we know that day that these two men were going to become household names in our home for years to come.

Dr. Flicker explained that David was going to have to spend several weeks in Jackson Memorial Hospital, and they were going to start chemotherapy and radiation treatments immediately. I tried to listen, but my mind simply didn't want to process what he was saying. I wanted so badly to wake up from this nightmare.

Then Dr. Flicker warned Doneata and me, "The months ahead are going to be extremely tough on the family as a whole, especially on you, Mrs. Vaughn, in your present condition."

In desperation, I asked, "Doctors, I know everyone is different, but how long do you think our son has to live?"

The doctors looked at each other. Then Dr. Flicker said, "Larry and Doneata, I can't tell you for sure how long David will live; no one can. But I'll try to give you an answer based on what I have seen and experienced. Some of the children with leukemia live only a few weeks, others for a number of months. But looking at David and his present condition, if I were you . . ." he paused momentarily, and then continued, "I would be thinking about having David with me for maybe two years."

As Doneata began to cry, I walked over to the two young doctors and said to them, "I know this meeting has also been very hard on the two of you. I would like to thank each of you for being so sensitive to my wife and me while presenting the facts to us about David's sickness and for being completely honest with us." We shook hands, and they left the room.

After that difficult meeting with our doctors, Doneata and I went straight to see David in his new room. When we first walked into the room, we thought we were in the wrong room—there were toys and stuffed animals everywhere! David was sitting up in bed having a wonderful time playing with his new cars, trucks, and all sorts of gadgets. Doneata and I were stunned.

"David, where in the world did all these toys come from?" I asked.

He said, "They came from Mr. and Mrs. Stern."

*David and Eddie Stern*

I showed Doneata the card: "Get well soon. With love, Aunt Jerry and Uncle Eddie."

Later that night, after we finally got David to sleep, Doneata and I left the hospital for the thirty-minute drive home. We got in the car, and she started crying. I put my arm around her shoulder and said, "Sweetheart, there is another family member that you are going to have to give some consideration to. You know who I'm talking about—our baby. I know it's going to be hard, but you must find some way not to get yourself so upset."

"Larry, two years! That's all we have, two years."

"No, that's all they think we have. Maybe they'll find a cure between now and then. David is a fighter. It's way too early for us to give up on him."

The next day I went in to the office. The support I received from Colonel Wolfson, Eddie, Stanley, Jack, and Marvin was overwhelming. Each of these men and their families were ready to do whatever they could to help Doneata and me during our time of need.

Betty buzzed me. "Mr. Stanley Stern wants to see you in his office right now."

"Okay, Betty. I'm on my way." As I was taking the short walk down the hall, I thought, "I just talked with Stanley an hour ago. I wonder what's come up so soon."

Stanley looked up when I entered his office, "Have a seat, Larry. I want to talk with you." Stanley got up from behind his desk, walked over to the door, and said to Martha, his secretary, "Hold my calls, unless it's the Colonel." He then closed the door and walked over and sat down in the other guest chair directly beside me. He turned his chair so he could have eye contact with me. Then he said, "Larry, do you mind if I pry into your personal life a little?"

I didn't know where Stanley was heading with that question, but I said, "No, Stanley, not at all."

"Okay, let's discuss your medical insurance. Since you've only been here a few weeks, I took it upon myself and checked on your coverage with ABC—which was not the best coverage, by the way, as you would have maxed out your major medical at only fifty thousand dollars. Leukemia is one of the most expensive types of cancer to treat."

Stanley smiled, "But I have good news for you, Larry Vaughn—and yes, maybe I had to pull a few strings—but I was able to work some magic and ensure that you and your family are enrolled in our executive plan. You and your dependents have individual coverage of up to $1,000,000. That should take care of a big part of your financial concerns."

As I walked to the door I stopped, looked back at Stanley, and said, "Stanley, I can't believe how good you folks have been to my family and me. We have been here less than a month and you, Eddie, the Colonel, and the rest of the company have been so kind to us. In only a few weeks, you folks haven't had the time needed to really get to know me."

Stanley interrupted me, "Larry, we know all we need to know about you. I have a feeling you're going to be with Wometco for a long time."

I found the best therapy for me was to get heavily involved in my work during the day. The busier I was at the office, the less time I had to think about what was happening just a few blocks away at Jackson Memorial Hospital.

Those next few weeks were terrible. Doneata might as well have been living at the hospital. The only time she left David's side was when I was there. After work I would go straight to the hospital for several hours, get home at midnight, and be up early to start doing it all over again. Doneata and I continually stayed tired, depressed, and frustrated.

The counselor at the hospital warned us, "We recommend that you both receive counseling because of what your family is about to go through." She then went on to give us facts and figures about the divorce rate among families who go through this type of hardship. We didn't take her advice, but I was starting to understand exactly what the counselor was trying to tell us. I noticed I was chain-smoking during the day and drinking several Tanqueray and tonics in the evening. I was trying desperately to escape from the pressures that seemed to be choking the very life out of me.

After three months we got some wonderful news. David's cancer had gone into remission! Shortly thereafter we got to take David home from "The Zoo." That's the nickname the three of us had given to Jackson Memorial Hospital.

On June 29, Doneata checked into Mercy Hospital for a much happier occasion. Doneata gave birth eight weeks early to our child, a 5-pound, 14-ounce, absolutely beautiful and petite baby girl. We named her Mentora Mary after two very special ladies: Mentora after Doneata's grandmother, and Mary after my mother. Sunshine and joy were starting to come back into the Vaughn family home.

# GOING OVERBOARD

*As long as we just keep a little friction between us, there's no problems.*
*– Christine Lahti, And Justice for All*

SINCE MENTORA ARRIVED EIGHT WEEKS early and had jaundice, she had to stay in the hospital two extra days. If Doneata and I had had any idea how much Mentora would cry when we took her home, we would have most certainly appreciated those two days of peace and quiet much more than we did.

When I left for work in the mornings, the last thing I would hear as I walked out the door was Mentora screaming, and she was the first thing I heard when I got home.

Sally Rosen used to come over at dinnertime and say, "I'll take the beautiful little monster for a stroll, so the three of you can at least enjoy your dinner."

Yes, Mentora was a beautiful baby, but her disposition was next to impossible to live with. She just about drove our family and our neighbors crazy during that first year.

One afternoon Doneata lost it. After spending all day at Jackson Memorial Hospital with David, waiting for hours to see a doctor; then having to listen to David scream as the doctors performed a very painful bone marrow and spinal tap on his lower back; she then had to contend with Mentora, who was known for her eight hours of nonstop screaming and crying. The pressure simply got to be too much. When Doneata finally got home late that afternoon, she immediately put Mentora down in her crib and David on the sofa, and then she walked outside and straight to the pool. There, fully dressed, she casually walked off the side of the pool into the six-foot-deep section of water. All the neighbors around the pool just ignored Doneata's unusual behavior. They knew she was totally stressed out. Later, some neighbors told us that, after Doneata left the pool area, they all applauded.

Things were going exceptionally well at Wometco. We were having a big summer at the box office, so I loved coming in every morning and looking at the box office receipts from the day before. Wometco had the premiere track of theatres in South Florida. All the film companies wanted to play their movies in a Wometco theatre, because of the grossing potential of the theatres. When I worked at ABC, their largest auditoriums could seat 600 to 700 people. Wometco's large auditoriums seated anywhere from 1,000 to 1,550 people.

Miami was a hot spot for the big national theatre circuits. The top three circuits in the country, General Cinema Corporation, Loews, and ABC Theatres, all had a strong presence in the Miami market. My job was to ensure that Wometco got the lion's share of the films—especially in Miami, since Miami was Colonel Wolfson's backyard.

Eddie called me in to his office one day. "Let's see, you've been with Wometco almost five months now. That's good, because I think you've caught on very quickly to how we play the game down here. Larry, Jerry and I are planning a trip to China in the fall. I'll be out of the office for three months. The booking department will be your responsibility."

"Eddie, that's great—a trip to China! I assure you that you need not be concerned about anything at the office during your absence. I'm looking forward to the challenge."

"That's good, Larry. You will have my itinerary, but I don't expect us to talk more than once or twice while I'm away. No point in my going away if I can't get away. If any fires get started, though, I expect you to reach me before the building burns down."

I thought a moment. Then I asked, "Eddie, who do I report to during your absence?"

"Well, the boys will all be around. Stanley and Jack, as far as I know, will be in and out, and the Colonel is there if and when you need him. However, I would prefer you to keep the other guys out of my department while I'm away."

"What about the bids? Who will approve my bids?"

"Larry, that's what I hired you for. You approve your own bids. Just work them up, sign them, and send them out. Miss Goldberg will be more than happy to type them for you." We both chuckled at that thought.

"Well, Eddie, I hope I don't make any costly mistakes."

"You will. That's part of being a film buyer. Just buy us several good movies at the right price to help make up for your mistakes. And don't let General Cinema, Loews, and your former buddies at ABC take all the marbles. Make them pay for what marbles they get! As far as traveling, take what trips you think are necessary. I would rather have you close to home while I'm gone, but you may travel as needed."

I went back to my office thinking, "This is going to be a wonderful experience for me, to show not only Eddie but everyone—the Colonel, Jack Mitchell, Marvin Reed, the film companies, and even my former boss, John Huff—the job I can do in a big market when left on my own."

The Wometco screening room is where Eddie and I would watch movies. The studios would send us prints of yet-to-be-released movies for our personal viewing. Most of the prints would be what was called a "work print," meaning the print came to us directly from the lab at the studio. The prints sometimes came in very rough condition. There might be discoloration in the film, no mention of title or cast, maybe a scene would be left out completely and the screen would just have "airplane crash" written where a plane was supposed to crash. Nonetheless, the print gave us an idea of what the finished picture was going to look like. I normally screened movies during lunch, two or three days a week. I averaged watching somewhere between 200 to 250 movies a year.

During those first months in Miami, I did very little gambling. Sure, I went to the dog track and the horse track a few times, but it was none of the serious gambling like I used to do in years gone by. For the first time in many years, other things in my life were taking priority over gambling.

Life was very difficult for David, both physically and mentally. He was a six-year-old boy who spent every weekday being taken by his mother and baby sister back and forth to Jackson Memorial Hospital for chemotherapy and radiation treatments. And when at home, he was tired, weak, and sick.

Three weeks after David started chemotherapy, he came in the house hot and sweaty after playing outside. Doneata took David's baseball cap off and, to her horror, his hair remained inside the cap and some fell to the floor. She tried to hide her tears as she calmly took David to the shower and washed off the rest of his hair. Doneata couldn't hold back the tears any longer and cried as she explained to David that he had just lost all of his hair. Baldness was extremely hard for David to accept because the other children, without realizing it, could be so cruel. David got to the point where he didn't want to leave the apartment. He would rather stay inside the apartment where he was safe from the ridicule of the neighborhood children than go to Burger King, or even out to play. To help David cope, we gave him the nickname Kojak, after the famous TV series that Telly Savalas starred in. David loved being called Kojak—sometimes little things make a big difference.

Every Friday night, I had a date with my best girl, Doneata. One of our favorite restaurants was the Rusty Pelican, a seafood restaurant on Key Biscayne, located right on the bay overlooking the Miami skyline. That was where we would talk, relax, and unwind from the many pressures of the week.

One Friday night, Doneata and I were sitting in a booth by the window. It was a beautiful night. From our seat we could see the gentle ripples on the water as they splashed up against the rocks laying against the weather-beaten building. The sun had almost set; only a dim ray of red light reflected itself as it glided across the top of the water. Across the bay, the tall glass skyscrapers were starting to light up. Miami nightlife was under way.

Doneata was quiet. I asked, "What are you thinking about?"

"You don't want to know," she responded.

"If I didn't want to know, I wouldn't have asked. Now tell me, what are you in such deep thought about?"

"God. I'm thinking about God, Larry."

I thought to myself, "She's right. I don't want to know what she is thinking about. Foolish me! Why did I ask?" I took a sip of my Tanqueray and tonic, lit a cigarette, and then said, "Okay, Doneata, tell me your thoughts about God."

"Larry, I don't want to talk about anything that will upset you. This is our time together."

"Doneata, if it's on your mind, you need to talk about it. Now, talk to me before I do get upset."

"Well, Larry, do you remember the church you told me that David and I could visit?"

"The church on the corner?"

"Yes, Wayside Church. Well, when I visited the church that Sunday, I filled out one of their visitor cards and dropped the card into the offering plate."

"Why did you do that?"

"I don't know. It seemed like the right thing to do at the time."

"Did you put any money in the offering plate?"

"No, I don't believe I did."

"Good. Go on, tell me more."

She took a deep breath and continued. "About a week later, a lady came to visit me."

I interrupted, "You haven't been back to the church since that one time, have you?"

"No, just once; but this lady, her name is Wanda, Wanda Glass, has come by to see me nearly every Thursday since my visit."

"I thought you weren't home every Thursday."

"Well, when I'm not at home, she leaves a note in the crack of the door as a way of letting me know she has been there."

"How long ago was it that you visited the church?"

"Oh, I don't know—two months maybe. It's been a while."

I thought to myself, "This Wanda sure is a persistent woman." Then I said to Doneata, "What else?"

"Wanda calls me sometimes, and we talk."

"Let me guess what you two talk about . . . church, going to church. How you, David, Mentora, and probably I need to be in church. Am I right?"

"Larry, Wanda doesn't say a whole lot about her church. What she has been talking to me about most is God and His Son, Jesus Christ."

"Doneata, did I ever tell you about the party I was invited to in Greenville, and the bad experience I had with one of those gung-ho Christians?"

"Honey, you have told me a lot of stories, but I don't remember that one."

"Well, it's so stupid that I have tried to forget it. Before we met, I was invited to a friend's home for a party. The person who invited me asked me if I would mind bringing a large bag of ice, as he knew I had access to all the ice I needed from the commercial ice machine at any one of my theatres. So, I brought a large bag of crushed ice, enough ice to take care of fifty people or more.

"Everyone was sitting down at the dinner having a good time. Of all the people to be stuck with, at my table is a guy who's on fire for the church. This guy dominated the entire discussion at the table. He spent the whole dinner telling everyone about his ministry, as if I cared one iota about his ministry."

Doneata asked, "Was he a preacher?"

"I don't know. I think he said he was going overseas to preach or something. I remember thinking, 'The way this guy is so gung-ho, he should be going into the Marines.' Anyway, he finally stops talking about himself long enough to ask me exactly what it is I do. I told him I was in the theatre business. You would have thought that I had said, 'I'm a hit man for the Mafia.'

"He proceeded to tell me about how all movies are evil, how movies corrupt peoples' minds, and how he personally would have absolutely nothing to do with a movie theatre or anything from a movie theatre. I said, 'Friend, do you know where the ice in all that ice tea you have been drinking tonight came from? One of my theatres.' When I said that, I thought he was going to throw up right there on the spot. He got up from the table, went to the sink, and poured his ice tea down the drain. Needless to say, the party was getting pretty much out of hand by that time.

"I went out on the back porch and lit up a cigarette. He came out behind me. He told me in so many words that I was totally lost and going straight to hell, if I didn't change my ways."

Doneata interrupted me. "And what did you say to him?"

"Honey, you really don't want to know."

Doneata said, "I knew I shouldn't have brought up the subject."

"Doneata, it doesn't bother me at all to talk about religion. It's just that it's a subject that I have very little, if any, interest in. I don't mind you thinking about God and having a lady friend who is a Christian, as long as you don't go overboard with it."

"Larry, I have already gone overboard."

"What do you mean?"

"Larry, this morning, after you went to work, I went into the bathroom and locked the door. I then got on my knees and cried out to God. I gave up the struggle that has been going on in my soul for some time now. This morning, I asked Jesus Christ to come into my life, to forgive me of my sins, and to make me a new creature in Him."

I just stared at Doneata a moment. Then I said, "How is this change, your being a Christian, going to affect our future relationship with each other?"

She answered, "Larry, what do you mean, 'affect our future relationship'? You're my husband, and I love you dearly. My being a Christian wife is only going to make things better between you and me."

"Okay, we'll see. Furthermore, I don't want you trying to convert me or bring any of those weird Christian people around our home."

"Darling, I won't. I promise. Larry, the only request I have is that the children and I be allowed to go to church on Sunday mornings."

"Okay, but that's it, period. And I won't budge an inch on anything else. I'll never change. Never, do you understand?"

Doneata smiled and said, "Yes, darling, that is fine. I love you just the way you are."

As we left the restaurant, I thought to myself, "Doneata has had a tough year. I guess she feels she needs religion in her life. As David gets better, this will probably pass."

The following Monday morning I was busy at my desk going over the receipts from the weekend when Marvin popped his head into my office. "You screening today?"

"Nope."

"Let's do lunch. I'm in the mood for some Cuban food."

Marvin and I walked to one of our favorite downtown Cuban restaurants. While waiting for our food to come, I asked, "Marvin, will you give me some of your beans and rice if I give you some of my steak?"

"No."

"Why not?"

"The last time we shared food, you gave me a little tiny piece of steak, and I gave you half my plate of beans and rice."

"Are you sure I did that?"

"I'm positive," Marvin said, "and I won't let you do it to me again."

"There's no way you'll consider sharing your beans and rice with me?"

"Yes, I'll give you some of my beans and rice if you'll let me be the one who separates both your steak and my beans and rice. Also, you have to throw in half your french fries."

"What? Half my french fries too? No deal. If you wanted french fries you should have ordered french fries. That's too much food for me to give away for just some beans and rice!"

"Okay! I'll throw in one of my fried bananas."

"Marvin, you have yourself a deal."

The waitress arrived with our much-anticipated and talked-about lunch. While eating, we started talking about the past weekend.

"Larry, how is David doing?" Marvin asked.

"All things considered, he had a good weekend. David is so happy to have his hair back. I believe being bald was harder on David in some ways than having to deal with the pain and sickness associated with the treatment of his leukemia."

"I'm glad your boy is doing better. How about Mentora? Is she still giving her lungs a good workout?"

"Marvin, that girl has the worst disposition and attitude that I have ever seen. If she weren't so pretty, I'd give her to you and Sadie."

"We'll take her only if you supply the ear plugs too." Marvin broke out in laughter. His freckles deepened beneath the pink flush of his rosy cheeks. "You know what's wrong with Mentora, don't you, Larry? She looks just like you, and when you were a baby, that's probably the way you acted."

"You mean what goes around, comes around?"

Marvin gave me that great-big Georgia smile and said, "That's right!"

"Well, if that's the case, then one day Miss Mentora will get herself married. Oh, and I can't wait to see her have to put up with her little terror of a baby." We both laughed.

Marvin continued, "And how's Doneata?"

I smiled at Marvin as I said, "Doneata and I had a rather strange conversation last Friday during our night out." Marvin stopped eating and asked curiously, "What's up?"

I explained, "Friday night, Doneata informed me that she had made a profession of faith in Jesus Christ. Well anyway, I'm not exactly sure how she worded it. The bottom line is she is now a Christian."

Marvin said, "Larry, this is wonderful news about Doneata. I can't wait to tell Sadie. She will be so happy to hear that Doneata is now a Christian." He paused a moment, and then he got a serious look on his face, and asked, "Larry, how do you feel about Doneata's being a Christian?"

"Marvin, to be quite frank with you, I have never cared to be around Christian people. Most of the experiences that I have had with Christians have not been good. Now, didn't you mention that you are a churchgoer?"

"That's correct. Sadie and I are both Christians." Marvin remarked.

"Well Marvin, I appreciate how you don't force your Christianity on other people. You're like—well, you're like a regular guy."

Marvin nodded his head in agreement with what I was saying. Then he said, "Larry, I think there is a time and place for everything. At work I try to work and on Sunday I go to worship. I try to keep a balance in my life; however, there are some Christians who don't."

I looked at my watch and said, "Speaking of balance, we'd best get back to work. It's almost one-thirty."

# TWENTY

# THERE ARE NO GENIUSES . . .

*Film itself is very technical, and I think you need this period when things are a little out of control for it to work right.*
– Jimmy Stewart

MY ADRENALINE GOT MORE THAN a good workout when Eddie and Jerry were in China. When it came to bidding for movies, I was throwing money around like it was play money. Sure, I made some great deals for the company, but I also bought my share of losers, just as Eddie had known I would.

One of my losers was a Mel Brooks comedy, *High Anxiety*. I felt optimistic about the grossing potential of *High Anxiety* because Mel Brooks was, at the time, one of the top comic actors and directors in Hollywood. His *Blazing Saddles* and *Young Frankenstein* were both successful box office hits. So I submitted bids for several theatres, totaling somewhere in the neighborhood of $285,000.

Well, I was awarded the picture in every single theatre that I bid. In other words, I had outbid all my competitors from every other theatre circuit. That result in itself gave *me* high anxiety, because it meant that I had in all probability put up too much money for the film. It was an insecure

157

feeling to be awarded a picture everywhere. When that happened, it made me wonder why the opposition didn't go after the picture.

*High Anxiety* was a big box-office flop. It only grossed, in all our theatres combined, a little over $100,000. That meant Wometco had to eat the other $185,000. Trying to guess what the public wanted to see could be unnerving at times. In the crazy world of film buying, that's called "playing hardball."

Then sometimes I got lucky. One afternoon Betty announced, "Larry, Joe Kennedy is on line three."

Joe was the Florida branch manager for United Artists. I had found out early on that Joe preferred doing business with our competitors rather than with Wometco Theatres. The majority of Wometco's problems with Joe Kennedy were self-inflicted. Joe continuously stayed upset with Eddie because Eddie ignored the United Artists' chain of command. Eddie was notorious for bypassing Joe and doing his business directly with UA's New York office. When Joe would receive a message from Jerry Esbin, the president of UA, informing Joe of a discussion that he and Eddie had, Joe would become aggravated at Eddie for bypassing him to buy film. When talking with Joe, I learned quickly to brace myself for a confrontation. Eddie and Joe, more or less, used each other only on an as-needed basis.

I leaned back in my chair, propped my feet on the edge of my desk, and took a deep breath before saying, "Good morning, Joe!"

"Hey, kid. How are things going with 'His Highness' being out of the country?" Joe abruptly asked.

Trying to ignore Joe's rudeness, I replied, "Well, I'm staying busy, that's for sure. What's doing with you?"

There was a pause on the line. "Kid, don't shoot the messenger. I received instructions from New York. We have to take *The Sunshine Boys* out of the Bay Harbor and move it to Loews Bal Harbour Theatre."

I swore and assured him that would not happen on my watch. I couldn't hold back my anger. "Joe, Eddie personally made that deal with your boss, Jerry Esbin, months ago. You can't up and pull the picture at this late date. You know the best gross in the state will come out of the Bay Harbor! The senior citizens love Burns and Matthau."

"Kid, you and Eddie need to be thankful that you don't bid our product on Miami Beach. Besides, I have another picture that was scheduled to play in Loews Theatre that I will gladly move to the Bay Harbor."

I thought to myself, "If Eddie found out that I let Loews steal *The Sunshine Boys*, he would kill me! Joe is taking advantage of Eddie being out of the country and doing a favor for his good friend Bernie Myerson, the President of Loews Theatres.

"Okay, Joe, let's cut to the chase. Who do I have to talk with at United Artists? I am not giving up the film."

"Kid, last time I checked it was not your film to give up. I believe United Artists made *The Sunshine Boys,* and not Wometco."

"I have a contract," I insisted.

Joe started laughing. "You know what you can do with that contract, don't you?"

"Joe, I am going to hang up and call Esbin and voice my displeasure at what you are trying to do."

"Kid, you don't get it, do you? Esbin is the man who told me to call you!"

I raised my voice: "Quit calling me kid! My name is Larry. Use my name when talking with me."

There was silence on the line. His behavior was close to being over the top. "Ummm, *La'rie*, do you want the other picture or not? The studio has seen some rushes[7] on it, and they like what they've seen. But it doesn't matter to me. It's your call. Do you want the picture or not?"

Frustrated, I replied, "Tell me about the film."

"It's one of those underdog films about a boxer who goes from nobody to somebody."

"What's the title, and who is in it?" I asked.

"Well, hold on a minute, *La'rie*! I've got the press information some-where." There was a pause as I heard papers shuffling. "Okay, let me see. There is no cast to speak of, but John Avildsen is the director."

"Wait a minute, Joe. Is this the film that was shot in twenty-eight days on a shoestring budget of a million-one? And the guy who wrote the story is also playing the lead in the picture? What's his name, Stalwart?"

---

7   A print of a film scene, "rushed" through processing for quick review by the director or producer.

"No, ummm, I don't think it's Stalwart." I heard a heavy sigh. "Hold on, here's his name. It's Stallone. His name is Sylvester Stallone. The movie is *Rocky*." Joe replied.

I thought to myself, "When Eddie gets back, I might be the next victim to go through that swinging door that I've heard so much about."

I mumbled, "Okay, Joe. Book *Rocky* in the Bay Harbor."

"Thanks, kid. I mean *La'rie*. Tell 'His Highness' I owe you one."

Well, the rest is history. *Rocky*, the little picture I was forced to play on its release date, turned out to be the biggest-grossing film of 1976. It grossed over two hundred and twenty-five million dollars domestically and was honored with three Academy Awards, including the coveted Best Picture of the Year.

Now as the late Paul Harvey might have said, "Here is the rest of the story."

Eddie returned from a trip to New York several months after the successful opening of *Rocky*. Later, during lunch with me, Eddie started laughing as he said, "Larry, have I got a funny story to tell you. I got this scoop from an attorney friend of mine, Jonas, at United Artists. Jonas said that when *Rocky* went into production, no one at the office had actually seen the actor, Sylvester Stallone. But Stallone really wanted to play the lead, since he wrote the story. Management asked to see some of his work. Stallone in 1974 had a supporting role in *The Lords of Flatbush,* with Perry King and Henry Winkler. When the guys at UA watched a reel of *Flatbush*, they got the actors mixed up. They took King for Stallone and, of course, Stallone for King. After watching the film footage, they agreed to move forward with the production of *Rocky* with Stallone in the lead role. Now again, they thought they were signing off on King in the lead role." Eddie had to pause to wipe the tears of laughter from his eyes.

"Larry, this is unbelievable! Are you with me?"

"Yes, I got it. It sounds too funny to be true."

"Okay, so later the brass wanted to see some rushes during the filming of *Rocky*. While watching the rushes, they asked, 'Where is Stallone?' They were watching Stallone on the screen, but they were looking for Perry King. They ended up having to call someone into the screening to identify Stallone." Eddie couldn't stop laughing. He tried to continue, "Some mix-up, huh! The studio thought Perry was Stallone, and they green lighted the film with the wrong man in the lead."

"That is one crazy story!" I replied.

"But, Larry, it is real! Jonas was a witness to it all." Eddie jokingly added, "Now, nine months later, one might ask the question, who is Perry King? And, as for Stallone, why every moviegoer living on planet Earth knows who Stallone is and what he looks like! I'm not sure who it was who first coined the phrase, 'There are no geniuses in the film business!' But whoever it was sure knew what they were talking about!"

Eddie smiled. "Larry, I asked Jonas what he would consider to be one of his greatest accomplishments, as he is one of the most respected attorneys in the business." Eddie opened his eyes wide as he remarked, "I thought Jonas would have to think about the question, but he didn't. He said, 'Eddie, back in 1962, almost as a second thought, I put one sentence at the bottom of a contract. It gave United Artists first rights of refusal if and when there were any future sequels.'"

Eddie asked, "Mr. Vaughn, would you like to guess what the film was?"

I shook my head, "1962? Hmmm . . . I don't know."

Eddie laughed, "It was the first James Bond film, *Dr. No*, with Sean Connery. Now, fifty-some-odd films later, I think old Jonas earned his pay that day, don't you!"

Sometimes I got lucky by doing a favor for someone, and that favor ended up making me look like a genius. 20th Century Fox came out with a so-called "space fantasy" film. The picture was screened for all the film buyers around the country, and nobody liked the picture. It was labeled a big risk—a question-mark film. It was what film buyers would call "two weeks and out," which meant it was a little picture that would play two weeks in theatres and then be gone. Fox wanted to open the film for the Memorial Day weekend in May of 1977 while the kids were out of school, but film buyers were concerned about the picture being released in peak play time. By opening the picture on Memorial Day weekend, it would be going head-to-head with the other studios' big summer releases. Film buyers were afraid the picture would get lost in the crowd of much-bigger, more-popular films.

I received a call from Charlie Jones. Charlie was the Florida branch manager for 20th Century Fox. I had known Charlie from my days in Greenville, working for Heyward Morgan. Charlie was one of Heyward's best friends. Charlie started the conversation.

"Larry, old buddy, old pal, you have got to help me out on this space fantasy picture. The home office will have my head on a platter if I open this picture in Miami without proper theatre representation. You and I both know that Miami is a highly visible and very important market. Now, Larry, please, what can you do for me?"

I said, "Charlie, I don't want to leave you hanging, but I already have the top theatres—the Dadeland, Miracle, and 163rd Street—booked with other important movies. I guess I could play it a couple of weeks in the Sunset."

"The Sunset? Larry, you can do better than the Sunset. The Sunset is where you play your foreign films."

"Sorry, Charlie, I have two or possibly four weeks available in the Sunset, and I will give you a play date in the Normandy on Miami Beach." I paused, "Plus, I will work out two more play dates. But one of them will have to be in the Coral Way Drive-In."

"Larry, the Normandy is old. Can't you give me the Bay Harbor? And a drive-in? Come on, Larry. Can't you do better than that?"

"Sorry, Charlie, I will hold four theatres for two to possibly four weeks, if needed. At least you will be able to get the picture dated in Miami. And Charlie, you need to remind Mr. Allen Ladd, Jr.[8] that we have your big summer film, *The Other Side of Midnight*, dated in all our top theatres."

"That's true. *Midnight* is the important picture, and you have it dated in the big guns." Charlie exhaled a sigh of relief as he said, "Well, I do appreciate the four play dates on my problem child."

The name of that little "space fantasy" film that no theatre circuit wanted to play was *Star Wars*. *Star Wars* went on to set industry records

---

8    The President of 20th Century Fox at the time.

in every theatre it played in. The two- to four-week engagement extended to close to a year in most of our theatres. It was great to see *Star Wars* shatter all box office records. But it was a film buyer's nightmare trying to back out of the commitments that were made with other films previously booked to play in those theatres. I sure was proud of my four play dates in Miami. I only wished I had been a better friend to Charlie Jones and had given him fourteen play dates instead of only four. The big disappointment that summer was the much publicized film, *The Other Side of Midnight*.

I might also add that Charlie Jones didn't have to worry about getting play dates in Miami or anywhere else when the bids went out on *The Empire Strikes Back*, which was the sequel to *Star Wars*. After the overwhelming success of *Star Wars*, every film buyer in the country wanted to play *The Empire Strikes Back*. I was fortunate enough to open *Empire* exclusively in Miami. That privilege didn't come cheap. I bid $175,000 in one theatre and $125,000 in another—that was a lot of money in 1980.[9]

I learned firsthand that the saying is true: "there are no geniuses in the film business." However, as in gambling, I had to figure out a way to stay on top of my game, as I was determined to keep climbing to the top.

---

9    In 2014, that would be like bidding $500,000 and $355,000.

# THE ACCIDENT

*Things are never so bad they can't be made worse.*
– Humphrey Bogart, *The African Queen*

SEVERAL WEEKS HAD PASSED SINCE Doneata told me about her Christian experience. I must admit that I liked some of the changes I saw in Doneata. It seemed as if she was going out of her way to be more patient and kind with the children and me.

But there were several things that she was doing that did bug me. At times she would leave little Bible leaflets throughout the house—in the bathroom, by the end table at the bed, or by my chair in the living room. And Doneata placed her Christian books—books she always seemed to be buying—out on the table in the den. But the biggest aggravation was when she would change the radio station in my car from talk radio to Christian radio.

I talked to her about every single one of those irritations, and she didn't even get upset. She just said, "You're right, honey. I'm sorry. I'll try to be more sensitive to you about my Christian literature and turn the radio back to the station you had it on when I leave the car."

She was so apologetic that I felt bad about complaining to her. Yes, most of the changes in Doneata I liked, but I wondered how long it would stay this way before she started wanting to pressure me to give up my smoking, gambling, drinking, and other wild ways.

In the months ahead, everything seemed to stabilize, more or less, in the Vaughn home. Maybe it was just because Doneata and I were finally acclimated to our circumstances and surroundings. David had leukemia; Mentora was a strong-willed child; Miami was beautiful, but offered a totally different lifestyle from living in the Carolinas; Wometco was a great company to work for. Still, Wometco was a company that demanded a strong level of performance in a highly competitive theatre market; and I also was very much aware that I was now married to a woman who claimed to be a Christian.

During this time, I became ill. I didn't miss any work, but I just didn't feel well. During a period of about three weeks, I lost about fifteen pounds, had no appetite, and had very little energy. Doneata thought it was time for me to have a check-up, but I wanted to hold off on the check-up until my Wometco company physical came due.

Most days, Marvin and I would car pool when possible. This particular day, however, Marvin was out of town on business, so the day before, I had made arrangements with my secretary to pick me up at the Dadeland Theatre and give me a ride to the office. We were driving down US Highway 1 when, all of a sudden, a car rammed into the back of our car. My secretary slammed on the brakes as we started spinning across the highway. Another car hit us on my side of the car. While I was sore, I didn't feel too badly, and, thankfully, no one else was injured.

After a two-hour delay with the policeman, we hobbled on into work. I went into Eddie's office to give him an update. While I was standing there talking to him, he said, "Larry, take off your coat. I want to look at your side."

Unbeknownst to me at the time, I had badly hurt my right side—it was bruised, swollen, and bleeding.

Eddie said, "That's it! We're going to the hospital. Frieda, call Dr. Ipp. Tell him I have an emergency and ask him where I can meet him."

We met Eddie's personal physician, Dr. Ipp, in the emergency room. Dr. Ipp not only looked at my side but, after making a brief examination, started asking me several questions about my general health. I guess he noticed how pale and sallow I was looking. He said, "Mr. Vaughn, I will put a bandage on your side, and while I have you here, I think it would be a good idea to go ahead and admit you and have some tests run."

I was never given the opportunity to speak. Eddie said, "That's fine. Go ahead and admit Larry. I'll call the office."

I interrupted, "Mr. Stern, don't I have any say in this matter?"

"No, you don't! Just lie there and be quiet."

I replied emphatically, "Yes, sir!"

My room looked more like a hotel room than a hospital room. The furnishings were very nice. I thought, "If I have to be in the hospital, the Miami Heart Institute is the hospital to be in."

Doneata came to see me, and she didn't look well herself. I was very concerned about her. After we talked about the accident and everything Dr. Ipp had said, Doneata commented, "I'm glad you're in here. I'm tired of worrying about you." I convinced her that I was going to be fine and told her to go home and rest.

Dr. Ipp wasted no time in drawing blood and having me go through a battery of tests. The tests were very tiring, and some of them were quite unpleasant to experience. I thought about David, and how he must have felt having to go through similar types of testing.

The next day, Doneata called me and told me she felt worse and was unable to get out of bed. I suggested she ask one of our neighbors to help her with the children. I assumed she had a virus or something. I felt so helpless. I knew Mentora required attention, and David was always in need of special care. I was banking on our neighbors to come to the rescue.

The following evening I called Doneata. She was still struggling. What disturbed me the most about our conversation was when Doneata told me that Wanda Glass was helping out at home. I thought, "Wanda, that's Doneata's Christian friend. Why couldn't Sally Rosen or someone else have helped out?" I knew some sort of payback would be in order, and I didn't want to be indebted to a Christian.

I ended up spending ten long days in the Miami Heart Institute. Dr. Ipp never really diagnosed what was wrong with me. He seemed to think that somehow I had picked up a foreign virus, most likely from someone who had recently been overseas. After thorough testing, though, he felt that the worst was behind me, and I was on the road to recovery.

During those ten days at the Miami Heart Institute, I was able to see Doneata only that first day. The rest of the time she was at home sick in bed. During our nightly phone calls, Doneata kept me up-to-date with the events at home and how, thanks to the Glass family, all our immediate needs were being met. As I feared, I owed a debt of gratitude to her friend Wanda and her family.

Eddie checked me out of the hospital and drove me home. "Larry, Dr. Ipp said you shouldn't work for a couple more days. So I don't want to see you at the office until you and I have talked—say, in three days. You understand?"

"Eddie, before I came to the company, everyone told me how hard you were to work for. When am I going to see that hard side of Eddie Stern?"

Eddie forced a frown, then he turned his head my way as he wrinkled his forehead as if offended and said, "Larry, my boy, you must not believe everything you hear. I've been good for you, just as you've been good for me."

I smiled to myself as I looked out the window, counting the palm trees along the way.

TWENTY-TWO

# THE PAYOFF

*I don't have anything to prove to anybody, which is a lovely place to be.*
– Edward Norton

IT WAS WONDERFUL TO BE home with the family. My agenda was a good one—relax for the next few days with Doneata and the children. Doneata was still under the weather, however, she was feeling better each day.

The very first thing on my to-do list was to send flowers to the Glass family. I thought flowers would be a proper way of saying, "Thank you for your kindness," without having to have any personal contact with them.

Doneata did not have to cook that week, because the women from the church brought us a meal every day. I asked Doneata, "Did you ask Wanda to have meals brought to our home?"

"No, honey, Wanda told me the women in her church wanted to do this for us. She promised that the ladies would bring the meals to the door, but they would not stay and talk."

I thought to myself, "Those people from that church sure give us a lot of attention, seeing that they don't even know us. Moreover, they're even playing by my rules! Hmmm . . ."

The next week, I started feeling guilty that I had not called the Glass family personally to thank them for all they had done for my family during my hospital stay and beyond.

That evening I went into the bedroom to call Charles, Wanda Glass's husband.

"Good evening, this is Larry Vaughn calling."

"Hello, Larry. This is Charles. How are you feeling?"

"Just fine, thank you. I'm getting back to my old self."

"Well, that's wonderful! We have been praying that both you and Doneata will have a quick and complete recovery."

I thought, "I wish he wouldn't start spiritualizing things with all that prayer talk." Charles was saying something. "I'm sorry, what did you say?"

"Wanda just told me to thank you for the flowers. They have been the centerpiece of our living room table."

"Charles, the flowers are the very least that I could do for all that Wanda has done for us. The purpose of this call is to thank you and your family for the overwhelming support you folks have shown to my family during our time of illness. I can't believe all the delicious meals your wife sent to us."

"Larry, those meals were not just from my family. They were also from concerned and caring families in our church."

"So I hear. I would appreciate very much if you would pass on my expression of thanks to the other families involved."

"Yes, I'll be sure to do just that. We are glad we were able to help meet a need in your home. Larry, would you mind if I dropped by to meet you? From everything Wanda has told me about you, I feel like I already know you."

"That would be fine, Charles. I also would like to meet you."

Charles arrived at our apartment the following Tuesday evening. He was a nice-looking man; I guessed his age to be mid-to-late thirties. I noticed that Charles had his Bible with him—the Bible I expected to see. Doneata brought us some coffee and lemon meringue pie. Then she left the room.

I started the conversation. "Charles, tell me about yourself."

"Well, let me see. You know I have a wonderful wife, Wanda. I also have three children: two beautiful girls and a very handsome son. Of course, the three of them got their good looks from their mother." We laughed.

"I work for Eastern Airlines. I spend a lot of time in the air going back and forth from Miami to our New York offices."

I asked, "Are you a pilot?"

"No, sometimes I wish I were. I'm the treasurer of the airline."

I thought, "Really!" I was impressed.

"Outside of my work and my family, I am active in my church. I teach a Sunday school class."

We talked for a good forty-five minutes. Charles asked me all about myself. I tried to sugarcoat some of my experiences in life the best I could, so that he wouldn't think of me as being too much of a heathen.

At eight-thirty Charles said, "Where has the last hour gone?"

I thought to myself, "It has gone by quickly. I've actually enjoyed talking to this guy. He's not your average Joe; he's treasurer of Eastern Airlines. I'm impressed that Charles took the time to visit with me."

"Larry, may I ask a favor of you?"

Reluctantly I nodded as I thought, "This is it—the payoff. He'll want me to go to his church."

"I would be honored if you would consider visiting my Sunday school class. There are only eight other men in the class, and they are all young married men like yourself. We have a time of Bible study. It lasts about forty-five minutes."

"I don't know. You know, I'm not really into church."

"I'm not asking you to go to church. I'm only asking you to visit my Sunday school class. You can leave as soon as the class is over."

"Let me think about it." I shrugged my shoulders as I answered, "Well, who knows? You may have a visitor on Sunday."

"Seeing you would make my day." Then, almost as an afterthought, Charles asked, "Larry, before I go, would you mind if I close out our time together in prayer?"

Charles then proceeded to pray a prayer of thanksgiving to God for having brought the two of us together. Charles also thanked God for answering prayers in meeting the health needs of our family.

When he left, I went into the bedroom.

"Well, honey, how did it go with Charles?" Doneata asked.

"I like him. He's a nice guy. You know he brought his Bible, but he didn't even open it. We just talked the whole hour. I did let him close in prayer, but that was no big deal. He asked me if I would come to his Sunday school class next Sunday."

"And?"

"I told him I would let him know. Doneata, if I go to Sunday school, though, you can forget about me staying for church, because I won't!"

"Honey, if you decide to go, the kids and I will leave after Sunday school with you."

It was great to get back to work. My first week back turned out to be very hectic—trying to catch up on the accumulation of paperwork that had built up during my hospital stay, and returning over two weeks' worth of telephone calls. Eddie, too, was doing double time trying to get everything off his desk, because he and Jerry were planning on taking a trip to Nassau.

Eddie called me into his office to inform me that during his absence his old friend, Joseph E. Levine, would be in Fort Lauderdale meeting with the press and giving interviews on his upcoming Anthony Hopkins film, *Magic*.

Eddie said, "Larry, this is important! I want you to plan to spend some time with Mr. Levine. He will be staying at the Jockey Club. Whatever Joe needs from you, give it to him. As you know, he's a close personal friend of mine."

I told Doneata on Saturday evening that I would plan on attending Sunday school that Sunday. She got excited and said, "Oh, Larry, that is just wonderful!"

I thought, "It sure doesn't take much to make Doneata happy these days."

We walked into the adult Sunday school department right before the bell rang. I had planned it that way. Doneata went to her own class, and Charles motioned for me to come into his classroom. He briefly introduced me to the other men. He proceeded to tell the men that my family and I had moved to Miami from Charlotte and that I was currently employed as the assistant film buyer in the theatre division of Wometco Enterprises. After I was introduced, Charles moved right into the lesson.

I was really too uncomfortable to actually understand anything Charles had to say. I tried to listen while I was there so I wouldn't waste my time, and I hoped that, by listening, time would go by faster. But I was glad when the bell rang, because I knew that the class would end in a matter of minutes.

After the class, Charles thanked me for coming and asked, "Larry, would I be pushing it to ask if I might drop by again this Tuesday evening to visit with you?"

Without giving much thought to what he had just said, I replied, "Sure, Charles."

He extended his hand saying, "Good, I'll see you on Tuesday."

Charles knocked on the door. I greeted him, and after a time of dessert and small talk, he asked, "Larry, have you ever had any interest in knowing God?"

"No interest at all, Charles. I have never felt a need for God or His people in my life. The only reason you are welcome back in my home tonight is because I like and respect you."

"Well then, Larry, let me ask you a question. Do you believe the Bible is the inspired Word of God? That there is only one God and that He has a Son, whose name is Jesus Christ? Or do you believe in some other religion? Or is it that you just believe in nothing?"

"Charles, to be perfectly honest with you, I have never given much thought as to what I believe. I think I believe mostly in myself."

"Well, that's a start. Tell me what you believe about yourself."

"Okay, I believe I am very good at what I do. One day in the not-too-distant future I am going to be rich and able to give my family whatever their hearts desire. Charles, I grew up in poverty. I am now sitting on the crest of wealth. I am a self-made man. I know all that sounds a bit arrogant, but you asked for it. I believe different people at different times in their lives do need God. For example, it happened to my wife recently. Doneata was going through so much with David's leukemia and our daughter Mentora that she needed something extra to draw on. Instead of turning to alcohol or something else, she chose religion. I prefer my gin and tonic." I paused, wondering if I should have shared that last part.

Charles asked, "Larry, what about after this life has been lived? Let's say that God allows you to live sixty more years, and everything you have just predicted comes true. What about your soul when you die? What is going to become of it?"

I smirked at the question and said, "Charles, sixty years is a long way off. Who knows what will happen between now and then?"

Charles said, "Okay, Larry, let's say you don't have sixty years. Let's say your death is tomorrow. Now what about your soul? Where is it going to spend eternity?"

I didn't respond to his question.

"Larry, everything that you say you have at your fingertips I now have. I have wealth, power, a big home, a beautiful wife, and three wonderful children. Did you know that, if God so willed it, I would never see my family again. I could have a heart attack on the way home tonight, or my wife and children could be killed in an automobile accident as we speak. I could lose my job tomorrow, and my house could burn down tonight. The only thing I have that can never be taken away from me is my salvation—my salvation in Jesus Christ. Larry, do you know how I know all that to be true? Because that's what God's Word says is true."

He held his Bible reverently in the palms of his hands. I thought, "He acts as if he held some precious jewel, or that all the knowledge of the world rested in its pages."

Charles continued speaking, "Inside the covers of this old, worn book are sixty-six books that were written by many different men: men who were all writing under the inspiration of the Holy Spirit. Many unsaved men have become Christian men of God while trying to find errors in this book."

He then told me what, while flipping through the TV channels, I had already heard the television preachers say: that you are only a prayer away from having your sins forgiven.

After Charles left I went into the bedroom and told Doneata about our conversation. She smiled but had little to add. Later, I turned out the light and lay there in the darkness of our room. For the first time in my life, I was concerned about what would happen to my soul if I died.

The next week I took Doneata with me to Fort Lauderdale to the Jockey Club to meet the famous producer, Joseph E. Levine.

On the drive to the Jockey Club, Doneata asked, "Okay, tell me once again some of the films Mr. Levine has produced?"

"Sweetheart, just remember two or three of his great ones. Last year, he produced the much anticipated war drama *A Bridge Too Far*, the most expensive independent film ever made. *Bridge* is good conversation for at

*Larry, Doneata, and Joseph E. Levine at the Jockey Club*

least fifteen minutes. As you will recall, Mr. Levine had an all-star cast in *Bridge*. Then there was the classic, *The Lion in Winter*. Plus the 1967 classic, *The Graduate*, and don't forget *Carnal Knowledge*. You can ask him about those. Plus, he was the producer or executive producer on another forty-five films. Eddie and Jerry dearly love him. Doneata, just relax. Eddie said he is very easy to talk to."

Eddie was right. It was truly a wonderful experience to meet the grand old filmmaker and to hear some of his larger-than-life stories. He had a beautiful ocean-front suite, and I spent most of my time drinking Tanqueray and tonics, eating the delicious hors d'oeuvres, and talking films with Mr. Levine. After a couple of hours, I looked over at Doneata and motioned for her to get ready to leave.

Doneata and I told Mr. Levine how much we had enjoyed meeting him. I also told him how I was looking forward to opening his film, *Magic*, during the weeks ahead.

He asked, "Larry, may I ask a special favor of you?"

"Yes, sir! You name it."

"Larry, I would appreciate it very much if you would give me a call during the opening weekend, and maybe you could give me some numbers on how my film is doing, if you're sure it won't be too much of an inconvenience."

"Mr. Levine, it would be my pleasure. Besides, Eddie gave me strict instructions to give Joe Levine anything he wants. And I don't want to get in the doghouse with Eddie."

"No, you don't, Larry. I've been there before!"

We both laughed at the thought of upsetting Eddie Stern.

Jack buzzed me: "Well hello there, buddy—ole pal—ole friend."

"You sure sound chipper. What's up?"

"Well, I received a call from Columbia Pictures publicity informing me that Suzanne Pleshette will be in Fort Lauderdale promoting her latest film, *Hot Stuff*. Has Columbia contacted you about a sneak preview on *Hot Stuff*?"

"Yes, I just set the showing; it's Friday evening at the Dadeland."

"Great! This is one of those producer's sneaks where the studio is looking for audience reaction." Jack hesitated, then continued, "With Miss Pleshette in the lead role, it's bound to get some good feedback." Jack cleared his throat. "Columbia publicity will have a brunch Friday afternoon before the evening screening in Fort Lauderdale. Miss Pleshette requested that Wometco have its film buyer come to the brunch along with Marvin and me. Since Eddie is out of town, will you be sure and make plans to be at the brunch?"

"Will do," I replied.

That Friday afternoon, Jack, Marvin, and I drove up to Fort Lauderdale to meet with Suzanne Pleshette aboard a luxury yacht. The three of us were becoming like the Three Musketeers, since we enjoyed each other's company so much. I noticed that Jack, who was driving, kept looking through his rear-view mirror at me. Then he would look at Marvin through the corner of his eyes. His grip would tighten on the steering wheel, and again he would look back at me. I knew that something was up.

As we entered the marina, Jack got very serious and said, "As soon as we get aboard the yacht, I would appreciate very much if the two of you would give me some breathing room around Miss Pleshette."

He paused, licked his lips, glanced in his rear-view mirror quickly, and then continued. "I have always wanted to meet her. She is one of my favorite actresses, and I love her television program, *The Bob Newhart Show*."

Marvin thought for a moment. Then, in a very professional manner, he looked over at Jack, snapped his fingers, and said very emphatically, "Jack, as soon as we get on board, would you like for Larry and me to jump off the side of the yacht and take a swim in the ocean? Would that give you enough breathing room with Miss Pleshette?"

Marvin was laughing; then I started laughing. I always loved to hear Marvin get going. He would get so tickled that his face would turn red and his eyes would start watering. I wasn't laughing so much at what Marvin had said, but at the way Jack reacted to what he had said. Jack was shaking his head from side to side, and I noticed that his grip on the steering wheel was less aggressive. I knew he felt better since he had told us what was on his mind. He had that look on his face that said, "Marvin is crazy."

Jack said, "Larry, whose idea was it to bring this guy along with us anyway?"

"It was yours, Jack. Don't you remember? You're supposed to be Marvin's boss."

We walked up the ramp to the deck of the yacht. The captain was standing there, all decked out in white, waiting to greet us. Jack introduced himself, Marvin, and me. The captain then ushered us into a stately room. The room was quite large to be on a yacht; however, I thought the yacht looked more like a ship. Inside the room was a plush off-white sofa, which could easily seat up to four people, and across from the sofa, in one corner of the room, was a fully stocked bar. I saw another person all decked in white, standing in the other corner of the room and holding a large silver tray filled with hors d'oeuvres for our enjoyment.

Then Miss Pleshette walked into the room. Marvin and I wanted to be sure to let Jack take the lead, since this was a meeting of special interest to the old fellow, so we hung back. Jack walked toward her to greet her. He extended his hand.

"Hello, Miss Pleshette. I'm Jack Mitchell, Vice President and General Manager of Wometco Theatres. It is a pleasure to meet you."

"Hello, Jack. It is very nice to meet you too. I've heard many good things about Wometco Theatres. I understand Wometco has the best-grossing theatres in Florida." Then Miss Pleshette looked straight past Jack toward Marvin and me and said, in a very sweet, curious tone of voice, "Jack, which one of these men is your film buyer? That's the man I'm looking forward to spending some time with."

As soon as Miss Pleshette made that statement, Marvin got all choked up. He started coughing, and his face got very red. Then before I knew it, he was laughing along with his coughing. Marvin tried to stop, but he couldn't control his laughing. Marvin Reed had just totally embarrassed himself.

Miss Pleshette got an inquisitive look on her face, leaned over toward Jack's ear, and in a loud whisper asked, "Jack, what's wrong with that man? Did I say something funny?"

Jack replied, "No, ma'am. That's Marvin Reed; Marvin was our director of advertising. He's one of those guys who thinks everything is funny."

Then I smiled, wondering whether Marvin caught the *was* in Jack's statement. Miss Pleshette gave Jack a look as if to say, "Okay, I understand. You men don't want to let me in on your private joke." While Marvin was trying to regain his composure, I walked over to Miss Pleshette and introduced myself.

We stayed on the yacht for a couple of hours and had a wonderful time talking with Miss Pleshette. She told us about her upcoming movie, *Hot Stuff,* and made me promise to give Columbia Pictures, the company releasing the film, several play dates. She said that she was confident we would love her film and was looking forward to seeing us later that evening at the premier of her movie. Before we left, she had her publicity agent take several photographs of us as a group, as well as some individual photographs, and promised to have the photographs delivered to our office.

That evening at the Dadeland, I saw Miss Pleshette waving at me. She hurried across the lobby and asked me, "Why, Larry, you're not at work! What are you doing wearing a tie?" She pointed toward my tie and said, "You must remove that tie right now. This is going to be a fun evening, and what man can have fun in a tie?"

*Jack Mitchell, Suzanne Pleshette, and Larry on the yacht*

I started removing my tie as I introduced Miss Pleshette to Doneata. The evening was a special memory for Doneata and me, because we had the privilege of watching *Hot Stuff* with Miss Pleshette. As far as my true feelings about the film (it was just a picture), I kept my thoughts to myself, because I didn't want to spoil Jack's fun. After all, because Miss Pleshette was in it, the film was one of the best movies *he* had ever seen.

On the day the promised photographs arrived, one photograph of Miss Pleshette and Jack was proudly hung on Jack's office wall. Whenever I saw that picture, I thought of the "was" in Jack's comment to Marvin, and I wondered how Miss Pleshette would have reacted if Marvin and I had really jumped into the ocean!

Jack walked into my office and asked, "You ever met Walter Matthau?"

I looked up from surveying the weekend numbers, as I replied, "Yes, I met him back in the early 1970s. I happened to be in Hollywood at Paramount when he was filming *Plaza Suite*. I really enjoyed meeting him."

"Good. I have a surprise for you: Mr. Matthau will be in Miami this Thursday, and he wants to use our screening room to watch his latest film, *Casey's Shadow*. Will you take care of the arrangements?"

"Jack, it will be my pleasure. Doneata will enjoy meeting Mr. Matthau as well."

Doneata and I arrived at the screening room around 7:30 p.m., and Mr. Matthau arrived a few minutes later. I was surprised that he came alone. I introduced Mr. Matthau to Doneata and mentioned to him that he and I had met years earlier. He acted as if he remembered me, but I wasn't so sure. It's hard to tell when an actor is, you know, acting.

Doneata and Mr. Matthau hit it off right from the start. They talked a few minutes before the screening, and then, when it was time to take our seats, the two of them sat together and continued their conversation. I sat in my usual seat on the back row where I had a buzzer to communicate with the projectionist in the booth.

I noticed throughout the movie that the two of them kept talking with each other. I smiled to myself as I thought, "If we were in a theatre, someone would have to tell those two to hold it down!"

When the film ended and we had said our goodbyes, Doneata, almost as an afterthought insisted, "Walter, I must have your autograph."

The three of us stood there searching for a piece of paper, but none was to be found. Mr. Matthau came to her rescue when he opened his checkbook and took out a blank check. He wrote across the check VOID, and then he signed it. He then gave Doneata his famous grin and went on his way.

That evening, Doneata and I had walked into the screening room with only one of us being a big fan of Walter Matthau. When we left, I wasn't sure who was the bigger fan, Doneata or me.

# TWENTY-THREE

# THE DOVE IN FLIGHT

*Today, I consider myself the luckiest man on the face of the earth.*
– Gary Cooper, *The Pride of the Yankees*

CHARLES GLASS CALLED ME TO tell me about their new preacher. "Larry, I know you've never stayed after Sunday school for church, but I just want to let you know that our new preacher, Pastor Carey, will be in the pulpit this Sunday. It would be wonderful to see you and your family in church this special Sunday. Don't give me an answer now, just think about it."

Because of my friendship with Charles, I agreed to go.

The next Sunday I sat in a stiff pew, wondering why I agreed to go to church in the first place. I really didn't care about seeing the new pastor. When Pastor Carey walked up to the podium, I was immediately taken aback by his appearance. He wore brown alligator shoes and an off-white, western-cut, tight-fitting tailored suit. His shirt was expensive, with large French cuffs, and his tie was silk. I thought, "That tie seems a bit much for a preacher, but I guess it goes perfectly with his western attire." He had long blond hair that he combed straight back, without a part in it. I guessed him to be in his early forties. He had the chest of an athlete and probably a thirty-six-inch waist. With no disrespect to a South Dallas

183

used car salesman, that's what the preacher reminded me of. I wondered, "Now what kind of a car is the preacher driving? I would bet cold hard cash that he drives either a Lincoln or a Cadillac."

Pastor Carey preached for about twenty minutes. During his message, he kept walking very quickly across the stage, going back and forth. He had the audience laughing and crying. Everyone but me seemed to be having a good time. I thought to myself, "This guy is not a preacher. He's an entertainer."

As we left the church, I told Doneata, "Let's go by the pastor's parking space. I'm sure he has an assigned space."

Doneata asked, "Why do you want to do that?"

"Oh, I don't know. I'm just curious about something."

If I had made a bet, I would have won. The preacher drove a shiny, two-toned, red-and-white Cadillac Eldorado.

The experience I had that Sunday with the new preacher turned me off from ever wanting to go back to Sunday school or church. I thought, "I have seen enough movies to know how a preacher is supposed to look, dress, and act." I had gone to church that day expecting to meet a preacher who looked and acted like Spencer Tracy, or maybe Gary Cooper. What I found, however, was someone who looked and acted like Elvis!

Seeing Pastor Carey that morning reminded me of years earlier when I had tickets to see Elvis live in concert. Doneata didn't have any interest in going to see Elvis. After much persuasion, I had finally talked her into going with me. There were other good singers at the concert, and we enjoyed their performances. However, when Elvis had taken the stage, Doneata and I were in awe at his incredible voice. At the conclusion of the concert, Elvis sang "How Great Thou Art." Doneata and I both had goosebumps that evening. We were both convinced that we had just witnessed a miracle; while he didn't look like an angel, when Elvis sang, it was if heaven opened and an angel's voice was heard on Earth that day.

After that first Sunday with the new preacher, it seemed as if on every Sunday morning I woke up in a bad mood. I went through the apartment making excessive noise, looking for things to complain about. I found myself continually being short and rude with Doneata, and especially with the children. Half the time I ended up staying home from church.

One Sunday I decided I would go to church. While getting dressed, for no reason in particular, I became exceptionally rude with the family. Doneata came into the bedroom, shut the door, and said, "Larry, why don't you just stay home from church. No one is forcing you to go to Sunday school or church. Honestly, it would be best if you didn't go in the disposition that you're in."

I shot back at her very sarcastically, "Well, sweetheart, that's just fine with me. You and the kids go play church. I'm going up to the pool to get some sun and read the paper. When you get home, I might be here or I might not." On that note, I changed clothes, took the newspaper, and left.

When I got to the pool, no one was there. It seemed that on Sundays when the Christians were at church, everyone else chose to sleep in. I sat down at one of the empty tables and lit a cigarette. I looked around. It was a beautiful day. It was too bad I felt so miserable. I tried reading the paper, but I couldn't. I was too upset to concentrate. I was miserable on the inside.

I tried to analyze the situation. "What's wrong with me?" I thought. "Every weekend is becoming a bad weekend. I wish I had to work on Sundays, so I wouldn't have to decide whether to go to church or not. I've always been a black-and-white kind of guy. I just need to figure out the root of my problem before I let it ruin another beautiful weekend. Why do I seem to be at my worst when it's time to make the decision to go or not to go to church? I like Charles, and I also like supporting Doneata. And it's a lot of work for her to get the kids to church by herself. I guess it just bothers me that I have to sit under someone who looks and acts like Elvis every Sunday. So for now, I am going to make the decision to go to church. Yes, I guess it's the right thing to do."

I left the pool and went home, and started trying to figure out a way to get out of the doghouse with Doneata and the children. In honor of my decision, I humored myself by playing an Elvis record. When the family returned home from church, I had lunch on the table and a new countenance about me. I apologized for my conduct earlier in the day, and we ended up having a good Sunday afternoon together as a family.

For the next few weeks I went to Sunday school and church every Sunday. It was nice not to have to make a decision about whether or not to go, but I was still uncomfortable with Pastor Carey. I guess there are some people who just rub you the wrong way, and he always rubbed me the wrong way. I remember one Sunday morning, Pastor Carey made this statement from the pulpit: "I have noticed how hard it is for you people to get to church on time on Sunday. It amazes me that you men can get to the office on time Monday through Friday, but when it comes to getting to church on time on Sunday—well, that's another story."

That particular Sunday we were late to church because, just as we were about to leave home, Mentora had spit up on my shirt, and I had to change shirts before we could go. On the way out of church I stopped to speak with Pastor Carey. I said, "You know, Pastor Carey, you're right in what you said about men not getting to church on time. I can get to work on time Monday through Friday with no problem, but I admit I do struggle to get to church on time on Sunday. Do you know what the difference is?"

He took a hard look at me and said, "No, tell me."

"Well, the difference is this—on Monday through Friday, my wife and children don't have to be up, bathed, dressed, fed, and in the car to ride with me to be at the office by 8:30. If they did, I'd probably be late for work too." The good Pastor Carey gave me his artificial smile, and I left. I thought, "That smile of his annoys me greatly. I'd like to knock his teeth in just once. Now, now, Larry, it's not good to think such things of a pastor. Behave yourself."

Overall, things were going well in the Vaughn household. David still had to have his weekly trips back and forth to the hospital, but he was doing much better than a lot of the other children with leukemia were doing. That was one of the sad parts about taking those trips to Jackson Memorial. Occasionally, David would have a brief time away from Jackson, but when they returned to resume his treatments, Doneata would often notice that a child they had met was missing. And when Doneata would ask one of the nurses about the child, she would be told that the child had relapsed and died shortly thereafter. Tragically, we saw many families fall apart as they watched their children die during those years that David was being treated at Jackson Memorial Hospital.

Meanwhile, at Wometco, it was business as usual. Eddie and I stayed busy working on bids, trying to figure out how much such-and-such a picture was going to do in a given market. Florida had what was called "blind bidding," which meant a film company could offer their picture out on bid before it was ever made. Many times, a company would bid a picture while it was still in production. That meant all we had to go by was a title, the cast, the producer, director, and a synopsis of the film. We might have to put up several hundred thousand dollars on a picture, sight unseen, and this could be six or nine months before the picture was even set to open! When we would finally have the opportunity to see the picture that we had put up so much money on, it might turn out to be a success—or it could very well be a flop.

So film buying is definitely not for the fainthearted. But as a gambling man, this was the aspect of my job that I loved the most; I got to gamble as if I were in a high stakes poker game except, instead of having to put up my own money—I got to put up my company's money! I had the best of both worlds.

On the flip side, we made some cheap deals going in, when bidding for the rights to play what looked like little films. I remember one of these "little" films in particular. It was the story of an alien who came to earth, spent some time with some kids, and then found a way to return home—the name of that little hidden jewel was *E.T.*

Cheap deals on a film were deals where we didn't have to commit up-front to large guarantees of money, high weekly minimum percentage terms, and lengthy playtime. In actuality, the majority of the box-office gross goes to the studios—anywhere from fifty to sixty percent, depending on the size of the picture. Since the lion's share of the box office receipts go to the film companies, the theatre owner has to rely on concession sales to make a profit. That is why, today, a moviegoer pays fifteen dollars or more for a Coke, candy bar, and box of popcorn.

Yes, Eddie and I had a grand time working together. He would want to put the farm up on some crazy hunch, and I would try to talk him out of it—or vice versa. We complemented each other. I enjoyed working under a man who could lay out, sight unseen, hundreds of thousands of dollars for a picture, go home and sleep like a baby, and then wait several months to see if he won or lost. Eddie had a saying, "If Wometco can find somebody who can run film buying better than I can, then why are they paying me all this money and not him?" Eddie believed that too. As Eddie told me the first day we met, humility wasn't one of his stronger suits!

I received a call from Royce Brimage, the Southern Division Manager of Paramount Pictures. Royce said, "Larry, I just found out that John Frankenheimer will be in Miami next weekend. He wants to screen *Black Sunday* for Joe Robbie, the Miami Dolphin players, and their families. We would like a private screening of the film, on Saturday morning in the 163rd Street Theatre."

"No problem, Royce. I will alert operations and be sure they have plenty of popcorn and Coke for the guests."

Joe Robbie was at that time the owner of the Miami Dolphins. The closing scene of *Black Sunday* had been shot at the Orange Bowl during a Miami Dolphins game.

On Saturday morning, I was at the theatre, as I wanted to see *Black Sunday* for myself. It had all the makings of a big picture: a big-name director, Frankenheimer; a big-name star, Robert Shaw; plus it was filmed in our own backyard, Miami. After seeing *Black Sunday*, I thought it was everything it was built up to be. Paramount even wanted the film buyers to see it before they bid for it, in order to whet their appetite.

Eddie was out of town the Saturday we screened *Black Sunday*, so when Eddie returned to Miami, I filled him in on the picture. "Eddie, this is going to be the big one of the season, especially in Miami. I want to go after *Black Sunday* in the Miracle."

"What kind of a figure do you have in mind?" Eddie asked.

"Eddie, I want to tie it up. The other guys are going to have their tongues hanging out for this one. In the Miracle, with 1,500 seats, I want to guarantee $150,000."[10]

"Ouch, Larry! That's a lot of dough. Do you really think we need to go that strong?"

"Yes, sir. I do."

He paused a moment, frowned and said, "Go ahead, it's only money. Send your bid in to Paramount."

A few days later I knocked on Eddie's office door. "Eddie, I need to talk to you."

"Sit down, Larry. What's up?"

"We lost *Black Sunday* in the Miracle."

Eddie jerked the bid rejection letter out of my hand. He looked at it, and then he cursed.

I exhaled a sigh of frustration as I said, "It looks like General Cinema took their two theatres, the Riviera and the Westchester, and knocked out our bid in the Miracle."

"Frieda," Eddie yelled, "get Al Stout on the phone." Al Stout was the Florida branch manager for Paramount Pictures.

A moment later, Frieda barked back, "Mr. Stout is on line two."

"Al, how could you reject the Miracle's bid on *Black Sunday* and award it to those two crap houses?" Eddie cursed again.

Al was calm in his reply. "Eddie, we had to go with the best bids." He paused, "I'm sorry, Eddie. Your bid came in second."

Eddie slammed the phone back on its receiver. He examined the rejection letter again. He then held up his finger and gave me a look as if he knew something that I didn't know. While nodding his head he winked at me and said, "We got screwed."

Eddie's next call surprised me.

"Frieda, call over and ask if the Colonel can see me."

Eddie spent the next hour with Colonel Wolfson. I thought it was odd for him to alert the Colonel to our problem, because Eddie was known for keeping a tight lid on the film department. However, this was the maddest

---

10   In 2014 dollars, equivalent of a bid worth almost $600,000.

I had ever seen Eddie. When he returned from meeting with the Colonel, I was taken aback by what he had to say. Colonel Wolfson had agreed with Eddie's argument, and he had asked Eddie and one of Wometco's attorneys to fly to Jacksonville, which was the branch city out of which the studios licensed film for Florida, to meet with Al Stout in person and insist on inspecting General Cinema's bids. Eddie met with Al, who in turn presented Eddie's request to his superiors, and Paramount agreed to allow Eddie and the Wometco attorney to review General Cinema's bids.

The Riviera and the Westchester had each bid $77,500 and twelve weeks playtime. Their combined $155,000 bid was $5,000 higher than the Miracle's $150,000 bid with twelve weeks playtime, and both theatres had requested clearance over Wometco's Miracle Theatre.

Eddie suspected that General Cinema had knowledge of our bid before submitting theirs, but there was nothing else he could do. At least General Cinema had been forced to pay top dollar to play *Black Sunday* in their two theatres.

*Black Sunday* turned out to be the disappointment of the season. General Cinema's Riviera Theatre lost approximately $50,000 of their $77,500 guarantee, as did the Westchester, so Wometco actually won by losing.

But the story didn't end there. While on a business trip to Jacksonville several weeks after the disappointing opening of *Black Sunday*, Eddie again stopped by Al Stout's office. When Al saw Eddie come in, he smiled, pushed a chair back from his desk, and motioned for Eddie to have a seat. Al then gave Eddie a sly grin as he said, "You see, Eddie: sometimes you don't know who your friends really are!"

When Eddie told me the story, I thought about the possible irony in Al Stout's statement. And I also thought to myself, "Larry, you just dodged a $150,000 bullet with your name on it. Somebody up there must be watching out for you."

Frieda Goldberg, Eddie's secretary, banged on the men's room door: "Mr. Vaughn, would you please hurry up! Mr. Stern is on the phone and wants to speak with you."

I opened the door and attempted to ignore Miss Goldberg's haughty stare. She acted as if my bathroom break was robbing Wometco of valuable work time. I often wondered how Eddie tolerated Frieda's behavior. Eddie and I both knew, though, that her cantankerous manner was more of an act than anything else. In actuality, Wometco was the only family that Frieda had left to call her own.

Eddie was in New York City in a meeting with Norman Levy, Columbia Pictures' President of Distribution. Our bids were due on *Close Encounters of a Third Kind*—the much anticipated film directed by Steven Spielberg. Industry scuttlebutt had pegged *Close Encounters* as the big holiday release film of 1977.

I picked up the phone, "Hello, Eddie."

Eddie sounded depressed. "Larry, I knew the other guys would go after this picture big, but I had no idea just how big!" He paused, and then he said, "Norman showed me the bids. If I hadn't seen them, I am not sure I would have believed it. General Cinema bid heavy to play *Encounters* exclusive in South Miami."

I interrupted, "Eddie, you didn't pass on the film, did you?"

"Larry, when I initially saw the bids, I told Norman I would pass playing the film in Miami—period!"

Before I could respond to that grim statement, Eddie said, "Norman looked at me and said, 'I don't understand you, Eddie. You play all my crap, and then, when I finally get a big picture, you pass on playing it.'"

There was a moment of dead silence.

I asked "So, where are we now?"

"It's another *Black Sunday* scenario." Eddie muttered. "Remember, we lost Paramount Pictures' *Black Sunday* on a $150,000 bid. General Cinema had the better bid, and what happened? They grossed peanuts. Now, General Cinema is forcing us to pay the piper if we want to play *Close Encounters*."

"Eddie, are you saying we have to cough up $150,000 to play the film?"

"Precisely, a $150,000 guarantee and sixteen weeks is what it will take to play the picture at the Dadeland Twin. Larry, we both know *Close Encounters* is not going to lay an egg like *Black Sunday* did. But, we also know that *Close Encounters* was not filmed in Miami at the Orange Bowl. Yes, it is a good film, but not a great film. And I agree with you: the film critics, most likely, will not be kind to *Encounters*."

I interrupted again, "Yes, but Eddie, *Close Encounters* is an audience film. Word of mouth should carry the picture."

Then Eddie abruptly interrupted. "The question is: will word of mouth carry the picture sixteen weeks and get us our dough back?"

"I don't know."

"Well, Norman has stepped across the hall for a quick meeting," Eddie continued, "when he returns, I have to give him our answer." He paused, and then, he asked the question as if he already knew the answer: "You want to take the deal, don't you?"

Without a moment's hesitation, I emphatically stated, "I do!"

I could hear Eddie's frustration as his heavy breathing echoed into the phone. "Well, after all, it's only money." He cursed, and then he reluctantly said, "I guess I will take the deal."

Well, Eddie and I were wrong about the critics not liking the film. *Close Encounters* received both rave reviews and box office success; it was the number two film in 1977. The top grossing film of 1977 was, of course, the mega-film *Star Wars*. And the top gross in Florida on *Close Encounters* came out of none other than Wometco's Dadeland Twin Theatre!

It was a brisk Sunday morning in February of 1978; the alarm clock buzzed at 7:00 a.m. I got up, went straight to the kitchen, and made a pot of coffee. While the coffee was perking, I lit a cigarette and went outside for the newspaper. At 7:30 everyone was out of bed and at the breakfast table. I commented to the kids, "Let's move right along. We don't want to be late to church."

Later, on the way out of church, Doneata said, "Mentora and I have to stop by the ladies room." While waiting on them, I casually walked over to the display table in the lobby and picked up one of the many tracts that were lying there. Without thinking, I put the tract in my shirt pocket, and then I just stood there in the lobby waiting on Doneata and Mentora.

When we arrived home, I was met with the wonderful aroma of the roast cooking in the oven. Sunday lunch was always my favorite meal of the week. Doneata would do most of the cooking for Sunday on Saturday afternoon. By Sunday I was always starving, just thinking about the rump roast, mashed potatoes, and all the trimmings.

After lunch, Doneata went to the bedroom for her Sunday afternoon nap, David went outside to play with some of the neighborhood kids, and Mentora was in her crib sleeping. I finished up the lunch dishes and then went into the living room. I sat on the sofa enjoying the moment.

When I pulled out my cigarettes from my shirt pocket, I noticed the tract I had picked up earlier at church. It was a small blue tract with a small picture on the front of a dove in flight. It took only a few minutes for me to read through it in its entirety. That little tract asked a very personal question that I had been asked before, but this time, for some unknown reason, it had my undivided attention. "Have you been born again? Have you experienced the spiritual rebirth Jesus said was absolutely necessary for entrance into heaven? This is the one thing, according to the Word of God, that will determine your eternal destiny."

I knew at that very moment what I had always known to be true—that I was an unsaved man. I knew that if I died that day I would spend eternity in hell. I continued reading from the tract. "The moment we open our hearts to the Lord Jesus and place our complete trust in Him—and Him alone—as our Savior, God promises to forgive our sins."

I sat there on my sofa with tears streaming down my face wondering, "Why has it taken me so long to understand what a wretch I have been?"

I got down on my knees and prayed a prayer and asked God to forgive me of my sins, to put a new heart in me, and to give me a desire to be more like His Son. That afternoon I became a Christian.

I went into the bedroom and woke Doneata up from her nap. I told her the good news.

"Doneata, your husband is a Christian."

# "LIFE SLIPS BY"

*The difference between a hero and a coward is one step sideways.*
– Gene Hackman

I WAS ELATED TO BE a Christian. I called Charles and told him the good news.

He said, "Larry, I felt like it was only a matter of time before you gave up the struggle. I knew God was dealing with you. You are now my brother, my brother in Christ."

Monday morning, first thing, I went over to Marvin's office. Marvin held up his coffee cup and said, "It's about time you get to work. I'm already on my second cup."

I laughed, "Marvin, I'm glad that it's you who has to be here early on Mondays and not me. Okay, listen, I'm not screening today. Let's get Jack and have some Cuban food for lunch. I have something I want to tell the two of you."

"Is everything okay?"

"Yeah, this is not bad news. It's good news. I'll tell you and Jack all about it at lunch. Buzz me when you're ready to go."

I walked over to Eddie's office to see how his morning was going. We talked about his weekend.

"Eddie, before we get busy let me tell you what happened to me this weekend."

He looked up from his receipts, gave me a pleasant smile, and said, "Sit down and tell me about it."

"Eddie, yesterday the most wonderful thing happened to me. I became a Christian."

Eddie had one of those "you-don't-say" expressions on his face. "You did?"

"Yes, sir, I most certainly did. Right in my living room at home I surrendered my life to Jesus Christ."

Eddie seemed interested. He said, "Larry, did you know I used to have a leadership position in the Presbyterian Church?"

I was really taken aback. I replied, "No, Eddie, I thought you were Jewish."

"I am, but my first wife was from the Carolinas, and she was a Christian. When our children were little, I used to go with her and the children to the Presbyterian Church. There was a period of time where I was quite active in the church."

"Well, Eddie, why do you now go to the synagogue and practice the Jewish faith?"

"Because I divorced the Christian woman and married a Jewish woman." Eddie gave me a silly grin and laughed when he said, "I guess you might say the woman that I am married to has a lot to do with what religion I believe." He thought a moment and then said, "Well, Larry, I am glad you and the family have found yourself a church."

Frieda stuck her head in the door, looking haughtily at both of us, as if we were cheating the company out of valuable time and money. "Mr. Stern, do you want to talk with Colonel Wolfson? He is waiting on line two." I felt that was my cue to get to work.

Later, while walking down Miami Avenue with Jack and Marvin on the way to lunch, I noticed that Jack's thoughts seemed to be a thousand miles away. I asked, "Jack, how's your day going?"

"Larry, they have me wearing too many hats around here. Stanley informed me this morning that I have to be in Japan in two weeks. It looks like our wax museum needs an overhaul. And guess who gets the project?"

I spoke up, "I didn't even know we had a wax museum in Japan."

"Larry, the company has so much going on that I can't keep up with what we have just bought or just sold. We have had the museum for some time now. I guess Eddie or Stanley failed to mention it to you."

I thought to myself, "I wonder if Walter Powell (my pal at New World Pictures who had recommended that Eddie hire me) knows that Wometco owns a wax museum in Japan." Then I responded to Jack, "How long are you expected to be in Japan?"

"Three weeks. Three long weeks."

We got to the restaurant and placed our orders. Marvin said, "Okay, Larry. Give us this good news you were talking about. I'm having a miserable day."

Jack interrupted, "You're having a miserable day? I need to go to Japan like I need a hole in my head. I don't know how I am going to get all the work done that needs to be done."

I said, "Fellas, take it easy. That's why you two get paid the big bucks, because you're so good at what you do."

Marvin said, "Oh, shut up! You and Eddie make all the money, and Jack and I do all the work!"

Jack chimed in, "You're right, Marvin. We should have been film buyers instead of gophers."

"Well, I had something important that I wanted to share with my two best friends, but now I'm not going to do it because you've hurt my feelings."

Marvin stood up, reached into his back pocket, and took out his handkerchief. He started pretending to wipe tears out of his eyes. Then he reached over and put both his hands on my shoulders. "I'm so sorry."

I looked around the room and wondered what all the other people must have been thinking right then, but of course Marvin was never one to care what other people thought. The food came, and Marvin divided the beans, rice, bananas, steak, and fries among the three of us, and we started to eat.

While eating, Jack said, "All joking aside, Larry. What did you want to tell us?"

I laid my fork down, took a sip of tea, and said, "The most wonderful thing happened to me yesterday. I became a Christian."

That statement caught Marvin's attention, as Marvin had shared with me before that he was a Christian. I could tell Marvin was all ears, but I wasn't sure about Jack's reaction. He continued eating while I was talking. I told them exactly how God had been working in my life and how, finally, on Sunday I gave up control of my life and surrendered my life to Jesus Christ.

When I finished talking, Marvin said, "Well, I would have never guessed that's what you wanted to tell us—not the Larry Vaughn I know. Hmmm, the anti-Christian, 'Mr. Independent Larry Vaughn,' surrendering his life to Jesus Christ! Larry, I am happy for you. I can't wait to tell Sadie."

Jack chimed in, "That is good news, Larry. I'm also happy for you." Turning to Marvin, he asked, "I don't think the meat was as good today as it usually is. Marvin, was your meal okay?"

Marvin laughed, "Jack, didn't you just hear what Larry said? This is a big day for him. I don't know if talking about food is appropriate at the moment."

Jack looked up innocently, "I am truly happy for you, Larry. I was just wondering if your food was as good as usual."

Marvin shook his head. "Larry, Jack just doesn't comprehend the magnitude of the moment."

Jack rolled his eyes.

I smiled as I replied, "My meal was great!"

Pastor Carey cornered me one Saturday morning during a church workday. Of course, the first thing I noticed was how the pastor was one to dress up, even for a so-called workday. He wore freshly pressed jeans (a bit on the tight side), expensive cowboy boots, a thick black belt with a three-inch-thick silver buckle, and an off-white western shirt. His long blond hair was combed back with not a single strand out of place. I thought to myself, "The only thing missing is a horse named Trigger."

"Brother Vaughn, I have wanted to talk to you."

He smiled at me while taking my arm.

"I've seen that smile before," I thought. "I need to try to appreciate it a little more—the smile, that is. Yes, as a Christian now, I should like my pastor's insincere smile. However, if I told myself that I liked it . . . well, to be frank, I'd be telling a lie."

He was speaking, "No, it won't take long. Why don't the two of us go over there and sit on the bench for a few minutes."

We made small talk a few minutes before he got around to what he really wanted to say.

"Brother Vaughn, you are now a Christian. The Bible tells us that once we become a Christian those old things—our old nature—die, and all things become new." He paused for emphasis, "Brother Vaughn, are those old things dying with you?"

"Why yes. I think so. My language is certainly cleaned up. I used to swear all day every day at work, but I don't anymore. Well, I have slipped on occasion, but the Lord knows I'm trying."

"What about your cigarette smoking? Are you trying to do anything about stopping?"

"Pastor Carey, I have tried to stop smoking on and off for the better part of three years now. It seems that whenever I try to cut back on my smoking I get nervous and actually smoke more."

"Brother Vaughn, your smoking is a terrible witness to other Christians and to those people who are unsaved who know that you are a Christian. You should really pray about that and stop that filthy habit."

I didn't like what he just said, but I nodded in agreement.

He crossed his leg, wiped some dust off of the top of his pointed-toe boot, and said, "Brother Vaughn, you're not going to like what I am about to say, but as your pastor and because I love you and want God's best for you, I am going to say it anyway."

As he started to talk, I felt a gust of wind lift my hair from its resting position. I put my fingers through my hair. I then looked at Pastor's hair. "Amazing," I thought. "Not one of his hairs moved against the force of the wind. I wonder what he uses on his hair. I bet it takes him longer than his wife to get dressed in the mornings. Now, now, Larry, first it was his smile, now his hair."

Pastor Carey looked at me as if to read my reaction to what he just said.

"I'm sorry. What did you say?" I responded.

"I think you should quit your job and get in another line of work. Christian men have no business messing with movies."

I thought, "What! I must have missed something while thinking about his hair." I stood up and said, "Thank you, Pastor Carey, for your suggestions. Is there anything else?"

He then stood and replied, "No, Brother Vaughn, that has been weighing very heavy on my heart, and I wanted to share it with you."

"Well, I guess I'd better get back to those weeds because I'll have to be leaving in a little while. I'll see you tomorrow, Pastor Carey."

For some reason weeds sounded wonderful. "At least weeds are susceptible to the wind," I thought. "I don't like things being so fixed that even the wind is unable to play its natural role."

I got off to myself and started feeling very frustrated. I am sure Pastor Carey would have been quick to tell me I was "sinning in my heart." I was thinking terrible things about him. I knew he was probably right about the smoking part. As far as his statement that Christian men have no business messing with movies, well, I felt he had no business messing with my business!

The following Friday night Doneata and I went to the Dadeland Theatre. There was a long line of people outside the theatre waiting to get in to see the 10:00 p.m. showing of a movie. As I walked past the line, going up to the entrance of the theatre, I saw familiar faces—the good Pastor Carey and his wife.

In light of our recent conversation, I stopped dead in my tracks and asked, "Pastor and Mrs. Carey, how are you doing?"

He wasn't even embarrassed for me to find him standing there waiting to go in and see an R-rated movie.

He said, "Hello, Brother and Mrs. Vaughn. We have heard that the acting is so good in this film that we thought we would take a night out and see the movie that everyone is talking about."

I thought to myself, "How dare you tell me to leave the business I love, when you are standing in line supporting the movie business yourself?" Doneata and I left them and went on into the theatre.

Within six months, Pastor Carey got caught in some indiscretions with several women in the church. The deacon board asked him to resign, and he left the church.

After my weekend, it was great to be back at work. Eddie Stern called me into his office. "Larry, can you free yourself up to be in Atlanta next Friday afternoon? Warner Brothers is having a private dinner and a producer's screening of a yet-to-be-released Burt Reynolds film. Warner is having some of their home office boys fly in from LA. I'm not sure, but I think Burt Reynolds is scheduled to be at the dinner. I think it important that you plan to be there to represent Wometco."

"Sure, Eddie, I will plan to be there."

Sitting in my seat on the jet bound for Atlanta, I let my mind start to wander. Looking out the window, I thought about how the church is upside-down. The men wanted Pastor Carey to leave, and the women wanted him to stay. What are the odds? Here I was, a new Christian, and my church was without a pastor, and in the process of a split. Pastor Carey had always given me mixed emotions. But for now, the popular saying rang true: "Elvis has left the building." And in all honesty, I was relieved he was gone.

I knew that I needed to have my family in church. I didn't think we had been but once in the last month. I was glad to be on a plane going to Atlanta. I decided I would take the opportunity to unwind and enjoy my trip.

Roger Hill picked me up at the Ritz Carlton in Buckhead, and we rode together to the restaurant. Roger was the Florida branch manager for Warner Brothers and, like me, was in his early thirties.

Roger looked over at me, "Listen, Larry. Here's what the two of us are going to do. Let's not eat anything at this dinner. Knowing Warner Brothers, they will probably serve steak and lobster. Larry, you can get steak and lobster in Miami. I want to take you to the best hamburger joint in the world—the Varsity."

When Roger said, "The Varsity," a memory from years gone by flashed across my mind. I thought of the Varsity in Athens, Georgia, where my mother and I used to eat two meals every weekend. I replied, "Roger, I have eaten at the Varsity probably more times than you have, except I used to go to the Varsity in Athens."

"Well, then I don't have to waste any time selling you on it. Are you game to do it? Now remember, Vaughn, no eating at the dinner. Just pick through your salad and no more than two bites of your meal."

"Can I have some popcorn during the movie?"

"Absolutely not, you are not to eat or drink anything during the screening."

"Roger, you're starting to sound like my mother. She would always worry about my snacking and not being hungry at dinner."

"Well, the difference between your mother and me is that she would spank you when you didn't listen. If you disobey me, I won't sell you any movies."

We both laughed at the thought.

The dinner was a typical Warner Brothers dinner. We started out with cocktails and conversation. Everyone was introduced to each other. After the dinner, we all walked across the parking lot to the theatre where the screening was to be held. After the screening, Roger looked over at me and winked as if to say, "It's party time." I went over and gave my thoughts and suggestions on the film to Bob Motley, the Warner Brothers division manager. Then I decided to go outside and smoked a cigarette while waiting on Roger.

About ten o'clock, Roger and I were finally on our way to the Varsity. Roger said, "I don't know about you, but I'm taking my tie off. You don't need anything but an appetite where we're going."

I did the same. During the drive to the Varsity, we talked about the film—what we thought it would do in a given market, and about Warner's upcoming releases. When we got to the Varsity, we loaded up on burgers and fries.

During the ride back to the hotel, things got quiet. I think it was because we were so full from our overindulgence of eating. After a few minutes Roger asked me, "Larry, what's this I hear going around film row that you have become a Christian? I've had two or three guys ask me, 'Roger, have you heard about Vaughn? He's gone and got religion!'"

You could have knocked me over with a feather! That was the last thing I was expecting to come out of Roger's mouth. I hesitated before I said anything. Then I said, "Yeah, I've decided it's time to settle down. I've got a wife and two kids. I've been burning the candle on both ends most of my life. I think it's time for me to get into church."

"Larry, why did you decide to become a Christian? Tell me more about it."

I was tired and full. I had probably drunk too much liquor and wine earlier, so I didn't want to talk about things of God. I was trying to use this trip to get away from the church and church-related problems in Miami. I responded, "Roger, sometime I'll tell you all about what I believe and why I believe in what I believe, but not now. I'm too tired to get into anything heavy tonight." We dropped the discussion at that and returned to the hotel.

I never saw Roger Hill after that night. Shortly thereafter, Roger was critically burned in a hotel fire in Boston. He spent his last few days on this earth in an intensive care room, where his body was charred black beyond recognition. When I heard the news, my thoughts went straight back to that night in Atlanta driving on I-85, and Roger asking me to share with him my faith. Yes, I remember it well. I was too tired—I was too full—I was too drunk!—to care. As soon as I heard the news, I called Roger's office and asked his secretary if there was any way the hospital would allow visitors. She told me that only the immediate family was allowed to be with him, and that in his condition he was not expected to live very long.

Roger died a few days later. The many people in the film community who knew Roger mourned the loss of such a fine young man at such an early age.

In May of 1981, Eddie called me from France. He was at the Cannes Film Festival, one of his favorite annual activities. "Larry, I couldn't wait until I returned home to tell you about a film I screened yesterday. The name of it is *Chariots of Fire*. Larry, you are gonna love this picture. It's about your kind of people!"

I interrupted. "Ummm, what do you mean my kind of people?"

Eddie laughed as he explained, "We'll, it's about a Christian," he paused, ". . . and a Jew! When the word gets out on this picture, it's going to stretch out and play. Call Warner Brothers and find out when *Chariots* is set to be released in Florida. Larry, we are going after this one. Oh, and the music is fantastic! Hugh Hudson has made a beautiful motion picture." Eddie added, "Jerry said to tell Doneata and the children hello! See you soon!"

The bids came in on *Chariots of Fire* with a February release date in Florida. I sat down with Eddie to discuss where we should go after the film.

"Everywhere, let's go after it everywhere!" Eddie exclaimed.

I dropped my pen and gave Eddie that "are you serious?" look.

Eddie understood my concern. "Larry, I've seen the film. You haven't. There is something special about this picture." Eddie smiled as he assured me, "This is one of those films that we have to open and leave it alone. The audience will find the picture."

"With all due respect, Eddie, from everything I have read on *Chariots of Fire* it will have limited box-office appeal." I paused, "I thought you would want to play *Chariots* in the theatre where we play all our foreign subtitled art films, the Sunset."

"Of course I want to play *Chariots* in the Sunset, but I also want the film in Orlando, Boca Raton, Hollywood, Gainesville, Fort Lauderdale, North Miami, and Miami Beach." Eddie tapped off his cigar ashes as he added, "*Chariots* will be the sleeper of the year!"

I exhaled deeply as I said, "Okay, Eddie. If you are absolutely sure, I will mail the bids out today."

Not to my surprise, we were awarded *Chariots of Fire* across the state in every single theatre. I knew why the other film buyers passed on the film: they thought it was too limited in appeal to play in mainstream theatres. I noticed when I told Eddie it was our picture everywhere, though, it didn't seem to bother him at all.

When I saw the movie, it immediately rose to the top of my list of favorites, just as it had with Eddie. I got chills when the Olympic runner Eric Liddell, played by Ian Charleson, said, "I believe God made me for a purpose, but He also made me fast. And when I run I feel His pleasure." And when the Master of Trinity College remarked, "Life slips by, Abrahams, life slips by!" I couldn't help but think of my deceased friend, Roger Hill.

*Chariots of Fire* opened in October in selected cities around America to fair, but not exceptional, business. It did receive a nomination for the coveted Best Picture of the Year award, but in 1981 there were several high profile films being nominated in the Best Picture category.

Paramount Pictures had two big budget films nominated: *Reds*, which starred Hollywood's favorite actor/director, Warren Beatty. *Reds* also had Diane Keaton and Jack Nicholson in costarring roles. Paramount's other nominee was the George Lucas and Steven Spielberg adventure film, *Raiders of the Lost Ark*, starring Harrison Ford. Industry scuttlebutt had *Reds* as the shoe-in favorite for Best Picture.

If that wasn't enough Oscar competition for one year, the film that had even the executives at Paramount nervous about a possible upset was Universal Pictures' *On Golden Pond*, which starred Henry Fonda, Katharine Hepburn, and Jane Fonda.

Out of all the pictures nominated for Best Picture, *Chariots* was by far and away the long shot to win. But Eddie wasn't worried. He stuck to his guns, saying that *Chariots* was certainly going to win Best Picture, and once it did, then everyone would be flocking to Womteco's theatres to see it.

When the results were announced at the Oscars, Eddie Stern once again showed his ability for picking a box office winner. The Academy voted against the industry favorites and instead awarded *Chariots of Fire* the 1981 Best Picture of the Year award. This recognition immediately gave *Chariots* exactly what Eddie said the picture needed, and *Chariots of Fire* became an instant must-see film for moviegoers of all ages.

*Chariots,* along with its famous soundtrack, played on and on and on! Barry Reardon, Warner Brothers' President of Distribution, called Eddie and complimented him on believing what even Warner Brothers had doubted—*Chariots of Fire* could play to the masses.

The following Sunday my family and I visited Immanuel PCA church. After the service, we stopped and talked briefly with the pastor, Terry Geiger.

Pastor Geiger was a quiet man, but there was a warmth about him that made me want to get to know him.

On the drive home from church that night I told Doneata, "Honey, this has been a wonderful Lord's Day. You know what I like about Pastor Geiger?" I didn't give her time to respond, "I like the way he preaches. I got a lot out of both of his messages today."

"Larry, I am so happy that you're happy." She paused, and then she said, "Darling, I just want us as a family to find a church that we can enjoy going to and being a part of." Doneata then laid her head on my shoulder and said, "I think you're right. Immanuel is going to be our next church home."

# TWENTY-FIVE

# A VAPOR

*Strange, isn't it? Each man's life touches so many other lives.*
*When he isn't around he leaves an awful hole, doesn't he?*
– Clarence the angel, *It's a Wonderful Life*

EDDIE CALLED ME INTO HIS office. He looked worried. "Larry, Stanley Stern[11] just left my office. He informed me that Jack has a tumor in his right kidney. Dr. Manos suspects the tumor to be malignant."

"What? When did all this come about?"

"Tuesday. After everyone had left, Jack stopped by the men's room and started urinating blood. This morning the hospital made some X-rays and found the tumor."

"Eddie, did Stanley say when they are going to operate?"

"The surgery is scheduled for Monday morning at South Miami Hospital."

"I'll be sure to remember Jack and Ann in my prayers."

"Larry, they're going to need them."

I went back to my office, called Doneata, and told her to call Ann and find out what we could do. Jack's illness shouldn't have come as a surprise, since he had been pale as milk for some time. I had noticed that at

---

11    Senior Vice President of Wometco Enterprises.

our lunches he seemed to be struggling with fatigue, but I thought Jack's health issues were stress related.

Marvin came into my office, looking tired and worried. "Have you heard about Jack?"

"Yeah, Eddie told me the news."

"Larry, I just left a twenty-minute meeting with Stanley. Guess who's the new acting general manager? Yours truly. Stanley wants me to fill in for Jack during his absence." Marvin was unnerved from his meeting with Stanley.

Wanting to be supportive, I said, "Marvin, I know your desk is going to be busy for the next few weeks. I'll try not to drive you crazy making any last-minute booking changes."

"Thanks, Larry. That would be most helpful." Marvin then said he'd better call Sadie, before she heard about Jack from someone else.

On the way home I stopped by the hospital to visit Jack and Ann. When I walked into the room, Jack was lying there in bed with his eyes closed. No one else was in the room. I tiptoed over to the bed, bent down, and whispered in Jack's ear, "Are you dead, or just sleeping?"

Somewhat startled, Jack opened his tired eyes and said, "I ain't sleeping, and I sure ain't dead! I'm just resting." He held out his hand. I by-passed it and reached over to give him a hug.

"Larry, don't you fret one little bit. I am going to beat this thing. Monday it will all be over."

"I'm not worried about you, old pal. Marvin is the one I'm concerned about. Stanley gave Marvin his marching orders today. I think Marvin is the one who's going to need a transfusion."

Jack started laughing. "This will be a good experience for Marvin. That is, if it doesn't kill him."

At that moment, the door opened, and Stanley came walking into the room carrying a large, brown box with at least a dozen bags of assorted Pepperidge Farms cookies. Stanley said, "Jack, I forgot which one was your favorite so I bought you a box of each." As Stanley found his resting place on the side of Jack's bed, I thought it was time I say my good-byes and head on home.

While driving home, I thought how quickly everything can change. My stepbrother Farrell had died so young. And my mother had died so suddenly. Roger Hill was alive in Atlanta and, shortly thereafter, died in Boston. My son David was healthy one day and diagnosed with leukemia the next. Now Jack was lying in a hospital bed about to have cancer surgery.

The next morning, Marvin picked me up. I asked, "Marvin, are you okay?"

"Sure, I'll be fine. I'm just a bit on the tired side."

"You were really upset yesterday. You shouldn't let your work get to you like it does. It's only a job, Marvin."

"Larry, to be honest with you, I didn't sleep much at all last night. I'm just stressed out."

"You've got to go with the flow, man. If you don't take it one day at a time, you're going to give yourself another heart attack. Stanley knows you're doing a two-man job. He'll give you some slack."

Marvin wiped a bead of sweat from his forehead as he replied, "Larry, I hope you're right. There is only one Jack Mitchell. I hope what I have to give is enough."

When Dr. Manos came out from surgery, he addressed Ann. "As far as I can tell, the surgery looks like a total success."

Ann shed tears of joy when she heard the good news. Dr. Manos went on to say, "I took out the right kidney as the tumor was completely enclosed in it. I feel confident that I got it all, but I still need to see the test results to be absolutely sure the cancer hasn't spread to any other parts of his body."

A few days after Jack got a clean bill of health from Dr. Manos, he went home to recuperate. For the next few weeks, Marvin didn't know whether he was coming or going, trying to do his work along with all of Jack's duties. There were days when I couldn't even get Marvin to take a break long enough for lunch. I didn't like what I saw happening to Marvin. I could tell the responsibility that was put on him was starting to unnerve him.

That year, Doneata and I decided we needed more space. We bought a large house with a pool. The norm for me when I arrived home from work was to change into shorts and a T-shirt. This particular day was no exception. Doneata followed me into the bedroom and sat down on the side of the bed. I had seen that look before. I knew Doneata had something she wanted to tell me.

I said, "Honey, anything special going on?"

She grinned. "Uh huh."

Doneata stood up, walked over to me, and put her arms around me. Then she whispered in my ear, "We're going to have a baby."

Immediately I put my hands around her waist and pushed her back so I could look straight into her face. "Doneata, are you joking with me?"

"Not unless Dr. Friedman is joking with me at my doctor's appointment today. I was shocked, too, when Dr. Friedman gave me the news."

"Honey, that is wonderful news! Are you hoping for a boy or girl?"

Doneata replied, "Darling, I don't care what it is as long as it's healthy and doesn't scream all the time."

I thought a moment when she said "healthy" and "scream." "Yes, we must pray that this baby will be healthy . . . and happy!"

One sunny Florida afternoon, Doneata and Mentora came home from their Bible study fellowship group to find the house a complete mess. Doneata assumed that her sister, who was staying with our family at the time, must have been looking for a phone book or something and then had left in a hurry, as drawers were left open and things were tossed here and there.

While in the bathroom with Mentora (who was four at the time), Doneata, out of the corner of her eye, saw someone walk by the bathroom door and go down the hallway. In shock, she walked out of the bathroom, holding Mentora's hand.

The next thing they knew, they were face to face with a strange man, who was holding a pistol. Doneata recognized the gun, a Lima .380 semiautomatic, the same one I kept under our mattress for protection. The man's eyes were darting back and forth, and it was instantly obvious to Doneata that he was on drugs. The man was starring at Mentora. Doneata could feel Mentora's hand shaking. She looked over at Mentora and saw that her whole body was shaking. Doneata, determined to get the intruder's attention, talked to Mentora but kept looking at the man. She told Mentora that God's angels were protecting them and that, because they belonged to Jesus, no one could harm them. The man backed up, still holding the gun in his hand and pointing it at Doneata and Mentora. When he got to the glass sliding doors leading to the pool area, he opened the door, turned, and ran away.

Doneata immediately called the police, and they were at our home within seconds. (A neighbor had seen someone enter our home and had already called them.)

The man was caught hours later. When he was caught, we found out the extent of God's protection, as the man who had invaded our home had previously raped a ten-year-old girl. He had served time in prison for his crime, and had later been released.

Miami was beautiful, but it was definitely a hard place to raise a family. Thankfully, God protected our family; however, being born Southerners, we had a hard time adjusting to the high crime rate in big city Miami. After this incident, poor Mentora had nightmares for what seemed like forever. The only way Doneata could cope with what had happened was for us to move into a gated apartment community, which gave her the security she needed.

On the bright side, on the fourth of May in 1981, Doneata gave birth to a 9-pound 15½-ounce baby boy. We named him Larry David Vaughn, Jr. I remember, the first time I saw him, that I expected to see a larger version of what Mentora had looked like when she was born. But he didn't look anything at all like Mentora. Mentora was the most beautiful baby, but this big guy looked just like Alfred Hitchcock, or possibly Winston Churchill. When we took him home, we were pleased to find our not-so-handsome baby was a good baby. He had only three desires in this life—to be fed, changed, and loved.

Jack called a manager's meeting on a Friday afternoon to discuss upcoming play dates on the new Burt Reynolds movie, *Cannonball Run,*

booked to open in several of our theatres. I was in the meeting along with Jack, Marvin, two district managers, and several theatre managers.

Since I had seen the Burt Reynolds film earlier in Dallas, Jack asked me to give the group a full report it. With as many play dates as we had on the film and the large guarantees, this one picture could make or break our month at the box office.

After I gave the group a good pep talk and hyped the film to the point that everyone was excited about playing the picture, Jack started dividing responsibilities for his advertising and promotion ideas. When Jack got around to Marvin, he told Marvin to contact a certain radio station and try to work a promotion on the film. Surprisingly, Marvin was very negative about using that particular station to the point that he started cursing. I expected Jack to call him down. From their body language, I could tell everyone else was shocked at Marvin's behavior too. I looked over at Marvin, but he acted as though I wasn't even in the room.

I thought to myself, "What has gotten into Marvin?" I was concerned for my friend. I thought, "That's it. I'm going to talk to Marvin. His behavior is not only uncharacteristic, but he's out of line."

I was sitting at my desk Monday morning looking at the box office receipts from the weekend. I really didn't have my mind on how much business the theatres were doing. My mind was on Marvin. All weekend I couldn't get him off my mind, and I knew I had to talk to him. I walked across the hall to his office. He was on the phone. I sat down across from him and propped my feet up on the corner of his desk. He looked up at me as if to say, "Who do you think you are?"

I yawned, stretched, and started rubbing my stomach. I whispered, "Let's do lunch today." He put his hand over the receiver and said, "I don't want no Cuban food."

"Me neither. Let's go down to Burdines. Just buzz me when you're ready to go."

He nodded in agreement, and I left. Going back to my office, I thought, "Perfect timing! He's in a good mood."

Burdines was one of the major department stores in Miami. On the ground floor of their downtown store, they had a restaurant. It was a good place to go for a piled-high turkey or pastrami sandwich.

While eating our sandwiches, Marvin told me about the meeting he had earlier that morning with Jack. "Larry, Jack's got me running from morning to night. You won't believe the schedule I have this week. He's got me doing everything but painting the theatres."

We both laughed. It was good to be able to catch a glimpse of the old Marvin. I wondered how long Marvin was going to stay that way once I started talking to him about this lunch's hidden agenda. I said a brief prayer that the Lord would give me those words that He would have me say to Marvin.

I took a sip of coffee, pushed my chair back from the table, crossed my legs, and rested my elbow on the table. "Marvin, there is something I must talk with you about. It has been weighing heavily on my mind all weekend, and to be perfectly honest with you, that is why I asked you to go out to lunch today."

Without showing any emotion Marvin looked straight at me, smiled slightly, and said, "What is it, Larry?"

"Marvin, it concerns me greatly to see how you have been behaving the last few weeks. I guess you don't realize it, but you are so negative at the office, and your demeanor is awful. Marvin, do you realize that the only Christ that Eddie, Jack, Stanley, and all the other people that we work and come in contact with might see is the Christ they see in you and me?" He didn't respond so I kept on talking.

"Marvin, if I were you, I would do one of two things. I would get right with my God today, or I would put my Bible in the attic and stop claiming to be something I'm not."

Marvin cleared his throat, pulled his chair closer to the table, placed his arm on the table, and started rubbing his wedding band with his fingers. He didn't say anything at first. Then he looked at me and said, "Larry, I needed to hear that. You're right! You're absolutely right in everything you said."

He then took a deep breath and exhaled loudly. "Larry, the problem is that the office is driving me crazy. I'm not sleeping at night. I'm angry. I have no peace."

He paused and continued. "Yes, I'm out of fellowship with the Lord, but Larry—" Marvin looked very sternly at me, "I am a Christian. I made things right with the Lord several years ago before I had my bypass heart surgery. I know Jesus is my Savior."

"Marvin, you can't see the forest for the trees. Look at all the ways God has blessed you. Look at your home for instance—it's beautiful. You and Sadie both have a clean bill of health. Financially, you've told me yourself that you're not hurting. I wish I had as much Wometco stock as you have. Why, I'd probably retire and take the family on a trip around the world." We both chuckled at that statement.

"Seriously, Marvin, the Bible says, 'Naked came we into the world and naked we shall leave.'"

Marvin replied, "You mean when I die I won't be able to have a U-haul with all my stuff going to heaven with me?"

We both laughed, and I continued. "Marvin, do you know what I would do if my job bothered me like you say your job bothers you? I would make a change. I would go to Jack and tell him we have a problem and ask Jack if there's any way we can work it out. If not, then I would leave Wometco and find employment elsewhere."

"Who would be interested in hiring a fifty-three-year-old man who has had open-heart surgery?"

"You won't know the answer to that until you've asked."

"Larry, you've given me a lot to think about today. I'm going to go home tonight and do some serious soul searching."

"Marvin, you are not only my best friend, you are also my brother in Christ. I am so glad we had this talk today."

Later that night Marvin called to let me know he wouldn't be busing in with me in the morning as he needed to put his car in the shop at Dadeland. He said he would catch the earlier bus downtown.

"Okay, Marvin, I'll see you at the office." When I hung up, I commented to Doneata that I should probably pick up Marvin in the morning and ride in with him. I got busy with getting the kids into bed and didn't make the call. The next thing I knew it was too late to call.

The next morning I catnapped during the thirty-minute bus ride downtown. When I left the bus at Burdines, I started the ten-minute walk to Wometco. After I got about three blocks up North Miami Avenue, I noticed two police cars and an ambulance parked alongside the street with their lights on. There was an old man, who looked rather shabby, sitting in the back seat of one of the police cars.

The police were using yellow tape to mark off a large section of the sidewalk. I also noticed a third car, an old model car with the front end smashed in, parked between the police cars. I thought, "That must be the car that old man was driving."

As I got closer, I noticed there was a man who looked to be dead, lying on the sidewalk face down without a shirt on. It looked like the police officer had partially covered the body with a piece of black plastic. There were tire marks where a car had run up on the sidewalk, and a storefront wall was damaged and cracked from what looked like an impact of some kind. The wall had fresh blood along the side of it. I thought to myself, "Most likely, that guy lying there without a shirt on is a derelict. I'd bet he was asleep on the sidewalk and somehow that old car ran over him and threw him against the wall." It was nothing to walk around downtown and see street people lying around literally everywhere.

A merchant walked over, and I said to him, "Probably a derelict lying there."

He said, "No, I don't think so. The police officer over there said the man was a businessman."

"What happened?"

"The old man driving that Oldsmobile ran a red light and was speeding. He jumped the curb and crushed the man against the wall. It seemed to me the pedestrian tried to throw himself against the building, but there was no place for him to go; he was just crushed."

"That's horrible!" I replied, as the merchant just shook his head.

I walked across the street from the accident and went the one additional block to Wometco. I went straight to my office, turned on the light, and laid my newspaper on my desk. I thought, "I think I'll go over and see Marvin and see how last night went." I walked across the hall to his office—it was locked. I thought, "That's odd. Marvin was supposed to be early today. He must be in Jack's office." I went on down to Jack's office and stuck my head in the door. "Hi, partner, what are you up to?"

"Good morning, Larry. I was just looking at the stock report. I sure wish I could exercise some more options. Wometco is going nowhere but up."

I interrupted him. "Jack, have you seen Marvin this morning?"

"Nope."

"That's odd. He told me yesterday that he would be in early today." I guess Jack noticed the concern on my face. "Larry, what's wrong? What are you thinking?"

"Oh, nothing important. It's just that, well, there was an accident this morning on North Miami Avenue about a block from here. I think one of the street people was killed."

"Why do you think it was a street person?"

"I could tell the guy didn't have a shirt on."

"Oh." Jack got up from behind his desk and said, "Come on. Let's walk down to the scene of the accident."

We walked outside the front door of our office building and started walking toward North Miami Avenue. I noticed Art Hertz, the Chief Financial Officer of the company, walking toward us with a very solemn look on his face. Art walked up to us and looked directly at me, but he started to talk with Jack.

I immediately interrupted Art as I pointed toward the scene of the accident and said, "Art, that body over there isn't Marvin Reed's, is it?"

Then I wondered why I had even blurted out such a statement. I thought, "Of course it's not Marvin." Fear gripped me as Art bit his bottom lip and nodded his head in agreement. All of a sudden I felt sick and weak. I started crying.

Jack took me back to my office. He then said, "Larry, why don't you go home. I'll have someone drive you. I would take you myself, but I have to go over and meet with Art and the Colonel to see how we are going to handle this. Someone has to tell Sadie."

"No, I don't want to go home. I'll be fine in a few minutes."

"Larry, when does Eddie return to Miami?"

"This afternoon."

"He's not going to believe it."

Jack left, and I instructed the girls to hold all my calls. I picked up the phone and called Doneata. "Honey, are you sitting down? I've got some awful news to tell you." I told Doneata the whole story. She couldn't believe it. She cried throughout the entire conversation. I told her I should have been with Marvin that morning. I had every intention of calling him the night before to tell him I would ride in with him.

"Oh Larry, I don't know what to say. Yesterday, the lunch with Marvin, everything that was said, and you could have been with him, what does all this mean?"

"Honey, I don't know what to think. I'm glad Marvin and I had that time together yesterday. Maybe God was preparing Marvin for his homegoing. Maybe, oh, I don't know! Only God knows."

"Larry, why don't you let me come on down and pick you up?"

"Honey, not now, but keep yourself available. I'll phone you later."

Jack and Stanley were given the unpleasant assignment of telling Sadie Reed that her husband was dead. When Stanley and Jack walked into her office, she knew something was wrong. Sadie got up from behind her desk and asked, "Jack, Stanley, is it Marvin's heart?" Upon hearing the news, Sadie collapsed. Jack and Stanley took her home.

About an hour later I received a call from Stanley. "Larry, are you up to coming over to the Reed home? Sadie wants to see you badly."

"Yes, sir. I can be there within the hour."

When I walked into the living room, Sadie stood up and ran over to me. She put her arms around me and just held me. She was crying uncontrollably. After a moment, I took her by the arm and said, "Come on, Sadie. Let's sit down."

"Larry, not in here; let's go out by the pool. I have something I must ask you."

We left the other people in the living room and went out by the pool. Sadie sat down in one of the pool chairs and motioned for me to sit down directly in front of her. She adjusted her chair to where we were facing each other. I noticed we were so close that our knees were touching. Sadie took both my hands and held them. Tears were streaming down her face, but she did not bother to wipe them away.

"Larry, I have one question to ask." Sadie paused and closed her eyes. Her lips were quivering. It was as if she were praying before she asked the question. "Larry, tell me. Larry, do you think my Marvin was a Christian?"

I looked into her sad, bewildered eyes and noticed how swollen her face was. She was a woman whose heart had just been broken in two upon hearing the news that she had lost the most precious person in her life. I thought about Marvin and his struggles. I thought about our conversation, and Marvin's declaration, "I know that Jesus is my Savior." It is so simple and yet profound. That is all one needs. I squeezed Sadie's hand and said, "Yes, Sadie. I believe Marvin was a Christian."

I was a pallbearer at Marvin's funeral. It was one of the saddest days of my life. I heard very little the preacher said that day, because my mind kept going back to the lunch that Marvin and I had had together just a few days earlier. I thought to myself, "There was something else that I wanted to say to Marvin on Monday. What was it?" I thought a moment, and then it came to me. "I know. I wanted to share with Marvin a Scripture verse. James 4:14, 'Whereas you know not what shall be tomorrow. For what is your life? It is even a vapor that appeareth for a little time, and then vanishes away.' Oh, how Marvin would gladly testify to those words today."

# LIFE GOES ON

*Don't let yesterday use up too much of today.*
                                    – Will Rogers

I RETURNED FROM LAS VEGAS to Miami early on a Friday evening. Doneata picked me up at the airport, and the two of us met Jack and Ann for dinner at an Italian restaurant in Miami Springs called Joe Peppi's. After spending the last three days in Las Vegas, I would have preferred to have had dinner at home with Doneata and the children. But I knew how important it was for Doneata to have an evening out, especially after having such a busy week at home.

Joe Peppi's was Jack's favorite restaurant. It was one of those little Italian restaurants that you had to have heard about before you would go there to eat. It was a favorite hangout for Dan Marino, Don Strock, and several other Miami Dolphins football players. Joe was a big Dolphins fan; he had pictures of the Dolphins players and Dolphins memorabilia scattered throughout the restaurant. Joe also had a picture that Jack had given him, of Jack with Burt Reynolds and Dolly Parton, which was framed and hanging on the wall right beside the front door. Every time I saw that picture it brought back a funny memory.

In 1982, Universal Pictures released their much anticipated big budget film, *The Best Little Whorehouse in Texas*. The movie was based on the Broadway musical, which was inspired by the real-life Chicken Ranch in La Grange, Texas. Both Eddie and I wanted to play the film in North Miami at the 163rd Street Theatre. We knew that we would have to pay top dollar to win what industry insiders felt was going to be one of the top films of the year. We bid something like twelve weeks with a hundred and twenty-five thousand dollar guarantee. Not to our surprise, we were awarded the film.

Fred Mound, the General Sales Manager for Universal Pictures Distribution, requested a benefit showing on the evening before the film opened. The evening of the premier, Universal placed two huge searchlights outside the theatre. There were network television cameras along with a red carpet for Florida dignitaries, local VIP's and, naturally, the movie stars. There were well over a thousand people standing outside the theatre hoping to get a glimpse of all the celebrities. It seemed like the Miami police department had camped out in the parking lot, as police officers were everywhere. The theatre auditorium had twelve hundred and fifty seats, and they were all occupied. The benefit played to a full house!

What I remember most about that evening, however, happened, of all places, in the theatre manager's office. Jack had Burt Reynolds and Dolly Parton holed up in the manager's office, awaiting their grand entrance

*Dolly Parton, Jack Mitchell, and Burt Reynolds at the 163ʳᵈ Street Theatre*

*Dolly Parton and Burt Reynolds talking to a customer at 163ʳᵈ Street Theatre*

into the auditorium to be seated with the other VIP's to watch the Florida premier of their film.

The office phone rang, and before the theatre personnel could answer it, Mr. Reynolds reached over and took the call. He said, "Good evening, Wometco Theatres."

The person on the other end asked a showtime question. Of course, she had no idea she was talking to Burt Reynolds. Mr. Reynolds asked the caller her name.

She asked, "Why do you want to know my name?"

He replied, "Don't you know my name?"

"No," she remarked.

In a cheerful tone of voice he said, "I'm Burt Reynolds."

"No, you're not!" the caller insisted.

"Am too," he said, laughing. "Hold on, I want you to say hello to Dolly Parton."

He then handed the phone to Miss Parton. When Miss Parton said 'hello' in her famous Southern drawl . . . the caller instantly became a believer. It was a very funny moment as Burt, Dolly, Jack, the manager, and a bodyguard had a few moments of comic relief. That's not to mention the lady who had called for the show times. She got one of those lifetime memories to share with her family and friends.

Joe Peppi was a big Italian man. In addition to being the restaurant owner, Joe was also the head chef and strolling musician. Quite often while the customers were eating their meal, Joe, accompanied by a guitarist, would stroll from table to table singing love songs in Italian. I remember on one occasion I was enjoying my dinner when Joe Peppi strolled by our table singing. Jack stood up and made his way beside Joe Peppi and started singing love songs with him. I could hardly believe Jack was singing in front of everyone with Joe. Jack did have a good voice, and Joe seemed to enjoy Jack's singing with him.

This evening Jack, Doneata, and Ann were enjoying their meal and talking softly. I thought of the conversation we had had on the way to the restaurant. We had talked about Sadie. Jack had said that she was taking Marvin's death very hard. We all agreed to reach out to her in the days ahead.

Jack was talking to me. I interrupted him. "What did you say, Jack?" He was asking me to bring him up-to-date with my Las Vegas trip.

I told Jack about my dinner with Wayne Lewellen, Paramount's President of Distribution. It was always a pleasure doing business with Wayne.

I sighed, "Honestly, it was the hardest trip to Vegas I have ever had. For the first time in my life, I had no interest in gambling."

*Eddie Stern, Jack Mitchell, and Larry at a movie premiere*

Everyone was quiet at the table. Finally, Ann spoke. "Larry, we are all missing Marvin."

Ann hit the nail on the head. I was depressed over Marvin's death.

I had rethought that lunch at Burdines until there was absolutely nothing left to rethink. I needed to leave it alone. I had walked past the spot where Marvin died just before I left for Vegas. I had promised myself that I would take the long way to the office from now on, so I wouldn't have to walk past that blood-stained wall again. I wished they would paint the wall or scrub it with bleach—anything to remove the reminder of my dear friend's death. There was no point in my trying to figure out why Marvin was dead and why he died the way and the time he did. My pastor was right: some things are not for us to know. It's just that I felt so miserable on the inside.

Trying to change the subject, Jack told me about his week at the office. "Larry, I hired an old friend of mine by the name of Bill Copley as Director of Advertising and Marketing. He's been in the business a long time."

"That's good, Jack. You're going to need a good man to take some of the workload off your desk."

"Larry, have you been keeping up with the stock this week?"

"I looked at it Thursday. Wasn't it up a quarter?"

"Larry, it closed today at twenty-eight." Jack took out his pen and started figuring on his napkin. "Larry, do you realize if this happens and that happens, that means I'm going to have this much money." Jack then held up his napkin with about twenty numbers all lined up in a row.

"Jack, you spend too much time playing with your Wometco stock. Everyone knows that when the Colonel passes on, the company will sell, and your stock will be worth trillions."

I thought about how much of my own Wometco stock I had sold through the years to pay my family's medical bills. If it weren't for my stock options, I would have been head-over-heels in debt.

As we were about to leave the restaurant, Ann said, "Larry, you and Doneata remember to pray for Jack next week. He goes back to see the doctor on Tuesday. The old boy hasn't felt that well this week."

I looked at Jack. "Are you okay?"

"Oh, it's nothing," he replied. "I've just had a lot of indigestion lately, and I have been tiring easily."

"Well, you'd best stay healthy, old buddy, because I'm not about to let Stanley send me over to your office and have me play general manager for you."

Jack laughed, "No, I don't think that would sit too well with Eddie."

One of the most embarrassing moments in my life happened one afternoon when I was walking to lunch downtown with Stanley Stern. Like Eddie, Stanley always dressed to impress. I thought it was ironic that they shared the same last name, because Stanley and Eddie were both class acts. On the way back from our lunch, I heard a voice calling, almost yelling, "Larry . . . Larry!"

Stanley and I both turned to see who was hollering so loudly, and there across the street, about fifty yards away, was a homeless man. He wore pants cut off above the knees with holes in them, and his shirt was just as bad: an old, faded, gray tank-top. His hair and beard looked like it had been at least a year, maybe two years, since it had last been cut. He was barefoot, and his feet were totally black from being unwashed. The man continued to holler as he waved his hand, "Larry, Larry! Jesus loves you, Larry, and so do I."

Stanley looked at me with the funniest look on his face; he looked as if he had just taken a big swig of castor oil. "Do you know that guy?" he asked me. The derelict was walking faster toward us, starting to holler again.

I said, "Stanley, excuse me; I'll be right back." I double-timed it across the street to the man, feeling in my pockets along the way for some "hush money." Fortunately, I reached the man before he started yelling again. I slipped five bucks into his hand and said, "Not now, Bernie. I'm with my boss. I'll see you later in the week."

Bernie gave me the goofiest smile and said, "Okay, Larry." As I hurried back to Stanley, Bernie yelled after me, "God bless you, Larry!"

Stanley was standing there with a look of complete disbelief on his face.

"Larry, do you honestly *know* that guy?"

I dropped my head and said without looking at Stanley, "Oh, sort of. I gave him a few bucks one day, and now he thinks we're buddies."

What I didn't share with Stanley is that since Marvin died, I had sure missed my lunch partner. Not a day went by that I didn't think about how Marvin and I used to go out to lunch together. Since I had the time, I decided I would start going over to the park on Biscayne Boulevard a couple of days a week. During that year, I shared the good news of Jesus Christ to many of the homeless people who came to the park to spend their days.

I had a system that seemed to work. Now that I look back on it, what I most likely was doing was paying the derelicts to listen to me give them the plan of salvation. I got to know many of the street people by name, as we would see each other several times a month. It amazed me that some of them seemed to have been, at one time or another, just ordinary people, but eventually something had happened in their lives that put them over the edge with society. Bernie was one of my regulars, whom I saw almost weekly.

While Bernie was obviously happy to see me, I could tell at that moment that Stanley Stern, the Executive Vice President of the Entertainment Division of Wometco Enterprises, was *not* impressed with either me or my derelict friend!

Doneata felt weak when she heard Ann's voice on the other end of the phone, "Doneata, they have found more tumors."

"Oh Ann, where?"

"They found three."

"Three?" Doneata pleaded.

"Yes, three. There's one on his lung, one on his spine, and another one on his liver."

"Oh Ann, I am so sorry!"

"We're taking them one at a time. Jack is in good spirits, considering the gloomy news."

"I'll call Larry. I'm sure he will stop by after work. Ann, do you need anything?"

"Just prayer."

"Our prayers you have."

I stopped by the hospital on the way home. On the elevator to the fourth floor, I was trying to get my thoughts together. "I must be very upbeat. Now is when I need to be an encouragement to Jack. He must not see my concern and my fear." I continued praying quietly to myself as I walked into the room.

When I walked in, Jack was lying in bed reading the newspaper. "Hey, partner. What are you doing back here? These beds are supposed to be for sick people."

As he dropped the paper down, Jack peeped over the top of it at me and smiled. "Larry, come over here and sit down, right here beside me on the bed. Ann said she told Doneata about my tumors. Larry, you know what the good news is?"

"No, but I'd love to hear some right about now."

Jack laughed. "There are only three tumors and not four."

I smiled at the dear man and shook my head. "Jack, you don't need to be in a hospital—you need to be in an insane asylum."

Jack straightened the blanket on his bed while I fluffed his pillow. Then he got very serious. "Larry, I might end up in a wheelchair or bed-ridden, but I'm not going to give in to this. I'll fight it with my last breath."

"Jack, I know you will. Let's take it one day at a time. Now, tell me everything the doctor had to say."

It seemed to do Jack good to talk about it. He tried to remember everything word for word. When he finished giving me all the details, I asked him if I could have prayer with him. He nodded his head in agreement. I prayed for Jack's health needs and for strength for Ann. After I prayed, Jack and I talked a little while, and then I left the hospital.

Driving home from the hospital I thought to myself, "Jack's favorite pastime is watching the Wometco stock go up and down, up and down. I doubt if he lives long enough to see any real financial fruit from all those years of labor." I wiped a tear as I realized that my good friend was dying.

# TWENTY-SEVEN

# TWO OUT OF THREE

*It's an extra dividend when you like the girl you're in love with.*
— Clark Gable

ON THE BUS RIDE TO the office one day, I passed a billboard advertising the Fontainebleau Hotel on Miami Beach. Now there was a good memory! How long ago was it? It had probably been four, or maybe five years before, when the National Association of Theatre Owners held

*Larry, Marvin Reed, and Jack Mitchell at the Fontainebleau Hotel*

227

a convention at the Fontainebleau. The Fontainebleau was one of the largest and most famous hotels on Miami Beach. In earlier years it had been one of the most famous hotels in the entire world. Even though we lived in Miami, Wometco put Doneata and me up in an oceanfront room for the entire week. All we did was eat, sleep, and spend time with the Hollywood elite. That week was like a paid vacation with all the trimmings.

I thought back to a breakfast Doneata and I had in the restaurant of the Fontainebleau. We were sitting there in a booth and Doneata said, "Larry, there's Steven Spielberg in that booth across the way. Do you know him?"

"No, I've never had the pleasure of meeting him."

"Larry, his food hasn't come yet. Let's go over and introduce ourselves to him."

"Honey, if it were anywhere but in a restaurant, I would. But I don't want to disturb Mr. Spielberg in a restaurant."

"Do you mind if I go over and talk with him?"

"Not one bit, Doneata. You do what you want to, but I'll meet him somewhere besides his breakfast table."

Doneata got up and walked over to Mr. Spielberg's booth. I admired her attractive figure as she walked. There was another man whom I did

*Doneata and Dudley Moore at NATO convention*

not know sitting across from Mr. Spielberg, who was propped up in the corner of the booth with his leg resting on the seat. All I could see of Doneata was her back, but I noticed that Mr. Spielberg straightened himself up in his seat and made room for Doneata to sit down. She sat down beside him, and they seemed to be in a heavy conversation.

I thought to myself, "Maybe I should go over and introduce myself. He certainly doesn't seem to mind Doneata interrupting their conversation. I wonder what she is talking to him about."

They talked for several minutes before the waiter brought their breakfast to the table. As soon as the food arrived, Doneata got up from the booth, shook both their hands, and politely left.

She returned to our booth with the cutest smile as if she were saying, "I know something that you don't know."

"Okay, Miss Jet Setter. Do you mind telling me what all that was about?"

"Oh, Steven was just inquiring if I would be available to star in his next film."

"And what did you say?"

"I told him I would have to think about it and would phone him later, after I check my calendar," Doneata said with the cutest expression on her face.

"All right, tell me what you two were really talking about."

"Larry, you could guess all day, and you would never guess what we discussed."

"What?" Doneata had my curiosity up.

"Well, when I introduced myself to him and told him that you were my husband, he talked at length about the various theatres in Miami. I was impressed that he was so knowledgeable about each theatre. His friend mentioned Columbia Pictures, and Steven wanted to know why Wometco Theatres is out of business with Columbia Pictures."

"You're kidding!" I could hardly believe my ears.

"No. He wanted to hear the whole story. That's what we have been talking about all this time."

"Well, I'll be. Doneata, you would think a man of Steven Spielberg's stature—you know, the most successful director in the history of motion pictures—wouldn't be aware of, or even concerned about, Wometco's problems with Columbia Pictures."

"No, honey, you're wrong. He said he would like to see Wometco back in business with Columbia, because he likes the way our Miami theatres can gross."

"Well, how do you like that!" I thought.

"Larry, I didn't think you would mind my telling Mr. Spielberg the story. So I told him about how one of the Columbia bigwigs insulted Eddie Stern's wife at a dinner one night in Los Angeles, and how since that night Wometco's and Columbia Pictures' relationship has gone downhill."

"Well, Doneata, there's actually more to that story than what you told Mr. Spielberg, but you were correct in the part that you told him. That was the spark that was used to dissolve our business relationship with Columbia Pictures. By the way, did you get his autograph?"

Doneata looked at me as if I had just asked the stupidest question. She then took out of her dress pocket a small sheet of paper and waved it back and forth as she said, "Of course I got it."

I smiled to myself as the bus came to a halt, and we reached my stop. It felt good getting off the bus that morning. "Yes," I thought,

*Larry and Dudley Moore*

"Doneata and I have both had some good times because of our association with Wometco."

Doneata made a doctor's appointment for Larry, Jr. He had periods where he would stare into the distance with a glazed look in his eyes and drool. We also noted personality changes. Sometimes while he was sleeping, the left side of his body would jerk uncontrollably.

Larry, Jr. was admitted to Miami Children's Hospital for testing. After the test results came back, Doneata and I met with a neurologist, Dr. Duschanney. "Mr. and Mrs. Vaughn, your son is having multiple seizure activity. While we don't know the cause, we have some very good medications that we have had positive results with when treating seizures of this type. We would like to start treating Larry immediately with a combination of medicines for a period of several months, combined with periodic inpatient testing."

Driving home from the hospital, I commented to Doneata, "Well, two out of three is not good."

"What do you mean two out of three?" She asked.

"I mean David having leukemia, and now Larry, Jr. having seizures. That's two out of three."

"Larry, we can praise the Lord that David is doing so well. The doctors were ready to give up on him and look at how well he is doing."

"You're right, Doneata. We really have a lot to be thankful for. Even Mentora is now a wonderful child. It's just that she stretched the terrible twos from the time of birth until she was three years old!"

Doneata squeezed my hand. The warmth from her hand made my heart feel like it skipped a beat. She smiled and her beautiful brown eyes sparkled as she spoke. "Now you listen to me, Larry Vaughn. We will get through this with God's help. We will have to stick together and not allow this trial to drive us apart, but instead draw us closer together. So don't you go getting depressed on me. You're a Christian now. This is your chance, and my chance, to have faith that God can do the impossible in our lives."

The last six months of Jack's life were spent, for the most part, in South Miami Hospital. I dropped by three to four evenings a week to see him. Many times he never even knew that I was there. I felt bad for Jack, but even worse for Ann. She was the one who was always there by his side, daily watching her husband's life slowly slip away. Ann knew it would be only a matter of days or weeks at the longest before Jack—her love, her husband, and her very best friend—would no longer be breathing and living on this earth.

It was during this same time that the legendary Colonel Mitchell Wolfson, the dear old gentleman who had started a business empire with only one small theatre, passed away. Some fifty-plus years earlier, Mitchell Wolfson and his partner, Sidney Meyer, had started the Wolfson Meyer Theatre Company—the giant conglomerate that is known today as Wometco.

TWENTY-EIGHT

# THE BEST JOB IN THE BUSINESS

*I pretended to be somebody I wanted to be until finally I became that person. Or he became me.*

– Cary Grant

IT DIDN'T TAKE VERY LONG after the Colonel's passing for Wometco Enterprises to sell. Several companies expressed interest in purchasing Wometco. The stockholders' best offer came from a group of investors out of New York City by the name of Kohlberg, Kravis & Roberts & Associates. Their billion-dollar offer was all the Wometco shareholders needed to hear in order to sell the company.

Arthur Hertz and Michael Brown represented Wometco in the negotiations of the sale. I'd had very little communication with either Hertz or Brown in my eight years with the company; however, I knew very well the reputation of each man.

Arthur Hertz was a stout man in his late forties or early fifties. He combed his slick, black hair straight back without a part. Mr. Hertz looked the part: a senior executive with a reputation for being an extremely tough businessman. Every time I saw Arthur Hertz walking to his Cadillac, he would have twelve to fifteen manila folders packed full of papers tucked under one arm. In his other hand, he would have his large leather brief-case, which was always bulging at the seams from being overstuffed with more documents.

I understood that in his early years, Art had worked nights at a super-market while putting himself through the University of Miami, where he graduated *summa cum laude*. His entire business career had been at Wometco. Art knew everybody, from national political leaders to gover-nors, senators, and those politicians in between.

Michael Brown looked to be the younger of the two men. Michael was a short man who reminded me of the actor Dustin Hoffman. Michael was married to a lovely lady, Janice.

I had always thought that Hertz and Brown complemented each other, with Hertz being the mouthpiece, the front man, possibly the risk taker of the two, and Brown being the quiet one, the man behind the scenes, the thinker. Together they made a great one-two punch for the Wometco team.

Eddie called me into his office to give me the news. "Larry, I just got off the phone with Stanley. He was over at the hospital. The doctor says it's only a matter of days with Jack."

"Eddie, that's so sad. The company sells, Jack finally gets his payment for his stock, and it means zero to him."

"Well, at least Ann won't have to be strapped financially."

"That's true. I am glad Ann won't ever have to worry about money."

"Larry, Jack is not what I called you in here to talk about. Have you heard through the grapevine who's trying to buy back pieces of Wometco from KKR & Associates?"

"No, what's the latest?"

"Art and Mike are trying to put together their own leveraged buyout, so they can buy back certain parts of the company from KKR & Associates."

"Which parts?"

"They're going after all the Wometco vending, the Baskin-Robbins, the Miami Seaquarium, plus the Puerto Rico and Florida theatres."

Eddie scratched his head as he smiled and said, "Larry, my man, things sure do keep changing around here. It doesn't matter to me personally who ends up with Wometco, because I've decided to go ahead and retire. I told you eight years ago that when the Colonel was no longer here, that I was leaving. Well, the grand old gentleman is gone, so I plan to announce my retirement Friday. I have a feeling Mr. Hertz and Mr. Brown will be very interested in talking with you about a film buying position with the new Wometco in the not-too-distant future."

That evening on the way home from work, I stopped by the hospital. Jack never knew that I was there. I spent a few minutes talking with Ann. I had prayer with her, and then I left. I had been home from the hospital for maybe an hour when we received the call that Jack had passed away.

Jack was buried a few days later. The thousands of people at Wometco, as well as the hundreds of people in the entertainment industry who knew and loved Jack, all mourned his passing. Jack had been a dear friend, and I knew in the days ahead I was going to miss him terribly.

After the funeral, Ann came over to me, and we gave each other a big hug. I looked into her sad eyes and said, "If you need anything, and I mean *anything*, you let me or Doneata know."

"I will, Larry. Life will be very different without my Jack." I thought about how true her words were: life changes greatly when a loved one passes on.

In the next few weeks I found myself having to fight off anxiety. Nothing seemed concrete, stable, or secure anymore. Jack was dead. Eddie had announced his retirement. Art and Mike were working twenty-four hours a day trying to put their deal together to buy Wometco. Larry, Jr. wasn't doing well on his medications, and the doctors felt that he needed to return to Miami Children's Hospital for more testing.

I walked into Art Hertz's outer office at 8:00 a.m. For some reason I was nervous—very nervous! But I put on my poker face and said to myself, "Okay, Larry, go in there with both guns blazing. Act as if you're John Wayne, and you'll end up getting exactly what you want."

I tapped on his door and heard, "Come on in." I opened the door. Art was sitting behind his desk smoking a cigar. His tie was loosened, and the top button on his pinstriped shirt was unbuttoned. His shirt sleeves were turned up to his elbows. He was working through several stacks of papers, one sheet at a time. His desk was covered with documents and files. Looking at him, one would have thought it was eight o'clock in the evening instead of the morning.

Michael was sitting at the end of the sofa with a legal pad in one hand and the telephone cradled between his chin, shoulder, and ear. He was writing as quickly as he could while listening to the party on the other end of the phone. Seeing Art and Mike busy at work, I felt out of place standing there all fresh from a good night's rest.

Art motioned toward an empty chair and said, "Sit down, Larry. Mike will be off the phone in a minute." I sat down and started rehearsing in my mind those things I was about to say.

Mike hung up the phone, made a comment to Art, then looked over at me and said, "Good morning, Larry. Welcome to the new Wometco."

I smiled as Mike walked over and sat down beside me. He flipped over the page on his legal pad to a fresh page and then prepared himself for taking notes. Art did most of the talking.

"Larry, it's almost a done deal. Mike and I, along with our lenders, are about to finalize the purchase of several properties of the former company, which will include the Wometco Florida and Puerto Rico theatres. Mike and I would like for you to stay on as our film buyer for the Florida theatres. How does that sound to you?"

"That sounds just fine to me. I was anticipating that I would have the opportunity to work for you men in the film department."

Art replied, "That's great. We're looking forward to working with you." Art looked at me and said, "Now, Larry, what else do we need to talk about?"

I thought to myself, "Here goes nothing!"

"We need to discuss salary and a contract."

Mike and Art glanced at each other, and then they both looked at me. Art asked as he puffed on his cigar, "What do you have in mind?"

"I think a salary increase of $25,000[12] the first year would be in line with the additional responsibility I will have once Eddie has gone. As far

---

12    Equivalent to $54,350 in 2014 dollars.

as a contract, I would like a one-year contract. That will give the two of you a year to know if you're pleased with my performance, and it will give me a year to get to know you."

Art asked, "Is that it?"

"That's it."

He looked at Mike. "Have a contract drawn up for Larry, you, and me to sign. Larry, your increase will start effective March 1, 1985."

As I stood to leave, Art motioned for me to sit back down. "Larry, your demands have been met. Now here are ours." He coughed, and then took another puff on his cigar. "Two of the largest and most aggressive theatre circuits in the country, American Multi-Cinemas and General Cinema Corporation, have both targeted the Miami market as an area of expansion. They are going to be building new state-of-the-art eight-plex and ten-plex theatres right in our own backyard. I'm paying you very good money to make absolutely sure we keep the important movies playing at Wometco's theatres. Eddie tells me you have an excellent reputation with the film community. You're going to need all the help you can get once AMC and GCC get their new theatres up and running. I'm not buying Wometco to lose money, but to make money."

I looked at Art as if I were John Wayne himself. "Art, I will not be able to guarantee you and Mike that Wometco will play every important picture every time and shut the other guys out completely—not when the other guys are AMC and GCC. That's impossible. It can't be done. No circuit has enough muscle to shut down AMC or GCC theatres. But this much I can promise you and Mike: as long as I am your head film buyer, Wometco will get, at the very least, its fair share of the important movies in all of the Florida theatres."

Art looked at Mike as if to say, "He's awful sure of himself, isn't he?" Then he stood up, extended his hand, and said, "It's going to be a lot of hard work growing together, but if we make money, then Larry Vaughn makes money."

I shook both their hands and left the room. As I closed the door, I sighed. I was relieved that the meeting was over. I thought to myself, "I went in there with both guns blazing just like John Wayne would have done. But now that it's all over, my knees are knocking, and I feel more like Woody Allen."

What did one do with a $25,000-a-year raise in 1985? I sold my condo and bought a new home in one of the up-and-coming areas of South Miami.

The film community threw a surprise going-away party for Eddie Stern. My job was to find a way to get Eddie to Jacksonville. Then a group of Eddie's closest friends would take over from there. I asked Eddie to take one last trip to Jacksonville with me to help solve a problem I was having with one of the film distributors. Thankfully, he took the bait.

We arrived at the restaurant for the so-called meeting. There must have been seventy-five to one hundred film people there to "roast" Eddie Stern. They sent him into retirement in grand fashion. It was a wonderful luncheon that I was sure he would not soon forget.

My first Monday at work after Eddie retired brought my mind back to the very first time I had stepped foot in Eddie's office. I remember having been so impressed with everything that day: Eddie's conversation with Joseph E. Levine, his larger-than-life office, the king-size desk, and, yes, Eddie Stern himself. Now, some eight years later, the office, desk, and responsibility that went along with it were all mine.

As I sat behind my desk, I looked at my large desk calendar and noticed that my first scheduled meeting was lunch with Mr. Hertz and Mr. Brown at the Standard Club.

The Standard Club is a private club located downtown on Biscayne Bay, right in the heart of the banking district, and it's where Miami's elite in the business community gather for lunch and special occasions. While I had eaten at the Standard Club many times with film executives, this was my very first luncheon with Art and Mike.

While the waiter was bringing our drinks, Art started the conversation. "Larry, Mike and I would like for you to enlighten us further about the process involved in purchasing film for our theatres. This is the one area of the theatre business that we have a general knowledge of, but not a thorough knowledge."

"Sure, let me start out by saying that the way I buy film differs with each film company. Let me give you an example. Tri-Star Pictures plays Wometco exclusively in Miami, except in North Miami. In North Miami, Tri-Star plays all their movies in AMC's theatres. Now, what this means is that every picture that Tri-Star releases, I play. That's great when we're opening a grand slam like Sylvester Stallone's new film, *Rambo*, in May. Yes, that's the good news. The bad news is that I also have to play their losers. Sometimes holding an auditorium for a loser keeps us from going after a more important and much bigger picture with another company.

"More and more of the film companies are getting away from offering their films out on competitive bid. The reason is, the film companies are making a lot more movies today than in past years. For example, Disney used to release four to six movies a year. Now they are talking about cranking out twenty to thirty movies a year. When a company is bidding their product, then we—*we* being the theatre circuits—can pick and choose what movies we want to go after. We will bid for what looks to be a money maker and express no interest in a questionable film. The film companies are now finding it in their best interest to stop the bidding process altogether, and simply allocate their movies to play in the theatres of their choice. By doing this, they are assured that they will get all of their movies played."

Art commented, "I heard that's what is starting to happen. Larry, my concern is this. Say the big national theatre circuits like AMC and GCC make a deal with the film companies to play their movies in their theatres everywhere. What does that do to circuits like Wometco?"

"That's a good question, Art. But it should not be a legitimate concern for you or Mike."

"Why not?"

"Because of our relationships, Art, that's why. I've been doing business with these companies for the past sixteen years. The way the film companies do business with theatre circuits changes every so often, but regardless of how they change, we always get our share of the pie. Sometimes we even get a bigger piece than we deserve.

"Take Orion Pictures, for example. We play Orion one hundred percent wherever we have a theatre. You know Orion is as hot as a firecracker. Yet, we play all of their movies."

Art asked, "Is that relationship on a solid footing?"

"Is cement good enough for you?"

Art nodded as if he understood, but I could tell he really didn't understand all the information I was giving him.

Mike spoke up. "Larry, do you think all the companies will eventually discontinue offering their movies out on competitive bid?"

"Yes, I do. As long as the marketplace is flooded with movies, the film companies would rather be ensured of a home for all of their movies than to bid the big ones and have to worry about getting their little movies played off."

Art asked, "Do you feel comfortable that you will be able to continue to get films from all the companies?"

"Art, there is only one fence that needs mending that I am aware of, and that is with Columbia Pictures. As long as Eddie Stern was the head buyer, my hands were tied. Now that Eddie is gone, I am going to make Columbia Pictures a priority. But you must be patient. You must remember that all those years that we have been out of business with Columbia Pictures, someone else has been playing their movies. You can't expect Columbia to walk away from their good, loyal customer that has been taking care of them all this time and start playing Wometco just because Eddie Stern is gone, can you?" Art stuck out his bottom lip as he shrugged his shoulders.

I continued, "Give me some time with Columbia, but remember, sometimes you have to crawl before you can walk. And this is going to be one of those times. As far as bids, I think once I have made the bids up, I should go over them with one of you for final approval. I do need some freedom. I don't want to waste your time or my time on the small stuff. Say on bids of $15,000 and up, we should talk."

Art looked at Mike and said, "That's fine."

On the way back to the office, I felt like the lunch had been a good one. These two men had stuck their necks way out in buying these theatres. I thought I had told them what they wanted to hear. Now I just had to be sure to deliver the goods, or within three months they might be using me as fish bait over at the Miami Seaquarium.

The next few months were high voltage months. Between screenings, traveling, and meetings, I had very little time for anything else.

I really enjoyed working for Art and Mike. They divided the responsibility of overseeing the various departments within Wometco between themselves. As far as titles, Art was Chairman of the Board, and Mike was President of Wometco Enterprises. The two of them literally lived at the office during those early months. Art chose to oversee the domestic theatre division, which meant he was my direct contact person. One of Mike's many tasks was to oversee our theatres in Puerto Rico.

Every Tuesday morning we had an executive meeting in the board room at 8 a.m. sharp, which I always thought was sixty minutes too early. I always kept that thought to myself, however. Art, Mike, Bill Copley—who replaced the late Jack Mitchell as General Manager—and I attended the meetings. Film was always first on the agenda. I would submit a report showing what each of our theatres had grossed at the box office over the weekend. On that same report I would show what the other theatre circuits had grossed that same weekend. By doing this we could look at each individual market and see exactly how our theatres were doing against the opposition theatres.

I always felt somewhat like a sports analyst in those meetings. I would have to try to explain why the theatre in Ocala had done so well over the weekend; why Orlando's numbers had been low that weekend, but why next weekend was going to be great in Orlando; why we were in trouble in Gainesville; why Miami and Ft. Lauderdale had done this, but the coming weekend in Boca Raton, well, you'd best prepare yourself for this. During some of those meetings I would think to myself, "I'm like a football coach. I'm only as good as last weekend's results."

# TIPPING THE SCALES

*I'm just one stomach flu away from my goal weight.*
– Emily Blunt, *The Devil Wears Prada*

ART AND MIKE SEEMED TO be sensitive to their need to lose weight, especially since it was near the time for them to have their company physicals. One day during lunch, Mike made a proposal to Art and me. As Mike rubbed his stomach and looked across the table first at my stomach and then at Art's stomach, he said, "Gentlemen, the three of us need to go on a diet."

I noticed Art immediately got a frown on his face as if to say, "Now, why did you go and bring up that subject?"

Mike continued, "I've got a suggestion about how we might encourage one another to lose some weight; that is, if anyone is interested."

I looked over at Art, who was still frowning, and then back to Mike, who was waiting with a curious look on his face. I said, "Sure, I'm interested." Even though I was a jogger, I still had allowed my weight to climb up to 210 pounds. I could stand to lose twenty to twenty-five pounds.

Mike and I both looked at Art. Art gritted his teeth, stuck out his bottom lip, and shook his head from side to side as if to say, "It's useless. I can't lose any weight."

I almost laughed, but then I thought, "I'd better not!"

Art exhaled a large gust of air in frustration at the thought and looked at his watch as if to say, "Time might be becoming an issue." Then reluctantly he replied, "Go ahead, Mike. Tell us what's on your mind."

Mike smiled, pulled his chair up closer to the table, and put both elbows on the table as he prepared to share with Art and me his well-thought-out proposal.

"First thing, gentlemen, is we need a new set of scales to weigh with. I am prepared to fund the cost of the scales with my own personal resources."

I glanced at Art. He didn't seem impressed with Mike's generosity.

"The scales will be placed in the closet in my office. They are to be used once a week, every Tuesday morning prior to our 8:00 a.m. meeting. Our first weigh-in will be next Tuesday morning. Each person's weight on that day will be his starting number. Now, here's how the rules will work."

I glanced over at Art again. This time the expression on his face was already one of defeat. Mike leaned over toward Art to explain the rules very carefully.

"During the week, if you gain a pound or more, it will cost you ten dollars to each of the other two players for each pound you gain. For each pound you lose during the week, you will receive $10 from the other two players. That's it. We will weigh in every Tuesday, add, subtract, and pay off. What do you guys think?"

I said, "Count me in. I need to lose some weight. I'll feast between now and Monday. Then on Tuesday I'll start on my crash diet."

Art started popping his knuckles. I thought, "I wonder if Art's popping of his knuckles in any way represents what he would like to be doing to Mike's neck at this moment!"

Art said, as if under duress, "Okay, count me in as of Tuesday."

With a big smile on his face, Mike said, "Great! This will be good for Wometco. You know, a healthy Wometco management is a happy

Wometco management." He then wrote out a contract that he had each
of us sign.

Art looked at me in disgust, signed the contract, and said, "Let's go."

Financially, Mike's weight-loss program turned out to be a windfall
for me. The show-and-tell every Tuesday morning amounted to anywhere
from thirty to eighty dollars cash for me. The ten-dollar swing gave me
all the incentive I needed to cut back on food and to jog longer. I lost
twenty pounds; Mike lost about fiftecn. And Art—well, he gained a few
pounds during the program.

Unfortunately for me, after a few weeks, Art humbly asked Mike and
me to dissolve the program; Art was tired of his wallet getting lighter
every time he tipped the scales!

Betty Woodall, my secretary of eight years, retired after the Wometco
sale. I hired a young Korean-American named Julie Evans.

Julie buzzed me one day: "Mr. Heffner on line one."

Bob Heffner was Warner Brothers' Florida branch manager for distribution. Years earlier, Bob had replaced the late Roger Hill when Roger
died from the burns he received in the hotel fire in Boston. Bob was a
no-nonsense veteran film man.

"Hello friend," Bob said.

I glanced at my watch. "Do you know what time it is? It's 3:30 on a
Friday afternoon. On Fridays, you're usually long gone by now."

I heard a sigh on the other end. "I just got off the phone with Barry
Reardon, my president. We have a problem in North Miami."

I unintentionally returned the sigh. I then asked, "What's the problem?"

"Larry, we have to make a switch on the Christmas film in the 163rd
Street Theatre. We have to move *Spies Like Us* to General Cinema's 170th
Street Theatre."

My thoughts immediately drifted back to a recent meeting I had had
with Art where I had gone over the Christmas play dates in the theatres.
Art had commented that *Spies Like Us* would be a good family film for the
holidays and should do a lot of concession business. With Art being so

new to the job, I didn't want to disappoint him by now telling him that *Spies Like Us* was moving to the 170th Street Theatre . . . along with some of Wometco's money.

I pleaded, "You can't just up and take what's sure to be a solid Christmas film with two of the top names in the business, Chevy Chase and Dan Ackroyd, out of the 163rd Street."

Bob was in no mood to argue with me. "Now, you hear me out. Barry got a call from Steven Spielberg. Spielberg wants *The Color Purple* in the 163rd Street." Bob paused, "Spielberg asked Barry to work it out. And Barry told me to call you and tell you we have to make the switch."

I voiced my concern: "From everything I have read, *The Color Purple* will have limited audience appeal. You and I both know the 163rd Street is not an art theatre."

I thought, "Man, I wish I hadn't told Art we had *Spies* for Christmas in the 163rd Street."

Bob continued, "My hands are tied on this one. And so are yours. I need to call Barry, right away, and let him know the switch is made."

"All right, Bob. What can I say? *Spies* is out, and *Purple* is in."

Driving home that Friday afternoon I thought to myself, "Between now and our Tuesday meeting, I have to figure out a way to sell Mr. Arthur Hertz on the idea that losing *Spies* and picking up *Purple* in the 163rd Street is a better deal for Wometco."

I learned from that experience to never underestimate Steven Spielberg. I knew he had the box office magic when it came to an event film such as *Jaws, E.T.,* or *Indiana Jones.* But I didn't know his box office magic extended beyond the big budget special effect films until I saw *The Color Purple.* The 163rd Street Theatre had the top gross in Florida on *The Color Purple.* The film opened December 18, 1985. It played for several months, and our engagement alone grossed over $750,000. Moreover, the film brought a relatively unknown actor to the forefront: Whoopi Goldberg. Oprah Winfrey also starred in the film. A year later, *The Oprah Winfrey Show* debuted.

Traditionally, the two biggest box office weeks of the year are Christmas and New Year's week. With this being my first year as the VP and head film buyer at Wometco Theatres, I was working overtime trying to book the top movies, especially in the Miami theatres. The Sunday before the Friday opening of the Christmas films, I received a phone call from my good friend and former boss, Eddie Stern.

"Larry, this morning I was pleasantly surprised when I saw the entertainment section of the *Miami Herald*. I can't believe it! You have all the top movies booked in the Wometco theatres."

"Thank you, Eddie. That means a lot to me, coming from you."

"What caused me to spill my coffee, though, is when I saw the full-page advertisement announcing Columbia Pictures' *A Chorus Line* would open in the Dadeland and 163rd Street in 70mm. Wow! Two runs in Miami and you have them both. You have got to tell me how you ended up getting back in business with Columbia Pictures so quickly. And how in the world did you talk them into letting you play their Christmas movie *exclusively* in Miami?"

"Eddie, I should have called and warned you before you saw the *Herald*. I bet it did shock you when you saw the ads."

"Well, it's a wonder I didn't have a heart attack: a Columbia Pictures movie in a Wometco theatre!" Eddie laughed, "Okay, Houdini! Tell me how you did it."

"Eddie, when you retired, *A Chorus Line* was in production over at Embassy Pictures. So last spring, I was on the weekly phone call with Mitchell Goldman, the General Sales Manager at Embassy, trying to get a commitment to play the film exclusive in Miami. Mitchell had a problem: he was also being pressured by both General Cinema and American Multi-Cinemas to play *A Chorus Line* in Miami. But finally, after weeks of going back and forth with Mitchell, he committed the picture to me exclusively in Miami."

Eddie laughed as he asked, "I wonder what Mitchell had to give them to let you play Miami exclusive?"

"That's a good question; I don't know the answer. But here is where the story gets very interesting. So, I now have my two best theatres booked for the Christmas season for twelve weeks with a big city musical in 70mm presentation, and guess what happens? Our *good friends* at Columbia Pictures up and buy Embassy Pictures."

Eddie cursed.

"So I immediately called Mitchell; he was cleaning out his desk. He said, 'Sorry Larry, but all bets are off. As of this Friday, I am unemployed. If I were you, I would call Terry Tharpe at Columbia Pictures pronto and try to seal the deal before the other guys get to him. That is—if they haven't already.'"

"Well, of all the sorry luck," Eddie lamented.

"Yeah, it was the worst of days. Anyway, I immediately put in a call to Terry. He knew why I was calling. I told him that, prior to the sale, I had a commitment from Embassy to play *A Chorus Line* exclusive in Miami; and I wanted to discuss the same deal with him."

"Terry responded immediately. He said, 'Larry, *A Chorus Line* is now being released through Columbia Pictures. Any prior commitments you or anyone else had to play the movie with Embassy are now null and void. When I receive notification from Jeff Blake, the President of Columbia Pictures Distribution, I will then start the negotiation process on setting the film. Until then, I have nothing else to say on the matter.'"

Eddie, anxious to hear the rest of the story, said, "Go on!"

"Well, you know I am not one to go down without a fight. Every few days I would put in a call to Terry, asking him to help both himself and Columbia Pictures by doing what's best for *A Chorus Line* and recommending that Wometco play the picture. I felt like my calls were a waste of time, but I figured I had nothing to lose. All the other studios had booked their Christmas films in Miami, and I was left with two dark screens in my two best-grossing theatres. Then, the unexpected happened: I received a call from Terry Tharpe."

"'Larry, it looks like today is going to be your lucky day,' Terry remarked."

"'What's up?'"

"'Mitchell Goldman has been hired as the producer's rep on *A Chorus Line*. He talked with the studio about Miami, and they agreed with Mitchell that the Dadeland and the 163rd Street would be the best theatres to play *A Chorus Line* in.' Terry paused, and then he said, 'The picture is yours exclusive in Miami. The deal is twelve weeks.'"

"Well, I'll be." Eddie remarked. "Richard hired Mitchell as his rep, and he trumped Columbia with where the film would play."

"Who's Richard?" I asked.

"Richard Attenborough: he produced *A Chorus Line*."

"Ummm Eddie, I believe Attenborough was the director and not the producer."

"Doesn't matter; you got the film."

Almost as an afterthought Eddie commented, "Larry, I see you have *The Color Purple* in the other auditorium in the 163rd Street."

"Yes, that's one I sort of backed into."

"Big picture, Larry. *The Color Purple* and *A Chorus Line*: somebody up there is watching over you!"

My second call that Sunday afternoon came from Art Hertz. He called asking about how the weekend grosses were. After going over some of the theatres grosses with him, I asked, "Art, have you had a chance to look at the entertainment section in today's *Herald*?"

"Yes, I have seen the ads for our Friday openings. It looks as if we will be okay this holiday season. But I hope you are not relying on your Christmas bookings to make Wometco healthy, but are looking ahead to next summer. General Cinema and American Multi-Cinema will have their new theatres up and running. If I were you, I would be preparing myself for their presence in the marketplace!"

I thought to myself, "That's Art; he keeps the pressure on me. But that's okay. He's a numbers man. He wants to make sure I continue to earn my pay at Wometco."

I had big shoes to fill, but things were looking up. My years of working under the best of the best—Heyward Morgan, John Huff, and Eddie Stern—had given me the tools I needed to make the big office and the large mahogany desk my own. After six months with the new Wometco, I was promoted to the position of Vice President/Head Film Buyer. I felt a real sense of accomplishment to know that, in just six months, Art and Mike had gained complete confidence in my film-buying abilities in the highly competitive Florida theatre market. The good Christmas bookings put me in a holiday spirit. I was thankful I knew that someone up there *was* looking out for me, and I could enjoy the true meaning of the holidays.

# THE UNEXPECTED BOUQUET

*Well . . . that's quite a story.*
– Jack Nicholson

AS I REFLECTED BACK OVER my first ten months of service with Art and Mike, I was pleased, as they were, with the December 1985 holiday box-office numbers. But the month of November was by far the most memorable to me. The limousine driver put the last piece of luggage into the trunk, slammed the lid down, and then we were on our way to the hotel. Art and Mike were sitting directly across from me, and Doneata was sitting beside me. Janet Brown was sitting on the other side of Doneata, and the ladies were having a good time just talking with each other about everything they wanted to do while "the boys" were busy working at the upcoming NATO convention.

NATO is short for the National Association of Theatre Owners. NATO annually holds a convention in a major city in the United States. This particular convention was held in Los Angeles, with around five thousand theatre owners in attendance.

We stayed in a beautiful old hotel that had been restored into a magnificent piece of architecture. Doneata especially enjoyed our room and our beautiful balcony view of Los Angeles.

That evening, Mike and Janet went to the convention dinner while Art, Doneata, and I had dinner with Bruce Snyder, the President of Distribution for 20th Century Fox, in a quaint little Italian restaurant. Down through the years, Bruce had been a good friend to me and the former Wometco, and I was excited about introducing him to Art and the new Wometco. The four of us had a most enjoyable dinner, and, afterwards, Bruce suggested we return to the hotel and have after-dinner drinks.

While we were sitting in the lounge at the hotel, Bryan Holliday, a newly appointed executive with Orion Pictures, walked up and said hello to me. I introduced Bryan to Art (he already knew Bruce and Doneata). Bryan chatted with us for a couple of minutes, and as he walked away, he made a statement loud enough for all of us to hear: "Larry, I hope you've enjoyed your past relationship with Orion Pictures, because it's about to come to an end." Smiling at me as if he knew something that I didn't, Bryan abruptly left the room, and I immediately felt a knot in my stomach.

There I am sitting with the President of 20th Century Fox, the Chairman of Wometco, and my wife, when this guy torpedoes me in the presence of them all. Art wasn't sure how to react. With Bruce sitting there, it was a rather awkward time to be discussing a potential problem with one of our best customers in front of another of our best customers.

I looked over at Bruce.

He asked me, "Larry, do you know what that was all about?"

I said, "No, tell me."

"Bryan is trying to make himself look important in front of me. That's all it was, Larry."

I said, "Well, Bruce, I wish it hadn't come up during our time together, but let's not let his actions ruin a wonderful evening."

Bruce shrugged his shoulders as if to say, "No big deal."

Later, Bruce said his farewells and left for the evening. Art couldn't suppress his concern with Bryan Holliday's statement one second longer.

Immediately, Art said very emphatically, "Larry, what's this all about with Holliday?"

"Art, I don't know why Bryan would say something like that, except for the obvious reason that, just before moving to Orion Pictures, he was working for one of our competitors. In markets where Wometco operates theatres, Bryan's company has never had the opportunity to play Orion movies, and Wometco's exclusive relationship with Orion was a real point of contention with him." I thought to myself, "Maybe Bryan doesn't realize that his allegiance is to Orion now, not to his former employers."

I could see the steam starting to come out from under Art's collar. "Larry, isn't Orion Pictures the company you told me we played 100 percent, and this is one of those relationships you said was sealed? I believe you said, 'sealed in cement.'"

"Art," I replied, "my relationship at Orion is not with Bryan Holliday. It's with Bob Cheran, Orion's President of Distribution, and with Charlie Jones, their Southern Division manager. You, Mike, and I are scheduled to have lunch tomorrow with the Orion people—Bob, Charlie, and the Executive VP, Buddy Golden. At lunch we'll see just how good our cement really is with Orion."

At 12:30 we met in one of the hotel's restaurants. I remember we were seated at a round table located in the center of the restaurant—Bob, Buddy, Charlie, Art, Mike, and me. My best friend at the table was Charlie Jones. He was my original connection with Orion, and we went back to the Heyward Morgan days in Greenville. For years, Charlie had worked for 20th Century Fox, and I had been the one to help him out in the summer of 1977 by giving him a few play dates in Miami on his "little space picture," *Star Wars*. Now Charlie was responsible for sales for Orion Pictures from Texas to the Carolinas. When I had taken a chance on *Star Wars* years earlier, I made both 20th Century Fox and Wometco a great deal of money. Now I desperately needed that relationship to hold strong.

This was *not* one of those luncheons where you have some small talk, then eat a hearty lunch before you get down to the business at hand. No, it was just the opposite. I started out telling them exactly what Bryan had said the night before. As I gave the specifics, it was obvious to everyone that Bob Cheran was becoming angrier by the minute. When I finished talking, Bob hit the table so hard I was expecting to see twelve waiters respond to his command.

Bob said, "Over my dead body will we sell films away from Wometco. Who does Bryan think he is, to come into this company and start messing with my customers?"

Buddy spoke up. "He thinks he still works for his old company."

Bob said, "Well, he doesn't. Larry, I want to apologize to you, Art, and Mike for last night. I'm truly embarrassed that happened, and I do wish Bruce hadn't been there." Then Bob looked me straight in the eye and said, "Larry, as long as I'm President of Distribution at Orion Pictures, you don't have a thing to be concerned about. We're there as long as you need us."

After the luncheon I asked Art, "Well, is the cement going to hold?"

Art gave me a reassuring smile as he winked and said, "Yes, Larry, I believe it will."

That evening we were scheduled to meet Sylvester Stallone at a private party. I was in the shower trying to get refreshed from the stress of the day when Doneata stuck her head in the bathroom door and said, "Larry, you have a telephone call."

From the shower I shot back, "Honey, see if I may call them back in ten minutes." I got out of the shower, dried off, put my housecoat on, and went into the bedroom. Doneata handed me a note that read, "Call Mr. Holliday in room 2307."

"Well," I said to no one in particular, "this is going to be an interesting conversation." I dialed the phone and heard a familiar voice on the other end.

"Hello?"

"Hi, Bryan, Larry Vaughn returning your call."

In a very cordial tone of voice Bryan said, "Larry, what are you trying to do to me?"

"I beg your pardon?"

"Larry, you've got the boys all upset with me. Bob called wanting to know what I was doing making threats to his customers. Larry, don't you know I was just joking with you last night?"

"Bryan, neither I nor anyone in my party found any humor in what you had to say."

"Well, I meant nothing in what I said. Of course you're our customer. I can't believe you took me seriously."

"Okay, Bryan, let's drop it at that," I responded.

"No hard feelings?"

"No hard feelings, Bryan."

I hung up the receiver thinking, "I sure hope Bob Cheran has a long-term contract with Orion."

That evening at the Stallone party, Doneata and I enjoyed meeting Sylvester Stallone and his bride-to-be, Brigitte Nielsen. They were only five weeks away from their December 15th wedding date, and the two of them made for a most attractive couple.

Since his *Rocky* fame, Sylvester Stallone had become one of Hollywood's top box office names. His opening of *Rambo: First Blood Part II* in May of 1985 had grossed over one hundred and fifty million dollars. Despite being so successful, Mr. Stallone was easy to talk to, and I really enjoyed talking about his success with *Rambo*.

While at the party, I saw Bruce Snyder, and I brought him up-to-date on the Orion luncheon and my phone conversation with Bryan Holliday.

*Larry and Sylvester Stallone in LA*

*Brigitte Nielsen, Doneata, and Sylvester Stallone in LA*

Bruce laughed as he said, "I'm glad it's back to business as usual with you and your friends at Orion." And that's just the way the balance of the week was—business as usual. That is, up until the Thursday evening grand finale.

On Thursday evening, prior to the convention's closing ceremony, there was a private party in a room adjacent to the grand ballroom of the hotel. The party was by invitation only to a select group of 150 VIPs. Immediately following the party would be the dinner for all 5,000 convention attendees and the closing ceremonies in the grand ballroom.

*Janet Brown, Danny DeVito, and Michael Brown at the VIP party*

*Ron Howard and Larry at VIP party*

I had tickets for Art, Mike, Janet, Doneata, and me to attend the VIP party. I told them to be sure to make it to the party, because there would be several studios heads there along with some big-name stars. Ron Howard, Danny DeVito, Michael J. Fox, and Clint Eastwood were all scheduled to be there, along with several other big names in the business.

We arrived at the party right at 6:30. The room started filling up with people, but somehow Doneata and I got separated. I found Ron Howard standing over in a corner by himself and walked over to introduce myself to him. I talked with him for several minutes, telling him how much I appreciated his last film, *Cocoon*, and how I had been a fan of his from his days as Opie on the *Andy Griffith Show*. Ron Howard is a genuinely nice man. For someone who grew up in front of the camera as a star and is now behind the camera as a respected director, he seems to have a lot of humility—and that's not something you see much of among the Hollywood elite.

I started looking for Doneata, but I couldn't find her anywhere. I ran into Danny DeVito and reintroduced myself to him. I had met him years earlier at one of the industry functions. We talked about his action adventure film, *The Jewel of the Nile*, with Michael Douglas and Kathleen Turner, which was scheduled to open for Christmas.

*Danny DeVito and Larry at VIP party*

While talking with Mr. DeVito, I looked across the room and saw Doneata standing beside Clint Eastwood. From his demeanor, it was obvious Mr. Eastwood was enjoying his conversation with Doneata. I couldn't help but notice his body language as he leaned in and whispered something in her ear. Doneata looked surprised as she turned and glanced up at him. She said something to him and then pointed toward me. He looked at me and nodded his head, as though he were agreeing with her.

I thought to myself, "I wonder what they are talking about? I'd best mosey on over to them and find out." It took me a minute to get there, but I finally made my way over.

Clint Eastwood extended his hand and said, "Hello, Larry Vaughn. Doneata and I have been talking about you. She tells me that you have been faithful in playing all my films."

*Larry and Clint Eastwood at VIP party*

"Mr. Eastwood, I believe that to be correct. I have done a lot of business with Warner Brothers down through the years, and I don't think I've missed playing many of your films.

As I am a big fan of western films, I congratulated Mr. Eastwood on his summer opening of *Pale Rider*. It was an excellent western that did a lot of business at the box office. In fact, *Pale Rider* ended up being the highest-grossing western of the 1980s.

I commented to Mr. Eastwood that one of my favorite western films of all time was *The Good, the Bad and the Ugly*. When I said that, Mr. Eastwood grinned, nodded, and said, "Oh yes, I've heard that comment before!"

As he and Doneata chatted, I thought of how, in the early sixties, Mr. Eastwood had played the cowboy Rowdy Yates on the TV series *Rawhide*. From there, the Italian director Sergio Leone had asked Eastwood to be in a low-budget, Italian "spaghetti" western (as they were called by their critics). When Sergio Leone cast the young American actor to play the lead role in the film, little did he know that decision would launch Eastwood's career. The *Dollars* trilogy made Clint Eastwood a household name and, well, the rest is history! Clint Eastwood went off to Italy as a young TV actor, but he returned to America as a full-blown Hollywood star.

After a most enjoyable conversation, Doneata and I stepped aside to let some other folks have a chance to speak with Mr. Eastwood.

I said, "Let's get some more food before we leave."

"Larry, if I do, I won't be able to eat any dinner."

"It doesn't matter. Dinner can't be as good as these scrumptious hors d'oeuvres. Let's get another plate and enjoy ourselves." Doneata agreed, so we filled our plates and found a resting place.

At this point, I simply had to find out what Doneata and Clint Eastwood had been talking about. I began, "Doneata, did you have the opportunity to meet all of the celebrities?"

*Michael J. Fox and Doneata at the VIP party*

"Yes, I did. I especially enjoyed meeting Michael J. Fox. Larry, I had no idea he was so young. He was very kind to me. We talked about his hit film, *Back to the Future*. Larry, he said *Future* was the number one grossing film for eight weeks in a row. Did you know that?"

I smiled at Doneata's *naiveté*—of course I knew that.

She continued, "He acted as if his time was my time, but I could tell he was exhausted."

"Honey, everyone is tired. These conventions will wipe you out. I'm glad you had the opportunity to meet everyone. Now, let me ask you a question."

"What's that?"

"What did Clint Eastwood whisper in your ear earlier?"

Doneata put her hands on her sides and gave me a very serious look. "Larry Vaughn, do you know what he asked me?"

"No, what?"

"He wanted to know what I was doing later this evening!"

My mouth dropped, and I stammered, "You're kidding?"

"No, I'm not!"

"And what did you say?"

"I pointed toward you and said, 'I'll be with my husband—that tall man right over there.' That's when I had the opportunity to tell him that you were the buyer for Wometco."

"Then what did he say?"

"He asked, 'Have I met him?' I said, 'I don't know. I'll call Larry over.'"

At this point, I thought to myself, "Humph! Clint Eastwood's trying to come on to my wife." We finished our hors d'oeuvres and moved on into the ballroom for the banquet.

Doneata and I ended up with fairly good seating. Our table was located about two-thirds of the way back, but it was situated directly beside one of the two main aisles which led in and out of the ballroom. We didn't feel the need to be seated near the dais, though, because we had talked with nearly everyone on the dais earlier.

The most interesting event of the evening, as far as I was concerned, happened at the closing of the ceremony. All the awards had been given out, all the speeches had been made, and all the stars were preparing to leave the dais to exit the ballroom. Clint Eastwood was

*Clint Eastwood and Doneata at VIP party*

the first to leave the stage, along with Barry Reardon and other Warner Brothers executives. Eastwood, being first in line, set the tempo for everyone behind him. He happened to exit the aisle closest to our table. A spotlight and television network cameras followed him as he walked the aisle toward the exit.

While walking toward the exit, Mr. Eastwood spotted Doneata. He immediately stopped on the spot, which meant that the twenty celebrities behind him also had to abruptly stop. He stepped over the crowd-control ropes and walked past the security guards, who were separating the people from the aisle, and walked the fifteen feet or more over to our table. Then Mr. Eastwood proceeded to pick up the bouquet of flowers that was being used as the centerpiece on our table . . . and graciously handed the bouquet to Doneata. He gave her a warm smile, then turned and walked back to the security guards and crossed back over the rope, where all the other celebrities and executives were standing waiting for him to return so that that they could leave the ballroom.

Doneata had nowhere to hide. She could only stand there, totally embarrassed, with five thousand people looking at her and her bouquet of flowers.

# MONEYBAGS

*For me, the cinema is not a slice of life, but a piece of cake.*
— Alfred Hitchcock

IT FELT GREAT TO BE back in Miami after spending the previous week in Los Angeles. Doneata and I spent Saturday with the children, and Sunday was our day of rest and worship. I had a busy week ahead at the office. I had bids due, screenings daily, a backlog of paperwork, and as always there were those unexpected and untimely meetings with Art and his investors. In addition, that week I had two important dinners scheduled with film distributors.

Wayne Lewellen, Paramount's President of Distribution, had requested a meeting in Miami with Art, Mike, and me. In prepping Art for the dinner I told him, "Art, Wayne Lewellen is not someone you make a commitment to and later break it. Wayne is known by his fellow distribution presidents as 'The Godfather of Distribution.' Wayne's word is his bond. And he will expect the same from you."

Art winked as he replied, "I got it."

I thought to myself, "The beauty of the film business is so much more than films, directors, and actors—it's relationships. Actually, it's more than *just* relationship—it is loyalty and trust." While not everyone followed the bond of trust, I learned quickly whom to trust and whom not to trust. Among those few loyal friends, our word was our bond. We worked together, day in and day out. I counted on them, and they, in turn, counted on me. We established a bond of mutual respect and loyalty for each other.

The meeting was held at Joe's Stone Crab Restaurant on Miami Beach. Art, Mike, and I met with Wayne and two of his top lieutenants. Wayne addressed, front and center, how Paramount was getting the cold shoulder from Wometco in Puerto Rico. This disturbed Wayne, as Puerto Rico was a high-grossing movie market, especially with the action films. Peter Moreno, our film buyer in Puerto Rico, was known for playing Paramount movies only when it suited Peter to play them.

Wayne made a proposal to Art and Mike. "I will take care of Wometco in Florida if Wometco will take care of me in Puerto Rico. I want assurance from you guys that all of my films will play in your top track of theatres in Puerto Rico. In return, my guys will work with Larry and give Larry what he needs in Florida."

Art and Mike knew enough about the film companies to know that Paramount Pictures was one of the major film studios. A relationship with Paramount in Florida would pay off in spades. With only a moment's hesitation, Art and Mike agreed to Wayne's most generous proposal. As they shook hands I thought to myself, "What is great news for me is going to be a nightmare for Peter Moreno." I also wondered why Peter wasn't invited to the dinner and the meeting.

In the months ahead, our relationship with Paramount Pictures was a sweet one. The only aggravation I inherited from the deal was my having to keep Peter Moreno in check with his unwanted relationship with Paramount Pictures.

The next big dinner on my agenda was with Charlie Jones. One Thursday afternoon, Charlie flew in from Dallas to settle the film rental payments on the box office mega-hit film, *Platoon*. As always, it was good to see my pal, Charlie. Down through the years Charlie had become one of my very best friends. A few years earlier I had been best man at Charlie's wedding when he and Thelma, the love of his life, were married.

Charlie was a tall, rugged guy who knew the film business inside out. He was a high roller when it came to placing a wager on just about anything: a game of golf, a blackjack table, a sports bet, or a high-stakes poker game. Charlie knew no fear when it came to a bet, and his reputation as a two-fisted drinker, however, preceded all of the above. He was known to make some of the best deals for Orion Pictures while nursing a vodka gimlet or two . . . or three or four. He was known as a very tough, nononsense, Southern division manager who did a very good job for Orion Pictures—in spite of his personal lifestyle. Like him or not, Charlie Jones had built up quite a reputation for himself.

I picked Charlie up at the airport at 4:30 p.m. and drove him to his hotel, the Grand Bay in Coconut Grove. I spent the remainder of the afternoon with him in the hotel's lounge. That evening, Charlie and I

*Larry, a film executive, and Charlie Jones, at a golf tournament*

were to have dinner with Art in one of the private clubs in the Grove. I was a bit concerned about Charlie, as he was already "totally relaxed" by the time we left the lounge. Then the first thing Art did was order him a drink. I could see this was going to be another one of those long "Charlie Jones" evenings.

Art was hungry for industry gossip. He loved data, data, and more data. Charlie brought Art and me up-to date with everything that was going on in production at Orion Pictures. He discussed the industry as a whole and the latest news about what other theatre circuits were doing with their expansion programs.

Finally, Charlie held up his hands and pleaded, "Art, that's enough shoptalk. I came to Miami to see my good friends at Wometco. I'm here to spend money, to wine and dine you and Larry." Laughing, Charlie said, "I'm here especially to wine you."

I said, "Charlie, you can wine and dine us when we're in Dallas. As long as you're in our town, we do the wining and dining."

Art spoke up, "Yeah, who do you think you're having dinner with? We're not one of those other cheap theatre circuits. In Miami your money is no good, Charlie Jones."

Charlie smiled at Art, and then in a businesslike tone of voice he said, "I wish you guys were as friendly at settling the film rental payments on pictures as you are in picking up dinner checks."

Charlie then looked at me and stuck out his tongue. When he did that, Art looked totally dumbfounded at Charlie's most unusual behavior. Then Charlie said with a smirk on his face, "Larry, you're a miserable guy to settle film rental payments with. I think I'll make Bryan happy and start playing my pictures with the opposition theatres."

I looked at Art and said, "You see the type of character I have to do business with."

Charlie motioned to the waiter for a refill on his drink and said, "Larry, are you saying I have no class, or just low class?"

"Charlie, I didn't say anything about your class. I was talking about your character. I'll discuss your class tomorrow after we have finalized the film rental payments on *Platoon*."

Charlie nudged Art and said, "Art, how would you like to settle the film rental payments on *Platoon* with me right here and now, and leave Larry out?" Holding up three fingers as if to say, "Scout's honor," Charlie said, "Art, I promise I'll give you a better settlement than I will him." Charlie pointed toward me as he puffed his cheeks out and stuck his finger up in the air.

I thought to myself, "Charlie is getting stone drunk. Art is used to dealing with politicians and bankers, not people like Charlie Jones. It's going to be interesting to see how Art handles this proposal. We have about twenty theatres playing *Platoon*, which has grossed megabucks."

Art said, "Charlie, if I settle with you, then I will have Larry upset with me for not allowing him to do his job. I'd better let the two of you work out the settlement on *Platoon*."

I thought, "Very good, Art."

Charlie started waving at Art, "Tell your money bye-bye. I'm offering a one-time *Platoon* sale."

Art gave a very cordial smile and said, "No, you and Larry work out the settlement."

I don't think Art really knew how to take Charlie, but I knew that Charlie was just giving Art a hard time.

Then Charlie said, "Okay, Larry, let's settle the picture right now across the board. One percentage number, and it's done. Larry and I will write down what we think a fair film rental payment to be on a napkin. Then we'll place the two napkins in this cup, and Art will pick one of the two napkins. The napkin Art picks is the final settlement on *Platoon* for all the Wometco play dates."

Then Charlie held up his fist and looked at me as if to say, "But you'd better be fair." Charlie then paused to explain the rules, "The figures have to be in line with what I can get New York to approve and with what Larry can get . . ." Charlie pointed toward Art, "moneybags over here to be pleased with."

I leaned over the table and eyeballed Charlie. "Let's do it." The concern in Art's face was obvious. By his expression alone I knew that Art felt Charlie's method of conducting business was entirely inappropriate. No,

Art didn't appreciate or understand this haphazard way of settling the film rental on a film like *Platoon*. Art's pick of a napkin from the cup could mean literally thousands of dollars in Wometco's plus or minus column.

Charlie thought a few seconds, and then jotted down his number on his napkin. I did the same. We then placed the two napkins in a cup, and Charlie mixed up the napkins. He then handed the cup to Art and asked Art to hold the cup over his head. Then he told Art to pick one of the napkins. Art, with a look on his face as if to say, "I can't believe I have to do this," took the cup and raised it in the air.

Immediately, Charlie pulled the cup away before Art could take a napkin, and then Charlie looked in disbelief at me. Charlie said, "You were going to go through with it, weren't you?"

"Absolutely, why not?"

Charlie looked at Art and shaking his head from side to side, he pointed his finger at me as he said, "Art, you've got a dangerous man working for you."

While Charlie was talking, Art's hand dove for the napkins in the cup. He wanted to see the numbers that Charlie and I had written down. Charlie's number was fifty-seven-and-a-half percent. My number was fifty-two-and-a-half percent.

Charlie said, "Art, if I were you, I'd get me another film buyer, one who's not so hard on distributors." Then leaning back in his chair and placing both his hands over his heart, Charlie said, "And on their hearts! Now if you gentlemen will excuse me, I'm going to try to find the men's room."

Art did not try to hide from me his disapproval of Charlie Jones's shenanigan ways. When Charlie was out of sight, Art became very straightforward. "Larry, I haven't figured out exactly what all is involved between you and the film companies in the way you obtain films and settle film rental payments for films played in our theatres. One day soon, however, I expect to understand exactly what it is you do. Between now and then, I wish you would be more careful with the company's money."

I knew before Charlie ever left the table that Art was upset. I figured I'd best try to explain. "Art, I told you when I came to work for you, that I purchase films and settle films differently with each distributor. When you get back to your office tomorrow, look at your film rental settlement sheets with Orion Pictures. You will see right there in black and white that no one, I mean no one, gives us better film rental settlements than Charlie Jones." I knew I was now talking in crystal clear terms for Mr. Arthur Hertz—numbers, in black and white.

Art shook his head in disbelief and said, "Larry, what do you think you'll end up settling *Platoon* for?"

"It will average out somewhere between fifty-four to fifty-five percent."

"Well, if Charlie hadn't backed down, we could have ended up paying a bump of two-and-a-half percent on every one of our play dates on *Platoon*." Frowning as he shook his head from side to side, Art said, "Larry, that's a lot of money."

I shrugged my shoulders. "That's true. Or we could have ended up saving two-and-a-half percent. Art, this is all part of film buying. Don't let it get to you. Here comes Charlie."

The dinner came, and the three of us started enjoying our delicious meal. After dinner I took Charlie back to his hotel. Overall, I thought the dinner was a success. I had a feeling Art went home exhausted after spending the evening with Charlie, but I also think he came away with a better understanding of the complexities of film buying. Charlie Jones left the dinner satisfied because he had not only rattled Art's cage, but he had also given Art a nickname. And I came away from the dinner with a greater appreciation of the fact that there's only one Charlie Jones.

# THE GOLDEN OPPORTUNITY

*I'm going to make him an offer he can't refuse.*
– Marlon Brando, *The Godfather*

IT WAS MID-FEBRUARY, AND I found myself once again on an airplane, this time going to the ShoWest convention in Las Vegas. Upon arrival in Vegas, I took a taxi to the hotel. I asked the taxi driver, "What's the latest news in Vegas?"

"Mister, last week the strangest thing happened downtown. This guy walks into one of the casinos with two bags, one in each hand. One bag has five hundred thousand dollars in cash, and the other bag is empty. He walks over to the pit boss at one of the craps tables and says he wants to put the whole five hundred grand on the next roll of the dice.

"Now mister, a woman was rolling the dice at that particular table, so the guy said, 'I'll play her next roll of the dice.' So, the lady rolls the dice and comes up a winner. The guy had them put his winnings, five hundred thousand dollars cash, into the empty bag. He then left with two bags of cash totaling a million dollars. Now what do you make of that?"

I thought a moment, and then I said, "Well, either this could have been a very desperate man who had to have five hundred thousand dollars and was willing to lose just that much money to get it, or it could have been a great publicity stunt put on by the casino. See, that's all we've talked about for the last five minutes."

The cabby said almost angrily, "You know, I didn't think of a publicity stunt idea. I wonder if it was."

He pulled the cab up to the entrance of the Bally Hotel, and there were people standing around outside everywhere. I knew something was wrong. When I went inside, there was a long line at the registration desk.

A hotel receptionist said, "Sir, the computers are down. We're running two to three hours late on checking in." No problem, I could check in later.

That evening I met with Terry Tharpe, the Southern Division Manager of Columbia Pictures, for dinner at the hotel. After dinner I went back over to the registration desk, and the check-in situation was still impossible. The woman at the desk apologized and told me it would still be an hour or two before I could expect to get into my room. I turned around and thought, "Now what? I've got a couple of hours to kill. I might as well check out the action in the casino."

As I slowly walked through the casino, I heard a familiar voice say, "Larry Vaughn, get over here and sit down."

I turned to see my good friend Wayne Lewellen sitting at a blackjack table. I walked over and started talking with Wayne.

He said, "Come on, man. Get out some money, and let's get this table smoking." Optimistically, Wayne said, "Larry, my friend, tonight is our night. I can just feel it."

A few minutes later Jimmy Spitz, the former President of Columbia Pictures Distribution, stopped by our table. Jimmy sat down and talked to us as we played, but he didn't do any gambling.

Well, the old Larry Vaughn came to life. I started gambling like I had in years gone past. At one point I was up more than $20,000. On one hand alone I won $6,000. Jimmy left the table around midnight. Wayne and I stayed and gambled together until 6:30 the following morning. After all was said and done, Wayne had won about $4,500, and I walked away winning more than $15,000.[13]

Wayne looked at me as we cashed our chips into hundred dollar bills. "Larry, I knew last night we were going to have a hot streak. I'm sure glad you ran into me. Let's go celebrate our winnings over breakfast."

Wayne and I went to breakfast and talked about some of the many outstanding hands we had during our all-night blackjack game. Wayne made me promise that we would gamble together again before the week was over.

After breakfast I went over to the registration desk to see if my room was ready for check-in. The lady at the desk informed me that my standard room had been upgraded to one of the tower suites by the hotel management. I immediately thought back to around 2:30 that morning. That was about the time the casino boss asked me if I had checked into my room. I told him that the line was too long earlier, and I would check in after I left the blackjack table.

I thought, "They have marked me down as a high roller and upgraded me to a tower suite. This is like going back to the Heyward Morgan days." My room was a huge, beautiful suite that was reserved for high rollers. The casino boss at the Bally had wanted to make sure my stay with them was a pleasant one.

I looked at my watch and realized that I was supposed to meet Art and Mike in less than an hour. Getting no sleep the night before was going to make for an extra-long day.

I took a quick shower and changed into a fresh suit of clothes. In order to avoid pickpockets, I took a safety pin and pinned the envelope with over 150 hundred-dollar bills to my inside breast coat pocket. Then I hurriedly left the room to meet with Art and Mike.

I said absolutely nothing to anyone about how I had just spent the last eight hours, because I was hoping it would remain a well-kept secret between Wayne, Jimmy, and me. But it didn't. During the day it seemed like everywhere I went, someone had heard of my good fortune at the blackjack table the night before. Finally, I realized the consequences of

---

13    Equivalent to about $9,600 and $32,000 in 2014 dollars.

my actions. My all-night card game with Wayne Lewellen was the talk of the convention. By mid-afternoon, my winnings were being exaggerated by some people to be over twice what I had actually won.

That evening, in the quiet of my room, the reality of my all-night blackjack game became front and center in my thoughts. I was disappointed that I had allowed myself to get caught up in the thrill of the game and had lost control. I knew it was best, for all the right reasons, to put all my time and energy into my work during the remainder of my stay in Vegas. I then prayed for strength and help to overcome my desire for gambling.

I spent the rest of the convention meeting with various studio heads and going to industry luncheons and dinners. I always enjoyed the convention meals, and the evenings would be filled with entertainment. Hollywood's big-name actors would be seated on the dais, along with studio executives; the actors would talk about their upcoming films, and then they would show previews of their yet-to-be-released movies. Between the lunches and dinners, I would enjoy visiting the hospitality suites of the various studios, which were a more intimate setting, where one could have the pleasure of meeting and talking with actors, directors, producers, and other industry people about their upcoming films.

After that Vegas trip, the only other time I played blackjack in Vegas was to help out a buddy in need. I met Bert Livingston when he was the Florida branch manager for 20th Century Fox. Through the years Bert and I developed a close, personal friendship. We enjoyed each other's company immensely. When Bert was in Miami, he was always a welcome guest in my home; Doneata and the kids always loved seeing Bert when he was in town. And likewise, I always enjoyed spending time in Bert's homes—in Jacksonville, Dallas, and later, Beverly Hills—with his lovely wife, Janie, and their two children.

So I was looking forward to our dinner in one of the fine restaurants at MGM's Bally Hotel. After we were seated, I noticed right away that Bert seemed depressed, so I asked him, "Bert, what's wrong with you?"

He sighed, "Larry, this afternoon I arrived in Vegas. Man, I am already broke." He shrugged his shoulders in hopelessness as he continued, "I lost over $2,000 on the blackjack table."

Not wanting to ruin our dinner, I said, "Bert, let's enjoy our meal. As soon as we finish dinner, I will help you win your money back."

In years past, Bert had seen me in action on the blackjack tables. He excitedly asked, "Larry, do you think you can really win my money back?"

I nodded as I replied, "Absolutely! I know I can win two grand. Now, let's forget your earlier losses and enjoy our meal."

After dinner we went straight to the casino floor. I told Bert to go to the teller's window and get a $3,000 cash advance on his Visa card.

He asked, "How much?"

"Bert, trust me. Get *three thousand* dollars."

He asked again, "Are you sure we need three grand?"

"Yes, Bert. Please just get the cash."

With cash in hand, we walked over to a blackjack table where I picked a seat for Bert to play. I stood directly behind him. As the dealer dealt the cards, I instructed Bert when and how much money to bet. Within half an hour Bert had won back his earlier losses, plus the fee that Visa charged for the $3,000 cash advance.

As we walked to the elevator I remarked, "Okay, Bert, you are now even for the day. What you do from here on out is entirely up to you. As for me, I am going to bed."

Bert replied, "Larry, when it comes to a deck of cards, you are in a league all your own. I can't believe the way you made me play those hands. I could never have done it on my own. When it comes to gambling, you must have ice water in your veins."

I smiled as I replied, "Yes, I've heard that statement before." I paused as I continued, "Well Bert, here's what you have to remember when gambling: it's only money." I smiled as I added, "Besides, it was your money, not mine!"

That was the last time I ever played blackjack.

I spent the next few months staying very busy at the office. Wometco, like other theatre circuits, was in an expansion mode. The company as a whole was having a very good year, and Art and Mike were trying to protect our position in the Miami area by building several new state-of-the-art multiplex theatres.

One benefit I received from Wometco's new relationship with Paramount Pictures was working with John Hersker, Wayne Lewellen's newly-appointed Florida branch manager. Early on, John and I became close personal friends. One of my first negotiations with John was for our flagship theatre, the Dadeland Twin, where we opened the much anticipated *Star Trek IV: The Voyage Home* in 70mm presentation for Christmas in 1986. Playing a Paramount picture at the Dadeland Twin Theatre was, to my knowledge, a first for Wometco. In years past, the Dadeland Twin did not play any of Paramount's movies, as Paramount sold their movies to Wometco's competitors, Loews and General Cinema. Rather than bid for Paramount movies, we opted to fill our screens with other studios' movies. I felt a sense of pride to be finally playing a Paramount film in the best-grossing theatre in Florida!

Some of my fondest Paramount memories are from when John and I would talk for hours on the phone, working on Paramount's film release schedule and allocating which play dates worked best in each theatre. It was like solving a puzzle, and it was fun when all the pieces came together and we both were satisfied with the end result.

Julie buzzed me, "Mr. Vaughn, you have a Mr. Forbes here to see you."

I went out to meet him. Ever since his secretary had called and set up the meeting, I had been wondering why David Forbes would fly through Miami for such a brief meeting with me. I had seen David's picture in all the trade magazines and knew he had a unique look. He wore his salt-and-pepper hair short, and his hairstyle, coupled with his conservative suits and small, round wood eyeglass frames, gave him somewhat of an Ivy League look. He used to be associated with the actor, the late Steve

McQueen; David was Steve McQueen's press agent, or publicist, or something along those lines.

MGM/UA had recently appointed David Forbes as President of Distribution. MGM/UA was one of the oldest and most famous of all the major studios, but also one of the most troubled studios. In recent years, MGM/UA had been bought and sold several times over. The company had been struggling for some time in trying to get big-name directors and producers under contract. They desperately needed some big movies to help get MGM/UA back on track. The industry thought it was a move in the right direction when MGM/UA's board of directors brought David Forbes aboard to head up their distribution arm.

"Hello, Larry Vaughn. I have been looking forward to meeting you."

"Likewise, David. Please come in."

As I went to close the door, I told Julie to hold my calls. David Forbes looked just like he did in his photographs.

He sat down at the far end of my large desk. I bypassed my office chair and sat down directly across from him. We made small talk about Wometco, MGM/UA, and the industry as a whole. Then David got right to the purpose of his visit.

"Larry, let me tell you why I am here today. I wanted to meet you and talk with you about the possibility of your joining the senior management team at MGM/UA. I have two men I intend to interview for the position of General Sales Manager, Eastern Division, for domestic distribution. I guess you have figured by my being here that you are one of those men. I am going to interview the other man tomorrow afternoon. I shall make my decision when I return to the studio in LA on Monday."

David spent fifteen to twenty minutes talking about his plans for reorganizing the distribution arm of the company, and what my responsibilities would be. He said, "Larry, your responsibility would be the oversight of the placement of films in those theatres located throughout the entire Southeastern United States."

He concluded his introduction with, "Larry, this would be a golden opportunity for you. The sky would be the limit." Smiling, he said, "Well, have I whet your appetite or not?"

I sat back and gave him a warm smile of appreciation for his consideration. I then said, "You know, there are a lot of people who would give anything to have an opportunity to be a part of the new management team that David Forbes is putting together at MGM/UA. But David, in all honesty, I don't believe I'm your man."

He had a very inquisitive look on his face as if to say, "Really?"

I went on to say, "David, I am deeply honored that my name would even be brought up as a candidate to be a part of your team. There was a time when I would have given anything for such an opportunity. In all honesty, though, today I am content where I am. I enjoy working for Art Hertz." I paused as I smiled and said, "Even though, at times, Art Hertz can be next to impossible!" David nodded and smiled as if he understood. I continued, "At this juncture, I feel Wometco is where I am supposed to be. David, I give Wometco one hundred percent when I am on the job. However, Wometco takes third place in my list of priorities. When I leave the office, my time and energy are put into my family and my church."

I paused a moment. "Now, David, what I think you are looking for is a man who is going to be loyal to you and MGM/UA first, second, and third. And that's okay. It's just that, well, after what I have just told you, I don't see myself being that man."

While nodding his head in agreement, David said, "I think I understand." He thought a moment. Then he said, "Larry, thank you for being so open and honest with me. It's been a pleasure meeting you. On your next trip to LA, I'd like to take you to one of my favorite restaurants for dinner."

"David, that's a dinner I'm looking forward to."

We shook hands. I thanked David again for his consideration and wished him much success with his new challenge at MGM/UA.

THIRTY-THREE

# "LIVIN' ON A PRAYER"[14]

*Why love if losing hurts so much?*
*I have no answers anymore; only the life I have lived.*
— Anthony Hopkins, *Shadowlands*

STANDING AT THE FOOT OF the hospital bed watching the nurses go through the tedious process of hooking all the small electrodes from the monitor to Larry, Jr.'s head made me wonder if our medical problems were ever going to end. Dr. Duschanney was very concerned about the way the medications were having very little, if any, effect on Larry's continuous seizure activity. In a few short months, we had seen our three-and-a-half-year-old son's body digress back into infancy. Larry was back in diapers, constantly drooling at the mouth, and staying continuously doped up from medications.

I thought about my little boy, my namesake. Before these health issues, he had been such a happy child. When he smiled, he was all teeth. I had often wondered when he would grow into his big adorable smile. He loved people and would easily brighten any room. He also loved to dance. Whenever there was music playing, Larry was jamming. We didn't know

---

14    Bon Jovi, "Livin' on a Prayer," by Richard Sambora, Jon Bon Jovi, and Desmond Child, from the album Slippery When Wet, Mercury Records, 1986.

for sure where he got that talent from, but I knew it probably came from Doneata, not me. Now I didn't know if he would ever grow up to be a normal child, or if he would even grow up at all. I wiped a tear from my eye. I would have given anything to trade places with him. I wanted him to grow up and live a full life. I thought of David and all he had suffered. I had to be strong for Doneata. I had to be strong for Larry, Jr. I knew I needed help—help that only comes from God.

After two long days of watching Larry, Jr.'s brain cell activity being monitored on a moment-by-moment basis, Doneata and I finally met with Dr. Duschanney. He gave us a very sympathetic look. "Mr. and Mrs. Vaughn, the results of our tests confirm why Larry's behavior has been the way it is. Every medication or combination of medications that we have tried on Larry has been totally ineffective. His brain is continuing to have uncontrollable multiple-seizure activity."

After a moment Dr. Duschanney sat up erect in his chair and took off his reading glasses. "Mr. and Mrs. Vaughn, I think we should now consider the possibility of your son having a surgical procedure that will, hopefully, alleviate the seizure activity in his brain. However," Dr. Duschanney paused before continuing, "I must warn you. Having this operation does not in any way guarantee that Larry's seizure problem will be rectified. It is an alternative consideration, only to be used when medi-cation has proven to be completely ineffective. Let me explain the surgery to the two of you so that you may weigh your options."

I thought to myself, "I wish Doneata were at home, and I could spare her from having to hear this firsthand. It would be easier on her if I could sugarcoat the bad news to her, rather than have this guy give it to her point-blank."

"The first thing you need to be aware of is that this particular surgical procedure has been performed only sixty-six times in the United States. The majority of the operations have been performed in two hospitals up north, but one operation was performed here in South Miami within the last two months."

Doneata interrupted, "How is that child doing?"

"I'm sorry to report, not well. The child is still in a coma." Dr. Duschanney coughed and cleared his throat. "If we perform this surgery on your son, our intent will be to go into the front right side of the brain and remove a portion of the temporal lobe area. This is the area where all of Larry's abnormal cell activity is coming from. By removing this area of the child's brain, it should enable us to anticipate one of the following results."

Dr. Duschanney emphasized each number as he spoke, "One, the child could be totally free from abnormal cell activity—in other words, normal. That's the best case scenario. Two, by having this surgery, Larry would *not* be free from experiencing seizure activity. However, we would then be able to control Larry's seizure activity with medications. That's still a good result. Three, the surgery would have no effect at all on Larry's condition. His abnormal seizure activity would not be affected by the surgery. Of the sixty-six surgeries performed so far, those are the results we have received. Larry's odds would be evenly split, which is a thirty-three percent chance for each outcome.

"Now let me give you the possible side effects: blindness, paralysis, and death. All three are possibilities with this type of brain surgery." Dr. Duschanney paused, dropped his head, and said, "I'm really sorry that I don't have better news for you, but all I can do is give you the facts as they are."

I smiled and nodded as if to say, "We understand. None of this is your doing." Honestly, however, I didn't understand. How does one process this kind of news? I felt numb. I wanted to run into my son's hospital room, pick him up, tell the doctor he had made a big mistake, and take my little boy home.

Dr. Duschanney relaxed in his chair as if he had just finished a very unpleasant chore. Doneata's eyes were full of tears and concern, and yet she did not cry. But I knew it was all she could do to try to hold her composure.

I looked at short, white-headed Dr. Duschanney. He looked his part: a surgeon, a thinker, one of the intellects of our society. I thought to myself, "If this were a poker hand, I would fold and ask for a redeal. I don't like having to play this hand that I have been dealt."

282    HOLLYWOOD'S CHOSEN

"Dr. Duschanney, you have given Doneata and me a lot to think about. Let the two of us sort through all of this information and get back with you. If we decide to have you operate, when would you want to schedule the operation?"

"Within the next three months. Actually, a surgeon from the Northeast who specializes in this procedure will fly down to do the surgery. For the child's sake, the sooner we operate, the better off he will be."

I thought to myself, "So much for weighing our options." Then I continued, "Okay, thank you for your time. You'll hear from us by the first of next week." I was amazed at how calm and collected I was.

Doneata's sister, Mentora, met us at the hospital. She noticed how exhausted Doneata and I both were, so she insisted we both go home, and said that she would take care of Larry that night, so Doneata and I could get a much-needed break. We felt very blessed to have her help in our time of crisis.

Driving home from the hospital, I wanted to ignore the fact that we had just received terrible news only moments earlier. Sitting there at a red light, I looked over at Doneata, and I reached over for her hand. It's like we both knew, somehow, that we had to get beyond our emotions.

"Doneata, I think God is going to heal Larry's brain completely, and He is going to use the surgery as the means by which He heals Larry. Honey, I believe with all my heart that the surgery will not be done in vain. God is going to use Dr. Duschanney to perform a miracle in our son's life."

Doneata squeezed my hand and said, "Oh, Larry, what would we do in times like this, without the Lord?"

"Honey, I would be on my way to get drunk as a skunk."

Doneata laughed and said, "Honey, I feel encouraged. I know God is in control, and I also believe we are going to have a victory."

"Good. Now, let's work on getting some prayer support before the day of the surgery."

That afternoon Doneata called our dear friends, Wilf and Nancy Bellamy, to ask them to remember Larry, Jr. during their prayer time.

Prior to Larry, Jr.'s scheduled surgery date, Doneata started going around to various churches in the Miami area, showing ministers a

picture of Larry, Jr., and asking the minister to share with his congrega-
tion Larry, Jr.'s upcoming surgery.

Doneata and I checked Larry, Jr. into Miami Children's Hospital four
days before his scheduled surgery date. Dr. Duschanney said, "Because
of the seriousness of the surgery, we must put Larry, Jr. through this test
one more time, just to make absolutely sure all the seizure activity is con-
tained in the temporal lobe area of his brain." Larry was put in a brand-
new room in a new wing of the hospital. The nurses came in, carefully
placing each electrode in its proper place on Larry's head, and then began
the long process of monitoring his brain activity.

A few hours later the nurse came in to report that there was a problem
with the equipment. The nurse said, "Mr. Vaughn, I need to switch monitors. There must be something wrong with the monitor that we are using.
Everything is showing up normal on the screen. You know, this is a new
room, and it is going to take time for us to work the bugs out."

I responded, "That's fine." Larry, Jr. gave the nurse one of his irresist-
ible smiles.

The following morning the nurse and Dr. Duschanney came into the
room together. Dr. Duschanney was the first to speak, "Mr. Vaughn, we
are going to have to move Larry, Jr. into another room. We can't get the
equipment on track in this room. We spent all this money for the best
equipment money can buy, and what happens? It doesn't work properly."

"I understand. Larry, Jr. didn't care for the wallpaper in this room anyway." We all chuckled as we started packing to move to another room.

Later that afternoon, Dr. Duschanney came into Larry's room. He
looked worn out. He sat down in the chair located across from Larry, Jr.'s
bed. He took his reading glasses and propped them up on his forehead.
He took in a deep breath of frustration as if to say, "What a day!"

"Dr. Duschanney, you look like you've seen better days."

Dr. Duschanney held his arms out with his hands open wide and said
emphatically, "Mr. Vaughn, your son is making me out to look like a fool."
I sat up, because I was really curious about what he was talking about. "I
know what I am about to say is going to make absolutely no sense, but
for the past day and a half, your son has had no abnormal brain activity."

I just stared at the man, trying to figure out if I had heard him correctly. "Mr. Vaughn, I'm telling you there is absolutely nothing wrong with Larry. He has gone from continuous long-term multiple-seizure activity to zero seizure activity."

As if embarrassed, Dr. Duschanney continued, "We can't operate where there is no problem. The surgeon we flew in for this surgery is waiting to perform the surgery and now has arrived with no surgery to perform!"

I thought to myself, "What's wrong with me? Why didn't I see it before now?" Gathering my thoughts, I replied, "Dr. Duschanney, I can explain exactly what has happened."

Rubbing his eyes and acting as if he wasn't really interested in my uneducated theory, Dr. Duschanney said emphatically, "Tell me. I'm looking for an answer."

"It was God. God has healed Larry, Jr." Dr. Duschanney looked at me as if I were talking about the Easter bunny. I thought, "I must get that smirk of disbelief off his face."

"Dr. Duschanney, let me explain. My wife and I are Christians."

He raised his eyebrows as if to say, "Here we go."

"We have been calling Christian people all over the country—over two hundred churches—asking them to pray that the Lord would use this surgery to heal our son. Dr. Duschanney, your equipment is not broken, and Larry, Jr. is not sick. I thought God was going to heal Larry, Jr. through the surgery. Don't you see what has happened here? God has performed a miracle right before our very eyes."

I could tell the good doctor was not buying what I was selling. "Now, Mr. Vaughn, let's not get carried away with God performing some supernatural miracle just yet. There is a very good possibility that your son's seizure activity will return in the very near future."

"Dr. Duschanney, with all due respect to your medical expertise, you're wrong." That statement produced a frown on the doctor's face. "When God does a healing of this nature, it is permanent. Isn't God good? He spared us from having to go through the surgery."

Dr. Duschanney was just sitting there with a frown on his face, only halfway listening to what I was trying to tell him. I could see his wheels spinning. His mind was searching, searching for an answer.

After a while Dr. Duschanney came up with his own theory. "Mr. Vaughn, what could have very well happened is that your son, at the eleventh hour, realized the seriousness of the surgery. His body could have reacted by healing itself, rather than going through the trauma of the surgery. So, don't be surprised if the seizures return. When that time comes, we'll re-evaluate our position and act accordingly."

I was getting irritated with his disbelief. "Dr. Duschanney, God healed my son. You won't see Larry, Jr. again in this hospital for seizure problems."

That day was the end of Larry's seizures. It took Doneata several months to wean Larry off his medications, but within a few months he was a totally normal child. My family and I witnessed a miracle that day, a miracle I will never forget.

While in New York at a dinner, I met a very interesting man. His name was A. Foster McKissick. Mr. McKissick and I had one very special thing in common: we were both from Greenville, South Carolina.

The first time I heard the name Foster McKissick was some twelve years before, when I worked for John Huff at ABC. I was told at that time that Foster McKissick was one of the wealthiest men, if not *the* wealthiest man, in South Carolina. He was an entrepreneur on a grand scale.

Mr. McKissick was broadly diversified in his business holdings. He had vast real estate properties and was also into banking, car dealerships, credit companies, etc. He owned and operated an oceanfront resort, Litchfield by the Sea, which is a planned community at Litchfield Beach, South Carolina, located a stone's throw away from Pawley's Island, South Carolina. At Litchfield Beach, Mr. McKissick also owned and operated a hotel, three 18-hole championship golf courses, and the Litchfield Country Club. And last but by no means least, he owned a twin theatre.

Recently, Mr. McKissick had sold all but a few of his theatres to United Artists Theatres. At that time, United Artists was the largest theatre circuit in the United States. I was told by several people that the theatre business was Foster's true love. But one day United Artists came knocking at Foster's door with a pocketful of cash, and Foster just couldn't say no.

Upon meeting Foster, I thought, "He's not at all like what I had expected him to be." I had heard so much about Foster McKissick down through the years that I was expecting to meet a man who carried himself like a Mitchell Wolfson, or maybe even an Eddie Stern. But Foster was just the opposite. Everyone at the dinner, except Foster, was in a tuxedo. Foster sported a blue oxford shirt, a blue tie with the Litchfield logo, and khaki pants. I noticed there was a pipe tucked between his belt and his slacks. He looked to be in his mid-to-late fifties. He had a full head of brownish-gray hair that went well with his silver-framed glasses.

Mr. McKissick, at best, looked just like one of the guys, not the A. Foster McKissick he really was—a man of great wealth, vast power, and much fame. There was something intriguing about him, something that made me want to get to know him better.

# THIRTY-FOUR

# THE CONTROVERSY

*What we do in life echoes in eternity.*
– Russell Crowe, *Gladiator*

IN JUNE OF 1988 ART and I went to New York City to attend a black-tie dinner in honor of Wayne Lewellen. While in the city, we were riding down Fifth Avenue in a limousine on the way to the private dinner party. I had a few free minutes alone with Art.

"Art, I need to run something by you."

"Shoot."

I looked at Art sitting there all decked out in his tuxedo. He seemed to be enjoying smoking his fine Cuban cigar immensely.

"Art, there is a movie we need to discuss. It's going to be a very controversial film, especially among the Christian community. The name of the film is *The Last Temptation of Christ*. It's being directed by Martin Scorsese. As you know, Scorsese is an excellent director. Personally, I am appalled that he would associate himself with this deplorable film. Art, in my opinion this picture should have never been made."

I felt it was also extremely important that I furnish Art with all the facts going in. "I'm also disappointed to inform you that one of our good

287

customers, Universal Pictures, is distributing *Last Temptation*. I haven't had any discussions yet with Universal about Wometco's playing the film, but I'm sure I'll be hearing from Phil Sherman within a few weeks. My intention is to tell Phil that we will not play the film in any of our theatres." I paused and maintained eye contact with Art, because I wanted to communicate the importance of him supporting my decision that Wometco would not play this picture.

Art cracked his window a little more to let some additional smoke out of the car. He then looked at me as if to say, "Why are you telling me all of this?" Then he began speaking. "Larry, you're my film buyer. If you don't want to play the picture, then we don't play the picture."

I breathed a deep sigh of relief, "Thanks, Art, for supporting me on this one."

Art looked down at the floor, wiped some spilled ashes off his pants, and shrugged his shoulders. He seemed to give the matter no additional thought. If Art had only known that night the agony that lay ahead of us because of that decision, I'm sure he would have spent further time and much deeper discussion about his position on playing *The Last Temptation of Christ* in his Wometco theatres.

Toward the end of that summer, the nightmare began. I'm not exactly sure who or what was used to ignite the spark. It could very well have been a phone call from a lady who was referred to my office, as she was inquiring when and in which theatre the film, *The Last Temptation of Christ*, would open in the Miami area. I informed the lady that the film would most likely open sometime during the month of October but that Wometco would not be playing *Last Temptation* in Miami. She demanded to know why the film would not play in our theatres and expressed her disappointment in Wometco for not playing the film.

About an hour later I received another call from a woman in reference to Wometco playing *Last Temptation*.

"Mr. Vaughn, Wometco plays all the important films in the Miami area. I can't believe you have already made a decision, and a bad decision

I might add, not to play such an important film as *The Last Temptation of Christ.*"

"Miss, I'm sorry to disappoint you, but that's the way it is. We book our theatres months ahead. We can't possibly play all the movies that are released by the film companies in our theatres alone. This is one picture that you will have to see in one of our competitor's theatres."

"Then they will play *Last Temptation.* Is that correct?"

"I can't speak for another circuit about whether they will play *Last Temptation* or any other film."

"Mr. Vaughn, may I ask your title?"

"I am Vice President in charge of film buying and booking."

"Thank you." She then hung up the phone.

Within half an hour I had another phone call with someone else inquiring about when *Last Temptation* was going to open in Miami and if Wometco would be playing the film. I was beginning to wish I had a taped message that I could play and not have to keep going through my spiel every few minutes. They say the third time is a charm, but that wasn't true with this call. This particular lady got so upset with me for not booking the film in Miami that she promised me she would never again patronize a Wometco theatre. Then she said some very harsh words to me before she slammed the phone receiver in my ear.

Julie walked in my office. I asked her, "Is there supposed to be a full moon tonight?"

"Well, I don't know, sir. May I ask why you have asked?"

"Julie, this afternoon I have received not one, nor two, but three strange calls from women, all inquiring about the film *The Last Temptation of Christ.*"

"Well, Mr. Vaughn, I hate to be the bearer of more bad news, but I have two more messages on my desk for you to call in reference to that film."

I sighed, "Well, just hang on to them for right now. There will probably be more as the day goes on."

I started doodling on a piece of paper, trying to figure out why all of a sudden there was such an interest in *The Last Temptation of Christ.* Doodling has always been a great help to me when trying to figure things out and in making important decisions. I didn't think all these calls in one day were just a coincidence. I thought to myself, "I'm sure glad I had that talk with Art. At least I have the company backing me up on this one."

That night I shared with the family the five phone calls I had received that day in reference to *Last Temptation.* We prayed that the Lord would give me wisdom in handling the public in the days ahead, as I felt the calls of the afternoon were only the beginning. I didn't sleep very well that night. I kept tossing and turning and thinking about the potential problems that might come up because of that movie.

The next day I received another call on *Last Temptation,* but this call was from one of the local talk-radio stations. The city of Miami has many radio stations, but unfortunately for me this call came from the secretary of Mark Powell. Mark Powell was one of the most popular and outspoken radio personalities in the Miami market. His show was always right at the top of the rating surveys . . . and he was known for his controversial subject matters and his abrasive behavior.

Mr. Powell's secretary asked some very pointed questions about the film and my company's position on playing the film. I answered all of her questions, even though her tone was very aggravating. I felt I did well, because I kept my cool.

Then after a long and tedious conversation, she concluded, "In my opinion, *Last Temptation* is a must-see film. Mr. Powell and our station management want to make absolutely sure that those persons who live in the Miami area have the opportunity to see the film, if they so desire. We would be greatly disappointed in Wometco Theatres if Wometco would not play the film because of the subject matter. Why, Wometco would be taking away our First Amendment rights. Mr. Vaughn, don't you think Wometco owes the community the right to decide for themselves what they can or can't see?"

I replied, "Wometco's decision not to play *Last Temptation* is in no way an attempt to say what you or anyone else can or cannot see. We are operating our theatres as a business, not a public service—just as your station operates as a business. I doubt Mr. Powell would appreciate it very much if I called him and demanded he speak on a certain subject because I felt the community should be able to hear about the subject in question. I doubt that anyone tells Mark Powell what he should or should not speak on."

There was silence on the other end of the phone.

Then she asked one last question, "Mr. Vaughn, are you a Christian?"

Once I told her I was, she didn't try to hide her animosity toward me. As I hung up the phone I thought to myself, "I hate to do it, but I'd better listen to the Mark Powell Show today."

I don't know how bad I was expecting Mark Powell to be that afternoon, but he was worse than I could have possibly imagined. He was irate that Wometco would take such a position on not playing *The Last Temptation of Christ*. He went on to say, "Just who do Larry Vaughn and Wometco Theatres think they are to tell us what we can and cannot see? Wometco has taken away our First Amendment rights, and I'm not going to stand for it. And neither should you!"

Powell went on to say, "Good people of Miami, let's jam Wometco's switchboard with complaints of our displeasure because of their actions. If they won't let us decide what we can and can't see, then we'll boycott not only Wometco Theatres, but the Miami Seaquarium, and whatever else Wometco owns and operates. Who needs Wometco? I'll tell you who, good citizens of Miami—you don't!"

Driving home having to listen to Mark Powell spew off at the mouth almost made me sick. Wometco Enterprises was a household name in South Florida. This negative publicity was going to really upset Art and Mike. They were good men. I felt terrible that they were going to have to go through all of this controversy. I thought, "Tomorrow is going to be a very tough day at the office."

When I got home, I went over all the events of the day with Doneata. I told her, "Well, one thing good about all of this is, my decision is made. I will not be associated with the film. If Art and Mike cave in to the pressure, then I'm out of a job. If they support me, then I'll hang in there because I know God will give me the physical and mental strength to endure the storm."

We went to bed around eleven that night, but I might as well have stayed up. I found it impossible to get my mind off the events of the day. I lay tossing and turning in bed for the better part of the night. When I finally got up at three in the morning, I could tell from my nausea and sour stomach that my ulcer was active.

I knew my church and friends were praying for me, but I still couldn't sleep. I went to the kitchen table and started figuring the bills and my monthly overhead. I put the pencil down, leaned back in the chair, stretched my arms at length, and yawned. I thought, "Tomorrow at this time I may very well be out of work, with not a penny coming into the home."

I looked at the clock. It was 4:25 a.m. I thought, "I should go back to bed and try to get some sleep."

Somehow, two hours later, I mustered up the energy needed to get out of bed, shower and shave, and be at the office by 8:30. There was a message on my desk that Art wanted to see me.

I walked into Art's office. Mike was also there, along with Albert Stringer. Albert was the recently appointed Executive Vice President of Wometco. The three of them looked at me. As I expected, no one was in a very good mood.

Art bit his bottom lip and pointed his finger at the telephone. "Larry, look at the telephone."

I noticed that all the lines were lit up.

"All of our phones are ringing off the hook with moviegoers irate at us over our decision not to play *Last Temptation*. Mark Powell is making us out to be some sort of communistic dictators. Have you heard what he's asking people to do?"

I frowned as I nodded my head. "Yes, Art, I have heard every word."

Albert spoke up. "The decision about playing *Last Temptation* should have been discussed, in detail, among the four of us before now."

I looked at Albert. "Albert, I talked to Art about this film months ago. He and I discussed it in detail."

Albert looked at Art.

Art said, "Larry, that's true, but I had no idea about how negatively the community would react to our position of not playing the film."

Art lit up a cigar, made a ring of smoke in the air, and then looked directly at me.

"Larry, the calls started coming in nonstop yesterday afternoon. Our girls are getting told off and cursed at because that radio station keeps encouraging people to call. Mr. Powell has done a very good job at getting the citizens of Miami up in arms over our decision not to play the film."

Art turned his back to us and looked out the window.

Albert said, "I think we need to re-evaluate our position on playing the film."

I jumped in. "Albert, the decision of whether we are going to play *Last Temptation* has already been made." I said with complete confidence, "We are not playing the film."

I held my breath and started praying, "Lord, I need Art and Mike's support now more than ever."

Albert was ready to roll up his sleeves and slug it out with me when Art interrupted, "I don't like Mark Powell or anyone else telling me what I can or can't do with my theatres. Let's leave it alone for now and see if maybe it won't just blow over in time."

I thought, "Thank you, Lord, for answering my prayer."

I looked at Albert—his anger was showing in his eyes. I knew there was much more that he wanted to say about our decision not to play the film.

That afternoon the *Miami Herald*, one of the leading newspapers in the country, called and asked me basically the same questions that Mark Powell's secretary had asked the day before. The next morning I read an article in the paper stating something to the effect that Larry Vaughn, the Christian film buyer for Wometco Theatres, announced that Wometco will not be playing *The Last Temptation of Christ*.

I wondered, "When I get to work this morning, should I go to my office or go ahead and do the inevitable, which is to go on over to Art's office?"

Sure enough, I was back in a meeting at 8:30 with the three of them. Art held up the paper. Oh, he was fit to be tied.

"Larry, I'm sure you've seen this article."

"Yes sir. Art, while we're on the subject of newspaper articles, I might as well tell you, yesterday I also talked with one of the New York newspapers."

Art shook his head in disbelief of all the happenings around him and said, "Is this nightmare ever going to end?"

I spoke up, "Art, if you had agreed to play the film, you would have the same repercussions—only the negative calls and mail would be from the Christian community."

In an act of total frustration, Art threw the newspaper across his desk. I felt really bad for Art and Mike having to go through this trauma because of not playing a picture that they knew absolutely nothing about. They really didn't understand what all the controversy was over.

Albert wanted to pick up with where he left off yesterday. He appealed to Art. "Art, I believe you and Larry were too quick in your decision not to play the film. For the record, I think it would be in the best interest of the company for us to reconsider and play the film."

I looked at Albert. "Well, you're not the film buyer—I am. And the decision has already been made. We're not playing the film." If looks could kill, I would be a dead man.

Art interrupted my thoughts as he said, "You two stop it." He turned to me and asked, "Larry, what does Universal Pictures have to say about all of this?"

"I haven't heard a word from them on the subject."

Art raised his eyebrows and gave me that look as if to say, "You will."

During these rather testy meetings, all Mike seemed to do was look at whomever was talking and take all the information into his memory bank. That's the way Mike was. He was the quiet thinker. I knew when he finally did make a statement it would carry a lot of weight in how Art would look at things. After a few minutes, Art suggested we all get back to work and table the immediate problem at hand. I felt blessed that I was able to leave the meeting still in one piece. I knew Albert was after my head.

That afternoon I received the expected phone call from Phil Sherman, the Assistant General Sales Manager Eastern Division of Universal Pictures Distribution.

Laughingly Phil asked, "Larry, what's going on in Miami?"

"Phil, I don't know exactly how all this got started. I think it started with an inquiring customer who talked to me and, after not liking what I had to say, went to one of the top talk-radio stations. Then they got hold of it, and everything started snowballing in the wrong direction. I can tell you one thing. I wish that picture, *Last Temptation*, had never been made."

"Larry, I haven't even asked you to play the picture, and Miami's already national news."

"Yeah, I know."

"Larry, do you want to hear the good news?"

"Phil, I'd love to hear some good news right about now."

"Controversy sells tickets, lots of tickets. Because of all the adverse publicity already received on *Last Temptation* in Miami, I think Miami has the chance to be one of our better engagements on the film."

Phil paused a moment. "Larry, the studio wants you to play the picture on an exclusive-run basis in Miami. Fred told me to tell you he wants the Miracle Theatre."

"Phil, tell Mr. Mound to forget it. I'm not playing the film."

"Larry, I have seen the picture. It's a very good film. I'll tell you what I'll do. I'll put a print on a plane today. You look at it tomorrow morning and call me after you have seen the film."

"No, Phil. I am not interested in playing the film."

I could tell Phil was getting aggravated with me.

"Larry, does this hold true for all the other Wometco markets in Florida?"

"Yes, it does."

"You know, Larry, Florida is a very competitive theatre market. Universal Pictures has a lot of important films coming out in the months ahead. Wometco needs Universal far, far more than Universal needs Wometco."

"Phil, I don't see how I could keep my theatres booked with good playable movies without the support of Universal Pictures. Wometco Theatres needs Universal Pictures like Larry Vaughn's lungs need air. Phil, if you walk away from me over *Last Temptation*, the results would be devastating to me as well as to my company. However, I am not going to play *The Last Temptation of Christ* in any Wometco theatre as long as I am in charge of the film department."

He paused a moment. "Okay, Larry. If that's your final decision, then I guess we have no more to talk about on that subject."

Phil hung up, and I felt sick to my stomach.

It was another sleepless night.

All this happened in the span of four weeks. Finally, Art called what was to be the final meeting on *The Last Temptation of Christ*, except this time I was called into the meeting last. The meeting had started earlier with Art, Mike, and Albert.

Art started out doing the talking. "Larry, we as individuals and as a company have gone through several weeks of sheer agony over our decision not to play this film, *Last Temptation*. I personally can't go anywhere without the subject coming up. My phone at home rings off the hook with friends calling me, telling me they don't understand Wometco's position. And to be frank, I don't understand it either. The same thing is happening with Mike, Albert, and I'm sure with you. I was hoping the whole controversy about us not playing the film would blow over within a few days, but it hasn't. Now, my question to you men is: where do we go from here?"

Albert was quick to speak. "I'm embarrassed and disappointed that we're not playing the film. All along I thought the decision not to play *The Last Temptation of Christ* was the wrong thing to do. It has definitely hurt our image in the community. It could affect our long-term relationship with Universal, and I personally think the picture is going to do very well at the box office."

Albert then turned from Art to me. With a smirk on his face, he eyeballed me and spoke in a very sarcastic tone. "I think we all know what I have just said is the truth. The question is—what is Larry going to do if we have a change of heart and play the film? Well, they won't ask you, Larry, so I will. What will you do if we decide to have a change of heart and play the film?"

Before I could reply, Art looked at Albert and said, "Mister, you're out of line. That question is not yours for the asking." Then in a moment of built-up anger and frustration, Art slammed his fist down on the conference table. "Enough is enough!" he shouted. I glanced down at the table to see if it had cracked.

Looking straight into Albert's eyes, Art said, "I don't want to hear another word on this subject again. We are not going to play the film, and that is final, over, done with, period! Does everyone understand?"

I went back to my office thinking, "I have just experienced a true miracle. God touched Art Hertz's heart and mind to have him support his Christian film buyer, when the circumstances would seem to dictate that he do the opposite."

I breathed a deep sigh of relief. I knew in my heart that now I was up for anything.

It's hard to believe, but many good things came out of that bad experience with *The Last Temptation of Christ*. Because of all the publicity, churches all over the country got wind of the situation in Miami. Christian people by the thousands were praying for me and the company. Letters of appreciation poured in to Wometco from everywhere. People were thanking Art, Mike, and me for not playing the film.

I remember walking into Art's office one morning. Art, puffing on his cigar, motioned toward a stack of mail on the floor as he said, "Look, Larry, more mail from your friends." The Christian thank-you letters were actually outnumbering the earlier hate mail.

The next time I talked with Phil Sherman, it was as if we had never had that conversation about *Last Temptation* in the Miracle Theatre. It was business as usual. My relationship with Universal was as solid as it ever had been.

Because of all the adverse national publicity Miami received on the film, the other major theatre circuits also shied away from playing *Last Temptation* in Miami. AMC played it in other cities, but not in Miami.

United Artists Theatres wouldn't touch it, nor would General Cinema Corporation. I was pleased later to hear that General Cinema's board of directors made a company decision not to play the film anywhere.

For a while it looked as if *Last Temptation* would actually end up not playing in Miami at all, but a small, independent theatre owner—eager to make a fast buck from the publicity—negotiated with Phil to play the film. After all the controversy and advance fanfare on the film, I was pleased to see that his engagement did only fair business at best.

Every decision in life has consequences. What started as a simple gust of wind, a question in a limo, became a huge storm that had all the appearances of becoming a destructive hurricane. Miraculously, not only I, but my company, weathered the storm. C.S. Lewis said it best: "Christianity, if false, is of no importance, and if true, of infinite importance. The only thing it cannot be is moderately important."

# THIRTY-FIVE

# WHAT'S UP?

*The bitterest truth is better than the sweetest lie.*
– Michael Stuhlbarg, *Men in Black III*

IN 1989, I STARTED MY fourth year of service with Art and Mike. For the most part it had been an exciting adventure being part of the management team at the new Wometco. During the previous four years the company had renovated several older Wometco theatres, purchased two theatres in Miami from Loews Theatres, and built several new multiplex theatres. As far as the stability of the company, things just couldn't have been better. Art and Mike believed in sharing the company's prosperity, so I was one of the best-paid film buyers in the country.

Julie buzzed me, "Bert Livingston is on line two."

In a low tone of voice, my good friend Bert asked, "Larry, are you alone?"

"Yes. Why, what's up?"

"Larry, I just got off the phone with Bob Keller, the film buyer for United Artists Theatres. Bob was at a dinner earlier this week with his boss, Salah Hassanein. Guess who else was at that dinner?"

"I have no idea, who?"

"Larry, Art was there. Do you know why Art met with Salah?"

"No, but I have a feeling you're about to tell me."

"Art wants to sell the theatres."

"What!" I was shocked by the news.

Bert repeated, "Art wants to sell the Florida theatres."

"Bert, are you absolutely sure of this?"

Bert said emphatically, "Larry, Bob was there. What's there to be sure of? Art told Salah he wants to sell the theatres. You make sure you are protected."

Before hanging up the phone, I thanked Bert for his call and his genuine concern for my well-being.

The next week I met with Art and Mike to discuss a site selection for a possible theatre location. One of the major responsibilities of a film buyer is his input on theatre locations. When a location is presented to the company, it is the film buyer's responsibility to submit a budget as to what he thinks a theatre would gross in the location in question and what the projected film rental would be. Giving the stamp of approval or the stamp of disapproval on a potential theatre location is a high-pressure call. When

*Art Hertz and Doneata at a theatre opening*

a theatre company commits to a site, the cost averages a million dollars a screen, in addition to a twenty-year lease.

After we had spent the better part of an hour discussing the pros and the cons of the site in question, I felt the timing was right to ask my big question. While gathering my charts to leave, I asked Art, "Art, I heard a rumor that you are shopping the Florida theatres." His body language told me nothing.

I continued, "I know how unreliable rumors can be, but I was just wondering if there was any truth to this one."

Art kept fiddling with his stacks of papers as he replied, "No, Larry. We are building theatres and not selling theatres."

"Well, I am glad to hear that. Obviously, the rumor had me concerned. Thanks for setting the record straight."

Walking back to my office I wondered why Art didn't tell me about his meeting with Salah Hassanein.

It was about three months later when I received a call from Frank Jones. Frank had been the assistant film buyer under the old Litchfield organization, before Foster McKissick had sold his theatres to Salah Hassanein at United Artists. Frank was a funny-looking guy—bald, with big, sagging brown eyes that always had dark circles under them. He had a deep voice, a big smile, and a jovial laugh; he was always the one called on at a film function to tell a wild story to get the audience laughing. Everyone in the industry who knew Frank liked him.

After a few minutes of small talk, Frank asked me, "Larry, are you happy at Wometco?"

I immediately replied, "Very much so, Frank." Then I hesitated as I thought about my earlier phone conversation with Bert Livingston. I inquired, "But, why do you ask?"

"Well, Larry, do you remember meeting Foster McKissick in New York?"

"Sure. How can anyone forget meeting Foster McKissick?"

Frank gave his famous big laugh. "You got that right, brother." Frank paused before continuing. "Larry, Foster is going back into the business. I might add in a very large way. His intent is to build a circuit with 750 screens. His expansion plan calls for an opening of one to two theatres a week."

"What? Frank, Foster better have a lot—I mean a *lot*—of cash to build theatres that fast."

Frank laughed. "He does."

I thought to myself, "At Wometco during a good year, we would open only one or at the very most two theatres per *year*."

Frank explained, "Foster needs a head film buyer. When Foster, Ulmer, and I started looking at the various film buyers out there, your name ended up being first on our list."

I thought a moment about what Doneata and I had been recently praying about—that the Lord would provide an opportunity for our family to get out of Miami, and maybe one day even end up moving back to the Carolinas.

"Okay, Frank. Tell Foster that I would like very much to talk with him."

Frank sounded surprised. "Well, Larry, you just never know. That's exactly what Foster was hoping you would say. I didn't think you would ever consider leaving Wometco, but we would love to have you as part of our team." Frank paused a moment. "I don't want to sound like I'm rushing you, but could you and Doneata make a trip to Litchfield Beach this weekend to meet with Foster?"

I thought a moment. "Frank, pending no problem with our friends keeping the children, this weekend will be fine."

"That's great, Larry." He chuckled. "This call is going to make Foster McKissick's day."

Doneata and I arrived at the Myrtle Beach airport on Friday afternoon. Frank was at the gate, waiting to drive us the seventeen miles south to Litchfield Beach. The company had made arrangements for Doneata and me to stay in one of the townhomes located on one of the golf courses.

After bringing in the luggage, Frank handed me a set of car keys. "These are for the car in your driveway. Here's a map of the area. Feel free to call me if you need anything else."

Frank looked at his watch. "We are to meet Foster and the gang for dinner at the country club at 7:00 p.m." Frank gave Doneata and me that big, genuine, caring smile of his and said, "I will pick you up at 6:50."

Frank, Doneata, and I walked into the beautiful Litchfield Country Club, which looked like a stately Southern mansion from a bygone era. I almost expected to see Rhett Butler and Scarlett O'Hara walk by on their way to dinner.

We went to a private room upstairs. Everyone was already seated, waiting for our arrival. Foster was the first to stand up. He walked over to me and shook my hand. I then introduced him to Doneata. After Foster formally welcomed Doneata and me to Litchfield, he introduced his lovely wife, Sophie; his Executive Vice President and General Manager of Litchfield Theatres, Ulmer Eaddy and his wife; Jack Jordan, his Director of Advertising and Marketing, along with Jack's fiancée, Carol.

Ulmer's wife has the unique name (for a woman) of "Bill," and she wanted to get her explanation in first, before we could ask. "My father had his heart set on a boy, and when I came along he gave me the name he had picked out for his son." Then, giving us a real cute smile, Bill said, "I've never wanted to change my name, out of love for my father."

We all laughed at the novelty of her story. One waiter came and took drink orders while another waiter brought in two trays of delicious hors d'oeuvres. We had a wonderful time getting to know one another. Doneata took a special liking to Bill Eaddy right from the start.

After an hour or so, we moved into the elegant dining room of the Litchfield Country Club for our evening meal. Foster insisted that Doneata and I have she-crab soup as our appetizer. He said very proudly, "My chef is the best cook in the area. His she-crab soup is the best in all of South Carolina."

Doneata and I were both glad that we took Foster's advice: the soup was delicious. The filet mignon and grits were also wonderful; in fact, the entire meal was scrumptious!

During the meal I noticed Foster kept taking his fork and eating off Doneata's plate. I thought to myself, "Foster should have ordered the red snapper, because he's eating most of Doneata's." Then, a few minutes later, Foster started eating off Bill's plate.

Finally, Sophie explained to Doneata and me Foster's most unusual behavior. "Foster McKissick does what he calls 'grazing' when having a meal. That means he would rather eat off your plate than his own."

Sophie shook her head and threw her hands up in the air as if to say, "I have given up on changing him."

Sophie smiled, "Doneata, maybe you can break him from that bad habit. No one else has ever been able to."

Foster held his fork up in the air and said, "Well, I don't know why it always happens that everybody else's food always looks better than mine. I just like to have a taste to see if your food is as good as it looks." We all laughed.

I couldn't help but notice how kind Foster was to the waiters and the waitresses. He seemed to know everyone's name, from the water server to the hostess. Foster asked the waiter to have the chef come to our table so he could thank him personally for such a fine dinner. After dinner we all caravanned over to the McKissick's oceanfront townhouse at Litchfield by the Sea.

By the time the evening was over, Doneata and I knew everyone much better. Sophie was a wonderful lady. Exactly what you would expect Mrs. A. Foster McKissick to be—a very cordial, pretty, and intelligent lady. She had polish and class, but she didn't have that air of being better than the rest. She complemented her famous husband well.

Ulmer Eaddy was Foster's right arm when it came to Litchfield Theatres. Ulmer was an older gentleman who had spent his whole life in the theatre business, and he knew every facet of the business. He could talk real estate, popcorn, or film buying; Ulmer was one of the key players in the Litchfield organization.

Jack Jordan was no stranger to me at all. Jack was in his late sixties. He and I had worked together for John Huff many years earlier in Charlotte, North Carolina, at ABC. Jack held the same position, Director of Advertising and Marketing, at Litchfield that he had at ABC many years ago. Jack had a wonderful personality, and he was also a hard-working company man.

Before leaving the McKissick's home that evening, Foster put his hand on my shoulder and said, "The Bishop (that was Foster's nickname for Eaddy) and I want to meet with you in the morning at 10 a.m. in my office. It's located on the ground floor of the Country Club."

"Foster, I am looking forward to seeing you and Ulmer. Thank you for a delightful evening."

When I arrived at Foster's office the next morning, Eaddy and he were busy going over some real estate information. They cleared off the desk, and the three of us started to talk.

Foster said, "Larry, I'm going to move the home office from Easley, South Carolina, to Litchfield Beach. These days all you need to get work done is a telephone, a screening room, a fax machine, and an airplane. I just so happen to have all four here near Litchfield."

Foster went over the expansion plan of the new company. I was surprised that he shared as much information with me as he did, without my having made a commitment to come to work for him. After he walked me through the new company, he said, "Larry, in the very near future I am going to need a film buyer."

I looked at Foster and Eaddy and said, "I am interested in hearing what you have to say."

Foster sat back in his chair and put the palms of his hands on the back of his neck. "Larry, I guess the only thing left to talk about is money." He looked at me with a curious look on his face. "What kind of money are you making at Wometco?"

I jotted down a number on a sheet of paper and slipped it across the table. Foster looked at the paper then at Ulmer. "Larry, we don't pay any of our people that kind of money."

I thought I might as well be honest. "Foster, that's just my base salary without any of the perks."

He pulled on his ear lobe as he said, "Larry, I want you, but the question is, . . ." He held his hands open, "can I afford you?"

"Foster, let me ask you a question. How many screens do you have up and running right now?" The movement of his eyes passed the question over to Ulmer who responded, "Not many, maybe thirty."

I thought for a moment and then said, "Well, gentlemen, let's not let money kill the deal."

Foster had an inquiring look on his face as he said, "Larry, what do you have in mind?"

"Maybe we will have to come up with some sort of a compromise on my salary, where it can grow as the company grows. Foster, you and Eaddy put your heads together and get back with me."

Foster looked at Eaddy and said, "You know, Bishop, I like the way Larry says things." Foster thought a moment. "Larry, Bishop will call you in the next few days and the two of you will talk further."

Doneata and I spent the better part of that Saturday afternoon driving around the area.

That evening the McKissicks, the Eaddys, Frank, Jack, and Carol, plus Doneata and I all went out to one of Foster's favorite restaurants for dinner, then back to his home.

Our weekend at Litchfield Beach was a wonderful experience. I tried to imagine leaving the hustle and bustle of a major city like Miami, Florida, and living and working in this little corner of paradise nestled between Myrtle Beach and Georgetown, South Carolina. Foster commented, "I never lock my house at Litchfield. We don't have any crime here. I also never take my keys out of the ignition in my truck or cars."

I said, "Foster, you make Litchfield Beach sound like Camelot. Does it also only rain at Litchfield Beach after sundown?"

"Well, I can't go that far, but Litchfield Beach is a great place to live and raise a family." I could tell that Foster really wanted to work it out for me to be a part of his team.

Doneata and I talked on the plane ride home. "Larry, I think this would be a good move for us and the children."

"Well, I do too. It's just that I have such a big job now, it's going to be hard for Foster to come up with a plan to make it work financially. But if he gives me a figure that's anywhere in the ballpark or near the ballpark, I'm going to take it."

Doneata put my hand in hers and squeezed it. "Larry, I wish we didn't have to wait so long to know what is going to happen."

"Me too, sweetheart."

It was about three weeks later when the call came in from Ulmer. "Larry, Foster and I want to fly down to Miami and meet with you this weekend. Would it be possible for the three of us to have dinner Friday evening?"

"Only if you let it be my treat. I've got to do something to reciprocate for that wonderful weekend you folks showed Doneata and me at Litchfield Beach."

"Well, we'll see. Could you meet us in Fort Lauderdale Friday afternoon? We're staying at the Jockey Club."

When I arrived at the Jockey Club, Foster and Eaddy were relaxing in two chairs at an outside table. After a few minutes of small talk, Foster looked at Ulmer and said, "Bishop, let's get the business out of the way before we go to dinner."

Foster sat up erect in his chair and said, "Larry, Bishop and I have come up with a plan that we think will work for both of us. There's got to be a little give-and-take on both sides, but how does this sound to you?"

Foster then looked at Ulmer. "Go ahead, Bishop, give Larry the proposal."

Ulmer took out his pad and pencil. "Larry, the bad news first: we'll have to start out by shaving your base annual salary by $10,000, but we'll give you a new Ford Crown Victoria to be used for your personal use as well as business use. While you're trying to sell your home in Miami, we'll furnish you with a completely furnished three-bedroom home located on the golf course at River Club to live in for six months, rent free, with all utilities paid. Larry, I'll grandfather you a full membership to the Litchfield Country Club. You'll have at your and your family's disposal all golf, tennis, swimming, beach, and country club privileges." Then Ulmer added, "Larry, we'll also pay all your moving expenses."

Foster then looked into my eyes. "As Litchfield grows, Larry Vaughn will grow." He leaned back in his chair and said, "Bishop, is that it?"

Ulmer, checking off each point on his list, said, "I believe it is."

"Foster, you have yourself a deal. When do you gentlemen want me to report to work?"

Foster said, "We thought we would leave that decision up to you."

I thought a moment. "Well, today is Friday. When Arthur Hertz comes into his office on Monday morning, my letter of resignation will be on his desk. I will give him a two-week notice. That's all he'll need, because the theatres are booked with very good movies for the next three months. The timing couldn't be better, leaving in the end of May with his theatres set for the summer. I would like to take another two weeks off and report to Litchfield on, say, the first of June."

Foster looked at Ulmer. "Bishop, have our attorney draw up a contract for Larry and me to sign."

I looked at Foster. "Foster, as far as I'm concerned, I don't need a contract. Your handshake is all I need to seal the deal."

Foster elbowed Ulmer in the side. "I tell you, Bishop, I like the way Larry thinks." That handshake consummated the deal.

We left the Jockey Club and went out to a delicious dinner at one of Fort Lauderdale's better restaurants, the Down Under. That night was the start of many memorable evenings I was to have with Foster McKissick and Ulmer Eaddy.

On Monday mornings, Art usually called me by 8:45 a.m. to get a quick update on the weekend receipts at the box office. This particular Monday I did not hear from him until nearly 11:00 a.m. Then the call came in.

"Good morning, Larry."

"Good morning, Art. How are you today?"

"Larry, I was fine until I opened my mail. Would you mind coming over here?"

"No, sir. I'll be right there."

I walked into his office. Art was sitting behind his desk, and Mike was sitting in the guest chair directly across the desk from Art. I sat down in the chair beside Mike.

Art spoke first. "Larry, Mike and I received your letter of resignation this morning."

"Yes sir. Well, I can't say I haven't had mixed emotions, but I think thirteen years is long enough for me to spend in one place."

Art stared at me and gave me that look as if to say, "Okay, Larry, quit beating around the bush. What is it that you're after?" Art took out a fresh cigar and started twirling it with his fingers. "Larry, why don't you tell Mike and me what it is that you want?"

"They think I'm here to negotiate," I thought to myself.

"Art, I don't want anything. I'm leaving."

Art said very emphatically, "Larry, you know you're not seriously considering leaving Wometco. Now, what is it that you want?"

"Art, I have already made a commitment with another company." Both Art and Mike had a surprised look on their faces. "I'm not trying to get anything out of you and Mike." I looked at Art. "You men know that's not the way I operate." I paused a moment. "It's just that I have taken a film-buying position with another theatre circuit."

Art was shocked. "Larry, you mean you have already made a commitment to someone else?"

"Yes, that is correct."

"Where are you going?"

"I'm going to work for Foster McKissick."

Art thought a moment. "Foster McKissick—I thought he was out of the theatre business."

"He was, but in the very near future Mr. McKissick is going back into the business. I have made a deal with him to be his film buyer."

I looked at the genuine concern on Art and Mike's faces. I figured I'd best say something positive. "Art, Mike, I have your theatres already booked with top films through the month of August. Whomever you bring in will have plenty of time to get acclimated to the Florida market without having to worry about having good, playable films in the Wometco theatres for the summer."

Art's mental wheels were churning. He stood up and started walking around the room. "What about the lawsuit that is pending with Eastern Federal Theatres? If it ever goes to trial, and it looks like it very well might, then we'll need you to testify."

"If and when that happens, I'll just have to fly back down to Miami to testify. If your New York lawyers need me to give any additional depositions, then have them call me, and I'll make myself available. Foster is very much aware of the lawsuit and the pending trial in Miami."

Art shook his head as if he were angry with himself. "Larry, I wish you had talked with Mike and me before giving Mr. McKissick a final commitment. Maybe we could have made it worth your while to stay on with Wometco."

"It's not the money, Art. You have always taken very good care of me financially. It's just, well, I want to go back to the Carolinas. It's a personal thing with me. I have enjoyed working for the two of you very much."

I smiled as I pointed my finger at them. "You two are demanding as all get out, but I always liked a challenge. You men have been extremely generous to my family and me. By the way, I had a talk with Foster about Wometco. Since Wometco is not presently in opposition to Litchfield in any markets, Foster doesn't mind if you want to call me periodically for information. If you so desire, I will be a consultant for your new film buyer for, say, four to six weeks. That will give him the time needed to get acclimated to the Florida theatre market."

I looked at the disappointment on Art's and Mike's faces. "There will be no charge to you men for this service."

Mike looked at Art, but the only comment he made was, "Art, I told you we should have told Larry of our intention to sell the theatres!"

Mike's statement felt like a bee sting. We each knew the truth behind his statement had weighed heavily in my decision to leave. That was a tough meeting not only for Art and Mike, but also for me.

Art and Mike gave me a wonderful going-away luncheon at Christy's, which is one of the finest Angus prime beef steakhouses in Coral Gables. It was at that time I was given a plaque of appreciation for my thirteen years of service with Wometco. The home office employees also gave me a very nice going-away party and a very special gift, a leather briefcase. I was pleased to be able to leave Wometco without any animosity between Art and Mike and me.

Most of the major film companies in California never really understood why or how I could leave a top film market like Miami, with all its visibility and power, to work in Litchfield Beach, South Carolina. Even though all the distributors had the utmost respect for A. Foster McKissick, they just couldn't understand my walking away from one of the top film-buying jobs for a position with much less recognition, power, and challenge. Many times I thought how my colleagues in Hollywood would really think I had lost all my marbles, if they knew that I had withdrawn my name as a candidate for the Eastern Division General Sales Manager at MGM/UA.

# THE LAWSUIT

*Never revisit the past, that's dangerous. You know, move on.*
– Robert Redford

THE FAMILY AND I MOVED to Litchfield Beach on the first of June in 1989. Living at a country club resort made Doneata and the children feel as if they were on an extended vacation. Every morning, they woke up in their beautifully furnished home overlooking the ninth green on a championship golf course. Down the street were two swimming pools and the Litchfield Tennis Club. And, if that wasn't enough excitement for them, across the street were the beautiful Litchfield Beach and the Atlantic Ocean.

I must admit I enjoyed the laid-back lifestyle. In Miami it had taken me an hour to drive to the office; it now took three to five minutes. I was home early every afternoon. The pace of life at Litchfield Beach was about as far from Miami living as one could possibly go and still be living in the United States. I had spent the last thirteen years working in a suit, and I always had to be mentally prepared at a moment's notice to have to deal with bankers or investors. At Litchfield, the dress of the day was a golf shirt, casual slacks, and loafers—and my Southern accent was viewed as an asset.

Foster liked to meet once a week in the afternoon with Frank, Jack, and me in the lounge of the Litchfield Country Club. During the meeting we would go through four to six baskets of fresh, hot popcorn, as we talked about the past weekend's business. Those Litchfield meetings were very different from Wometco's Tuesday morning meetings where Art, Mike, Albert, Bill, and I had gone over each theatre's gross—both Wometco's and the opposition's—with a magnifying glass, to see who had come out on top for the weekend.

At one of our meetings Frank asked me, "Larry, when you worked at Wometco, what was the most money you ever bid on a picture?"

I appreciated his question. I hesitated before replying, as my thoughts drifted back to my heavy bidding days. "Hmmm, I remember when Eddie was at Wometco, we put up $150,000 on *Black Sunday* in South Miami."

"No kidding?" Frank was shocked.

"Would you believe that our bid was rejected, and General Cinema was awarded the picture?"

Foster immediately chimed in, "Thank the Lord for small favors."

I continued, "We also put up $175,000 and won The *Empire Strikes Back* in North Miami."

Foster gave me a high five, as he enthusiastically remarked, "Now, that's more like it!"

Frank smiled as he glanced at Foster and said, "Larry, did you know Foster once tried his hand at film buying?" Both Frank and Jack started laughing, because Foster looked as if he had just eaten a sour grape. I knew there was a funny story on the horizon.

I remarked, "All right, tell me about Foster the film buyer."

Frank nudged Jack while grinning at Foster. Then he said, "Well, Foster here is a big fan of General Douglas MacArthur."

I knew where the story was heading.

Frank said, "Foster, why don't you tell Larry about how badly you wanted *MacArthur* in Pensacola, Florida, in the Cordova Mall?"

Foster nodded as he replied, "Can't do it, Slick." ("Slick" was Foster's nickname for Frank.) Foster wiped away a false tear as he continued, "The memory hurts too bad to talk about it."

Eager to spill the beans, Frank said, "Okay then, I'll tell the story. In 1977, the bids came in from Universal Pictures on *MacArthur*. Foster called Allen Lock, his head film buyer at the time, and told him to bid heavy on *MacArthur* in Pensacola. Allen runs the numbers and sends in a good, strong bid."

Frank glanced up at the ceiling as he tried to recall the figures. "I think the first bid was around $40,000." Frank explained, "Now Larry, Pensacola isn't Miami—$40,000 was a big guarantee in Pensacola. A few days later, Allen calls Universal to find out if the Cordova bid was accepted. Universal told him that it looked like the picture would be awarded to United Artists Theatres, since their bid was the best bid. Allen then called Foster and gave him what we all thought, at the time, was disappointing news.

Frank looked at Foster and giggled as he said, "Next thing you know, ole Foster is a film buyer. He bypasses Allen, calls Universal himself, and pleads with them to rebid the picture in Pensacola." Frank gave Foster a funny look as he remarked, "Be careful what you ask for, because the next thing we know, we get notice from Universal that *MacArthur* will be rebid in Pensacola. On the rebid, Foster the film buyer works up the bid himself, and naturally, he has to up the ante."

Continuing to rib Foster, Frank remarked, "I forgot what you bid on your rebid. Was it $50,000, or was it 75,000?"

Foster leaned back in his chair and closed his eyes, as if to say if he has to hear the rest, he certainly doesn't want to see anymore.

Frank concluded his story. "Well Larry, I guess you know the rest of the story. *MacArthur* was a box-office flop—and ole Foster retired from film buying."

Foster pointed and shook his finger at me as he remarked, "I am glad I now have *you* as my film buyer!"

During another one of our laid-back meetings, Foster commented about how much weight he had recently gained and how he needed to start an exercise program. (I smiled as I thought back to my windfall with

Mike Brown's weight loss plan.) He said, "I think this excess weight is hurting my tennis game."

I suggested, "Foster, with all the beautiful places to run around here, you should take up jogging."

"Larry, I have been a jogger on and off for years. It's just that here lately I've been mostly off more than on."

"Foster, jogging is something that I've been doing on a regular basis for the last twelve years. Why don't you and I start jogging together?"

"Larry, that sounds like exactly what I need. When do you want to start?"

I thought a moment. "I'll be out of town the next two weeks. Let's plan to start in three weeks."

A man of Foster McKissick's position and income could drive anything he wanted to drive, but Foster drove a pickup truck. In the back of his pickup truck Foster had, believe it or not, of all things, a trash can! Foster's truck was often seen parked in the grass along Highway 17 South at Litchfield Beach while he was out picking up trash and empty beer cans that had been tossed beside the highway by careless litterbugs. That was just one of Foster's quirks; he couldn't stand to see any litter at Litchfield Beach.

In addition to the trash can, Foster often drove around Litchfield with his faithful companion and friend, Petey, perched on his shoulder. Petey was a beautiful parrot. I think Sophie thought the bird was a little much at times (especially when Petey would relieve himself on Foster's shoulder!), but Foster would have it no other way.

The first morning we jogged together, I couldn't help but notice Foster's outfit. He had on a pair of old, faded gray shorts and a red striped jogging shirt that looked like it should have been thrown away years ago. I noticed the sock covering his big toe was sticking out of the canvas on his left jogging shoe.

I said, "Foster, those jogging shoes have had it!" Pointing toward the shoe I said, "Your toe is coming out of the shoe."

Foster gave me a look as if to say, "It doesn't bother me. Why should it bother you?" Then he answered me. "Larry, maybe you're right. Looks like I've just about got all the mileage out of these shoes that I'm going to get."

"Well, Foster, maybe Jack, Frank, and I could take up a collection and get you a new pair of running shoes. I know how tight your finances are right now with the cost of building these theatres."

Foster looked at me and nodded his head in agreement. He said, "That might not be a bad idea."

Foster's displeasure with litter played into his thoughts even while he was running. If Foster saw a piece of paper, he would have to stop jogging long enough to pick it up. Well, it's kind of hard to jog with the Chairman of the Board and not become conscious of those things that irritate him. So when I saw a piece of litter, I would stop, pick it up, and then go back to jogging. I don't know why I wore a stopwatch. This type of jogging was terrible on your time. On a two-mile run, we were running out of storage places to put our collection of litter, so Foster came up with a solution. One morning Foster walked out of his house with two empty plastic grocery bags. Immediately, I knew they were for us to put our trash in. He gave me a look as if to say, "Well, you can't hold all the trash in your hands."

For several months Foster and I ran together as our schedules permitted. It wasn't always easy though—especially for Foster. Sophie once told Doneata about how Foster acted one morning when it was my turn to come over to his house to jog. This particular morning was extremely cold outside. Sophie said Foster got out of bed and peeked out the window. The rolling clouds were so low and dark that it looked as if it were nighttime outside. The chilling wind was howling, and blowing the trees to and fro. Foster turned from the dreary view and looked at Sophie lying there in the warmth of their bed, and he said, almost angrily, "Sophie, I don't want to run today!"

After a moment Foster looked at Sophie and said, "I have an idea. Sophie, when Larry drives up, why don't you go downstairs and tell him that I am sick, and I can't run today."

Sophie said, "Oh no, Foster McKissick. I'm not going to do your dirty work for you. If Larry Vaughn can get up in this cold weather and come over here to run, then you'd better be out there to meet him."

Sophie told Doneata that Foster had the saddest expression on his face as he put his running shorts on. She said, "Doneata, I actually was starting to feel sorry for the old boy."

The next sound they heard was a tap on the door. Foster looked at Sophie with an expression of sadness in his brown eyes and shrugged his shoulders in despair as he said, "I guess we know who that is."

Sophie told Doneata how much fun she had watching Foster force himself out of the comfort of his bed that dreary morning.

After I heard the story, I thought back to that cold morning. As I recall, Foster gave me a very solemn "good morning" that day. I was wondering during our run if he felt okay, because he sure was quiet. I don't think he even picked up much litter.

Foster finally broke down and bought himself a new pair of running shoes. That was the same year Frank, Jack, and I went in together and bought Foster a very nice running suit for Christmas. Foster now had the equipment needed to get serious with his running. The only other thing he needed was me, his jogging partner, to get him out and going.

Four months after our family moved to Litchfield, I flew to Miami to testify for Wometco in the Eastern Federal Theatres lawsuit. In Gainesville, Florida, Wometco operated a three-screen theatre, the Plaza, which played "exclusive run" movies, or what you might call "one-run only." This meant that when Wometco played a picture at its Plaza Theatre, no other theatre in Gainesville could play that picture simultaneously. Wometco's Plaza was the only theatre that took the exclusive one-run position.

Eastern Federal Theatres took objection to Wometco's playing exclusive run on every film it played in the Plaza. The owner of the circuit, Ira Meiselman, phoned Art Hertz about Wometco's policy in Gainesville and asked Art if he would reconsider his position. Art informed Ira that he would check into the situation.

Art called me and asked me to brief him as to why I was not willing to play two runs in Gainesville.

I said, "Art, the problem is not with Eastern Federal Theatres but with AMC Theatres. If we agree to two runs in Gainesville, then that means we will also have to let AMC Theatres have the opportunity to play with our theatre. AMC has two new multiplex theatres. If we play a picture with AMC," I paused, "AMC definitely will get the lion's share of the business."

Art frowned as he said, "Playing with AMC would kill our theatre."

"Art, it would happen overnight. When one is given the option to ride in a Cadillac or a Chevy for the same price, he will take the Cadillac every time."

Art phoned Ira Meiselman and told him that Wometco would continue its policy of playing film on an exclusive-run basis in Gainesville. Ira then put Art on notice that the next call would be from his attorney.

Ira Meiselman filed a lawsuit against Wometco Theatres and Twentieth Century Fox Film Corporation. The multiple lawsuits were filed for restraint of trade and collusion, in addition to other counts. The gist of the lawsuit was that while I was employed at Wometco as the vice president/head film buyer, I was using the clout of Wometco's Miami theatres to persuade 20th Century Fox to adhere to my film demands in Gainesville, Florida.

There were megabucks at stake in this lawsuit—millions of dollars—but this multi-million-dollar lawsuit between two multi-million-dollar companies actually all boiled down to just one thing—me. It really all came down to Larry Vaughn, and the way Larry Vaughn had conducted his business practices in Gainesville, Florida, as the film buyer for Wometco Theatres.

Blake Frazier, the attorney for Eastern Federal, went through the proper channels to obtain a jury trial, and he petitioned that the trial be held in the Dade County Courthouse, which is located in downtown Miami. Mr. Frazier wanted the trial to be held right in Wometco's backyard.

This was my first, and I hope only, experience on a witness stand. I went on the stand at 1:30 in the afternoon. From where I was positioned, I noticed that there appeared to be a lot of people in the courtroom. That surprised me. I mean, after all, this wasn't exactly a murder trial. After being sworn to tell the truth, the whole truth, and nothing but the truth, so help me God, I was instructed to sit down. I looked at the judge, the jury, and then at Meiselman and his two attorneys.

Art Hertz and Michael Brown were sitting on the front row, in public seating. Art retained two New York attorneys, Eric Rosenfield and Jerome Hindermann, partners from one of the top law firms in New York, to represent Wometco. Directly behind Eric and Jerome were several attorneys from Los Angeles, who represented 20th Century Fox. I caught a glimpse of my good friend Bert Livingston seated with the Fox attorneys.

I thought back to two years earlier, when Bert had appealed to me to drop the exclusive run policy in Gainesville for just one picture. Fox had a big-budget Arnold Schwarzenegger action film, and the studio wanted to have as many theatres as possible play the film. Bert said, "Larry, for goodness sake, let's play two runs in Gainesville on this one picture."

"Can't do it, Bert. Two runs will open a door of opportunity for the opposition theatres that I need to keep shut. If you want the Plaza and its big auditorium, you have to play the picture exclusive." I knew Bert had to have the Plaza—it was the best-grossing theatre in Gainesville.

Bert gave me a cocky look as he stuck his finger in my face and said, "One of these days, you and your clearances are going to have us right in the middle of a lawsuit!"

Looking across the room, I remembered what Bert had warned me about that day. Sure enough, he was right. Here we were in court!

Blake Frazier was the attorney who questioned me the most. He drilled me for the better part of seven hours. When asking some of his questions, he didn't have his facts exactly correct. I even had some fun with one of his questions.

"Mr. Vaughn, isn't it true that you were the best man at Walter Powell's wedding?"

I replied, "No, sir."

Frazier looked at me, then at the judge, and then over toward the jury as he asked again, very emphatically, "Now, Mr. Vaughn, are you telling me that you were not the best man at Walter Powell's wedding?"

I thought to myself, "This guy has Walter Powell mixed up with Charlie Jones, but I'm not gonna tell him." I responded to his question, "That's correct."

Frazier looked irritated and somewhat confused as he shuffled through some of his papers. He then had a brief conference with his associate and Meiselman. After a moment he said, "Now think, Mr. Vaughn, are you absolutely sure that you weren't the best man at Walter Powell's wedding?"

Once more I replied, "That's correct." I looked at the judge, and then at the jury. I shrugged my shoulders and smiled as if to say, "Your Honor, why does he keep asking the same question over and over?"

The judge, looking over his reading glasses, spoke directly to Mr. Frazier. "Mr. Frazier, if my memory serves me correctly, that's the third time you have asked Mr. Vaughn that question. I also believe Mr. Vaughn has answered your question with the same response three times. Now, let's move on." I got tickled inside at Mr. Frazier's mix-up of names, but, unfortunately, that was one of the very few moments of comic relief.

During his seven hours of interrogation, Mr. Frazier tripped himself up on one other occasion. He said, "Now, Mr. Vaughn, isn't it true that while you were employed by Wometco, you used the strength of your buying power in Wometco's Miami theatres to get films for your Plaza Theatre in Gainesville, Florida?"

I replied, "Mr. Frazier, what strength are you referring to?"

"You know, Wometco's big-grossing theatres in Miami. Isn't it true that you used the Miami theatres as leverage to get Fox to comply with your demands in Gainesville?"

"Mr. Frazier, I didn't have any real clout in the Miami market."

He looked surprised and almost stunned as he said, "You didn't?"

"No sir. The better-grossing theatres in Miami are the newer theatres that have been built by General Cinema Corporation and America Multi-Cinemas. They had the clout, not Wometco. While I was working for Wometco, I was doing everything I could to try to keep top movies in the Wometco theatres and away from those two big national circuits and their new state-of-the-art theatres." I paused, "Mr. Dick King, the Southern Division Manager for Fox, commented to me more than once, 'Larry, I wish you would leave Wometco so we wouldn't have to play our films in Wometco theatres as much as we do. You do realize that it costs us money to play Wometco Theatres because of those crazy clearances you demand!'"

Mr. Frazier looked somewhat confused at my correcting his statement about Wometco having clout. I'm not sure, but I believe I heard his pencil snap when I was talking.

When the judge gave everyone a fifteen-minute break, I sat there thinking about how, in recent years, the film companies continuously complained to me about my clearances. With the rapid expansion of multiplex theatres, now both theatre owners and film companies wanted clearances eliminated.

When Buddy Golden, the Executive VP of Orion, was in Miami, I took him to look at theatres. When driving from one theatre to another, Buddy became confused.

He asked, "Larry, explain to me why you will not play the same picture with a theatre that is five miles away from your theatre in a heavily populated town like Miami?"

"Buddy, our auditoriums are huge. The Miracle in Coral Gables seats over 1,500. A few blocks away, General Cinema has opened a ten-plex theatre. Its largest auditorium may be 500 seats, but then the auditoriums start dropping in seat count from 400 to 250, to even some seating 150. That is why they are willing to play the same movie with a theatre just two to three miles away. They have ten auditoriums to fill and most of them are small auditoriums. I have to have the clearance to make the folks drive past the other theatres to come to the Wometco theatre to see the film. With my twin and triple theatres, I have to have the big gross to compete with these multiplex theatres."

Buddy said, "Crazy! I don't know how you do it. I have never heard of clearances like this." Buddy laughed as he surmised, "No wonder your theatres gross so much. You are the only theatre playing the picture."

Bert caught my attention as he stretched his arms. He smiled at me, tilted his head down slightly, and reached his right hand up and saluted me. His gesture affirmed that he was pleased with the way my testimony was going. His salute also brought back a funny Bert Livingston story from my Wometco days. I was attending a trade screening of a 20th

*Bert Livingston, Larry's good friend
at 20ᵗʰ Century Fox*

Century Fox film; Bert, at the time, was the Florida branch manager for Fox. I don't remember the movie that was being screened, but I do remember there were a lot of people at the screening. The lights in the auditorium dimmed, and the famous 20th Century Fox logo appeared on the screen, with its famous fanfare music. As soon as the drums started playing, Bert, who happened to be seated on the front row of the auditorium, immediately stood at attention and extended a lengthy salute that would have made a Marine Corps general proud. The audience broke into laughter, and then applause, as they enjoyed watching Bert give a wholehearted salute to his employer, the Twentieth Century Fox Film Corporation.

Bert's response was completely unlike that which I received from Art and Mike, who, without them realizing it, were making me very nervous. They were sitting on the edge of the front bench, examining every word. The two of them kept rubbing their hands as if they were cold. I was very aware that a loss in this trial would cost them millions of dollars.

Finally, my two days on the witness stand came to an end. I was free to leave and return to Litchfield Beach. As I left the courtroom, Mike and our attorney, Eric, rushed to stop me. Eric said, "Larry, if we made a training tape on how to act on the witness stand, you're the man we would want to be our example. Your answers were frank, honest, and from your heart. I watched the jury carefully while you were on the stand, and I sensed they knew you were telling the truth." Mike gave me a firm handshake and eye contact that expressed his appreciation.

Later that week I received a conference call from Art, Mike, Eric, and Jerome. They were ecstatic with joy. The verdict was in: Wometco and 20th Century Fox had been found not guilty on every single count. As for

Mr. Meiselman and his theatres, he just thought he had had problems before. He not only ended up having to pay a fortune in court costs, but now 20th Century Fox refused to do business with him in every single state that he operated theatres in—and Eastern Federal Theatres had many theatres situated throughout the South.

As for me, when I received the conference call, I was sitting on my back patio watching the golfers come and go. It was a little after five o'clock, and I was already home relaxing for the day. While my colleagues may question my decision, I for one was happy to be back in good ole, laid back, South Carolina.

# THIRTY-SEVEN

# THE BRIEF FRIENDSHIP

*Some things are more precious because they don't last.*
— Dorian Gray

SOME OF MY FONDEST MEMORIES at Litchfield are when Foster got the gang together, and we went out on the river for an evening cruise on the *Litchfield Lady*, a yacht that Foster kept docked a few miles north of Litchfield Beach. It was a beautiful piece of craftsmanship, designed for those few individuals who could afford and appreciate the very best in yachts. Foster loved cruising down the river on the *Litchfield Lady*. As the sun started to set, the music began. Foster loved for us to sing the old gospel hymns, especially his favorite, "Amazing Grace." I often looked at Foster and thought, "He has got to be the most unusual man I have ever known."

In those first few months, I spent an enormous amount of time traveling. Ulmer had me visit all the Litchfield theatres; plus, he wanted my input on the new and potential theatre locations. In my spare time I flew around the country and met with film executives and brought them up-to-date with our expansion plans.

When I was back at the office I was busy introducing our new theatres to all the film companies. I received much ribbing from the film community. I was continuously reminded of my Wometco days and my horrendous theatre clearances. The word "clearance," however, wasn't even in Litchfield's dictionary. Litchfield built beautiful multiplex theatres and agreed to play with most any theatre.

It was also during this time that South Carolina had an unwanted visit from a hurricane by the name of Hugo. Hugo gave Litchfield Beach a solid one-two punch, followed by a knockout blow. It took several months and several million dollars to get everything put back together like it was before Hugo blew through South Carolina.

After Hugo slammed into the Carolinas, I got a call from my old friend and former employer, Art Hertz.

"Larry, didn't I try to tell you not to leave us? Now look at what happened to you. You leave Miami after, how many . . . thirteen years? You go to of all places, South Carolina, and there you get nailed by a hurricane." Art was enjoying giving me a hard time.

I hung up the phone thinking, "Art is a good friend. I hope his new film buyer does a good job for him." I then laughed to myself, as I remembered Art and Mike's Tuesday meetings to discuss their theatres' weekend grosses. Why did I just think "hope?" They would make *sure* their new buyer did a *very* good job for them, or in three months he would be fish bait over at the Miami Seaquarium.

After several months, our house in Miami sold. We left our River Club home and rented a home in the exclusive Wachesaw Plantation. Our intent was to live in Wachesaw Plantation while we began plans to purchase property and build a home.

Shortly before Christmas, my family and I joined Surfside PCA church. We were glad to officially be a part of a church family again. We made many friends at Surfside and learned a lot under the direction of Pastor Mike Ross. One Sunday morning he preached a sermon on being chosen by God. The word *chosen* jumped out at me, and I thought back to my conversation years before with Eddie Stern. Eddie had emphasized the importance of being "chosen" for the film buying position. I sat there in awe as I realized God's hand of providence in my life; God had chosen me, Larry Vaughn, to be His child.

I looked over at Doneata and my children sitting there in church. I thought about how amazing God's grace truly is. I smiled as I thought about the prayer request Mentora had dropped into the offering plate earlier. I am not sure what the elders did with her request. Mentora had been fervently praying for snow, mainly because—living in Miami all her life—she had never seen snow. "Doubting Larry" had told Mentora not to get her hopes up, because I didn't want her to be too disappointed if it didn't snow. I even told Foster and the gang about Mentora's desire to see snow, and they all agreed that we would have to move further north before that prayer request would be answered.

Well, a miracle happened that Christmas—it snowed a record fifteen inches! Not only that, but the snow stayed on the ground for three solid days. That snowfall taught me an important lesson: be careful what you pray for, because God most certainly answers prayers—especially Mentora's!

In December, Foster, Eaddy, Jack, Frank, and I flew in the company jet to Atlanta for a retirement party for Mac MacAfee, an icon in the film community, who had spent the majority of his life at Paramount Pictures. The dinner, held in one of the large banquet rooms at the Ritz Carlton Hotel in Buckhead, was a grand affair that no one wanted to miss. And I nearly did. I had almost decided to stay at the beach and not make the trip, as I was fighting a terrible cough and cold. But I had been asked by John Hersker from Paramount to give the invocation at the dinner, and since I held Mac in such high regard, I let my emotions overrule my poor health.

By the time we arrived at the hotel, my body was aching all over, and I thought I must have the flu. After struggling through the dinner and ceremony, I spent the rest of the evening in bed. The really bad news is that the next morning Foster woke up sick—on the plane ride home he felt miserable.

In between his coughing and sneezing, Foster with his red, watery eyes looked over at me and said, "Well, Larry, one thing good came out of your going on this trip with us."

Sneezing and coughing, I asked, "What's that, Foster?"

Foster nodded as he spoke. "For the past seven months I have been trying to find a nickname for you. Well, I've finally found it."

I hesitated to ask, but I did anyway. "Okay, Foster, what is my nickname?"

As if he were King Arthur himself, Foster stood and said, "From this day forth, you shall no longer be known as Larry Vaughn, but . . ." He paused momentarily to allow every ear to hear, "you shall be known as 'Germ.'" Foster then sat down as everyone in the plane broke out in laughter.

Foster elbowed Jack as he pointed toward me and said, "Germ gave me the flu." That nickname, Germ, stuck. From that moment on, Foster called me Germ: that is, except when we were with businessmen who wouldn't understand why anyone would be named "Germ."

That February was an especially busy month for me, because Foster and I spent a week in LA sharing our rapid expansion plans with all the studio heads. True to his word, Foster McKissick was opening theatres almost weekly.

We were doing just fine, when all of a sudden a financial crisis hit Litchfield Theatres. Foster had a $50 million lawsuit filed against him by United Artists Theatres. United Artists sued Foster because of a theatre Litchfield had built in the Atlanta area, which UA said was competing with one of their existing theatres. When Foster sold his former circuit to United Artists, there was a non-compete clause in the contract of sale. The United Artists suit stated that Foster had violated the non-compete clause by building the theatre in question.

Litchfield Theatres suddenly found itself strapped for cash. We had difficult days just trying to keep the theatres open. All of this happened during a period of several months. We had tractor trailers with theatre equipment sitting parked, with no place to put the equipment. We were in the middle of a financial disaster.

I remember standing outside the office talking with Foster about the cash crunch. Foster and I had just finished a conference call with Wayne Lewellen over a large film payment that was overdue at Paramount.

In that conversation Wayne told Foster, "Foster, if I don't have the check, it will create a problem with my men in the field. Their bonus is based on having no outstanding collections due. Litchfield owes Paramount several hundred thousand dollars. What are you going to do?"

Without any hesitation, Foster asked, "Wayne, will you take my personal check?"

"Did you say your personal check?"

"I did."

"Yes, Foster, your personal check will be fine."

"Then I will overnight the check to you tomorrow!"

That day my respect for Foster McKissick went to a higher level. Most businessmen would have tried to explain the cash crunch and offered a partial payment, or tried to find the money internally. But when Wayne shared that his men in the field would be penalized if the money wasn't paid immediately, Foster opted to pay the film rental from his personal finances.

Foster looked at me and put his hand on my shoulder. He said, "Germ, for the first time in months I can see light at the end of the tunnel. I really feel optimistic that everything is going to be okay. I have to go to Greenville in the morning for a very important meeting. I will be back at the beach late tomorrow afternoon or early evening. We will go over everything once I return."

Foster gave me that warm assuring smile of his as he said, "Hang in there, Germ. Things are starting to look up." And almost as an afterthought, Foster smiled as he said, "I'll be sure to get Wayne's check out by UPS tomorrow."

It was around four in the morning when we received the phone call. Doneata woke up and answered the phone. I immediately came out of my deep sleep as I heard the concern in her voice.

She said, "What? Oh no! When? It can't be! What can we do? Okay, thank you for calling. Please call us if you hear any news."

I said, "Doneata, what's wrong? Who was that on the phone?"

"Larry, I've got some bad news to tell you." She paused a moment, then took a deep breath and said, "Foster's plane went down in the ocean last night."

I jumped out of bed. "What! What did you say?"

"Foster's plane crashed in the ocean last night. He was flying back to the beach from Greenville when the plane went into the ocean somewhere off the coast of Georgetown. Right before the crash, Foster radioed in, 'Mayday! Mayday! This is Foster McKissick. My pilot has gone to sleep.' Larry, the Coast Guard is out right now looking for them. That's all we know."

My body felt limp. I thought I was about to get physically sick, but I only cried.

A few moments later I said, "Doneata, let's pray about this. If Foster and the pilot are still alive, let's ask the Lord to protect them until they can be rescued."

That morning driving in to the office, I had plenty of time to think and pray. I thought to myself, "Why is it that I have had to experience so much death in my life? My father, Farrell, my mother, Roger Hill, Marvin Reed, and Jack Mitchell—they are all gone, and now Foster . . ."

As I pulled into the Litchfield parking lot, the sky was littered with helicopters that were flying far out over the Atlantic Ocean in search of a downed airplane and, hopefully, two men alive and in need of rescue.

Eventually, plane parts were found resting on the floor of the ocean. Neither of the bodies were ever recovered. Foster McKissick, the man who was known and loved by all who knew him, was never to be seen again. As for me, I had lost a man whom I had come to know and love in a very personal way.

Mystery often follows death of this nature. The strangest thing happened the day of Foster's death. Petey, Foster's beloved parrot, was missing. He had been in his cage when Foster left on the plane, but after all the horrific events of the day, Sophie came home to an empty bird cage.

There was a memorial service for A. Foster McKissick held that weekend at Litchfield Beach. The funeral service was held two days later in Greenville. Friends and relatives gathered by the hundreds to pay their last respect to the man who had played such an important part in so many lives through the years.

The morning after the funeral, I awoke before my alarm clock went off. My joints ached as I got out of bed. I looked outside at the dark clouds and could see the slight drizzle of rain, but I still put on my running shorts and shoes. My thoughts ran wild this morning, and I was too tired to stop them. Each time my feet hit the pavement, I thought about how much harder it is to run by myself. The only thing good about the rain is it hides my tears. As a Christian, I don't fear death, but death separates us from our friends and loved ones. The person left behind wants so badly to be knocking on their friend's door, dragging their friend out of their warm bed on a dreary rainy morning, rather than finding themself, or rather finding myself, jogging alone.

# THE ROBBERY

*Nowadays people know the price of everything and the value of nothing.*
*– Johnny Depp, The Rum Diary*

I HEARD THE PHONE RINGING, but I was in such a deep sleep that I really didn't want to wake up to answer it. After several rings, Doneata came dashing from the bathroom, talking to me as she hurried toward the phone.

"You'd better wake up and get at it. I've already had my shower."

I heard Doneata answer the phone and say, "Hello, good morning Ulmer. . . . Yes . . . he's right here."

Doncata handed me the phone as she motioned to me that a cup of coffee was on the way.

As I reached for the receiver, I looked at the clock. It was 7:05. "Hello, good morning, Ulmer. You're up mighty early. Is everything okay?"

Ulmer's voice was trembling, and he spat out words that, at first, I couldn't comprehend. "Larry, we had a robbery in the Westgate Theatre in Spartanburg last night. Two of our employees, the assistant manager and an usher, were killed."

The fog of sleep left me as the reality of Ulmer's words rocked me. "What! Two men killed. Oh no, Ulmer, I can't believe it." I jumped out of bed, put on my housecoat, and started walking toward the den.

"Ulmer, this is like waking up in a nightmare! Tell me exactly what happened."

"Larry, during the last feature, two men came out of an auditorium into the lobby. The lobby was empty except for one nineteen-year-old usher who was walking around waiting to close. The men jumped the usher, took him outside the theatre, and put a bullet in his head."

Chills went up my spine. "Ulmer, why would they execute the usher?"

Ulmer sounded heartbroken. "Larry, who knows why evil men do those evil things they do? My guess is the men knew that the usher could identify them, so they killed him."

I felt like I was going to throw-up! I hated to ask, but I did, "Then what happened?"

There was a long pause on the other end of the line. I could tell Ulmer was having a very hard time telling the gruesome facts. "Well, Larry, you won't believe it, but," he hesitated, "next, the two men took all the cash in the safe and made James Greene, our assistant manager, leave with them. The three of them left the theatre in the man's van."

I interrupted again. "They actually kidnapped James? How do you know all of this?"

"As they were pulling away from the theatre, the son of the manager of the Westgate Theatre drove up and saw the two former employees driving away with Greene in the van."

I interrupted him. "Ulmer, you mean the killers were former employees?"

"Larry, I'm afraid so."

I felt sick at my stomach as I asked Ulmer, "Then what happened?"

"Charlie's son knew something was wrong because the theatre was left unattended while features were still playing. He went inside and couldn't find any employees. He started looking everywhere for the usher. He eventually found the young man's body outside the theatre by the air conditioning units, so he ran back inside and phoned the police.

"The police arrived at the theatre within a matter of minutes. Charlie's son told the police that he saw Greene in the van with two former employees. He then gave the police a description of the van. The assailants drove away from the theatre and stopped the van on a deserted road."

Ulmer paused again. "Larry, it was there that they executed James by putting a bullet in his head." Ulmer paused and said, "They found James on the ground with his hands together. He was either praying or begging for his life."

From his tone of voice I could tell Ulmer was emotionally as well as physically exhausted from telling me about these horrible double murders. "Larry, that's all I know right now. It's a terrible story, but that's what the police told me."

As impossible as it may sound, I wanted to find some words of encouragement to give to Ulmer. "Ulmer, this is going to be a long, hard day for you, Charlie Hopkins and his theatre staff, Charlie's son, and the families and loved ones of those young men who were killed last night. Doneata and I will be sure to pray for everyone affected by this awful tragedy." I thanked Ulmer for the call and told him I would be available as needed.

I told Doneata the unbelievable story just as Ulmer had relayed it to me. Together we prayed for Ulmer and the families and loved ones of the two young men who were murdered that night.

The two men who committed the heinous double murder at the Westgate Theatre in Spartanburg, South Carolina, were both caught and convicted. Both men were executed; one in 1999 and the other in 2005.

The brutal murders at the Westgate Theatre reminded me of how fortunate I was that I was never shot during the years I managed theatres. Back when I managed theatres we accepted cash as the only means of payment. On a busy day it was not unusual for my nightly deposit to be $10,000 or more. The deposit was all cash and small bills. When I managed the Astro Theatre for Heyward Morgan, I was robbed at gunpoint on three separate occasions.

The first robbery took place right after the box office closed at 9:30 p.m. My teen cashier turned from the ticket counter toward me. My desk was behind where the cashier sold tickets. She had tears in her eyes as she begged me to come to her. I stood and walked the ten feet to her station. There I saw a man with a gun. He demanded I give him the money. What frightened me were his eyes—I could tell he was on drugs.

Nervously, I opened the cash drawer and started counting out the money to him. He cocked the gun and said, "Don't count the money! Just give it all to me." From the glazed look in his eyes, I thought he was going to shoot me right there on the spot. He crammed the money inside his jacket, however, and ran. As far as I know, the thief was never caught.

The second robbery happened several months later and believe it or not, the same cashier was on duty. Again, with her eyes swelling up with tears, she turned to me and begged me to come to her. I knew we were being robbed, except this time it was a heavier man. He told me to open the office door and let him into the office with us. Our office safe was large and heavy. At installation it was anchored to the floor in the office closet. The thief made me open the safe, and he took the cash along with the cash in the cashier's drawer. He then told us to get in the closet, and he turned off the lights. We were both afraid that he was going to shoot us.

We stood there in the small closet in the dark for what seemed like forever, but in actuality it was only a minute or two. I listened carefully but heard nothing, so I walked out of the closet and turned the lights on. The robber was gone. The cashier and I went to the police station and looked at pages of mug shots, but like the previous thief, he could not be identified.

The very next day, I stopped by a gun shop and purchased two guns: a Lima .380 semi-automatic pistol and a twenty-two caliber derringer pistol. I kept the Lima in my car, as I had to take the nightly cash deposits to the bank's outside drop box. The derringer was small enough that I could literally conceal the two-barrel gun in my hand.

Meanwhile, Mr. Morgan installed a buzzer beneath the center drawer of my desk. If something happened, I was to hit the buzzer, and the silent alarm would sound loudly at Mr. Morgan's bowling center, which was next door to the theatre. They were to immediately call the police. Mr. Morgan also hired an off-duty police officer to work on the weekends. He patrolled the outside of the building and the parking lot.

The third robbery happened on a Friday night. This time the cashier had gone to the restroom, and I was alone in the office. The box office had just closed, and from the ticket window I saw a tall man standing there pointing a gun at me. He said, "Money! I want all the money!"

For a split second I acted foolishly: I hit the alarm and dropped to the floor behind my desk. Startled, the thief started to run away. I chased him, but I forgot my derringer. I stayed a good distance behind him, but I wanted to be sure I didn't lose sight of him. He shot at me, and I dropped to the ground. He ran behind the theatre, but then he stopped and didn't move. I was wondering what he was thinking by just standing there. He started running again and ran around the other side of the theatre; I was a good twenty-five to fifty yards behind him.

As he ran to leave the parking lot and enter the busy highway, a policeman yelled, "Stop, or I will shoot."

The man glanced back to see a policeman taking dead aim on him with a shotgun. The robber stopped, dropped the gun, and put his arms in the air. As they put him in the police car, he saw me standing a few feet away. He cursed and spit at me. He gave me a weird stare as he bellowed, "Mister, I will deal with you later!"

Later that night, I found out why the thief had run to the back of the theatre and then just stopped and stood waiting. That is where his getaway car was supposed to have been parked . . . but his driver was nowhere to be found. Our off-duty police officer had seen a man urinating on the street, arrested him for indecent exposure, and taken him to the theatre lobby to be held for police pickup. As it turned out, this man was the driver of the getaway car. That was one time the bad guys didn't get away!

# RAINY DAYS

*You pray for rain, you gotta deal with the mud too. That's a part of it.*
– Denzel Washington

THE NEXT FEW WEEKS WERE filled with uncertainty as to the future of Litchfield Theatres. The company was faced with $30 million of defaulted debt, two foreclosures, numerous lawsuits, and a negative net worth.

The board of directors appointed Douglas D. Richardson as Chairman of the Board for both the Litchfield theatre division and the Litchfield real estate division. Prior to Foster's untimely death, Doug had been brought into the company as a consultant. Doug's background was finance. Ulmer Eaddy remained on as the Executive Vice President of the theatre division.

Doug immediately sold several theatres. He took the cash and paid it on the outstanding debt. It hurt having to sell theatres to our opposition, but by doing so, it gave us the cash needed to keep the company going until we could decide the next move.

As unstable as things were at work, things began to spiral out of control at home as well. It's amazing how quickly life can change. Although I should have been used to changes in life by now, I found myself at a loss when I received the news.

Doneata called me from Dr. Lindsey's office. I sensed the urgency in her voice, "Larry, Mentora has type 1 juvenile diabetes."

I felt my heart sink and pleaded, "Honey, is Dr. Lindsey absolutely sure?"

"Yes, he is admitting her into the hospital."

I grabbed my coat and said, "Doneata, I'm on my way. I will meet you at the hospital."

On my way to the hospital, I thought about Mentora and how, since she was three years old, she had had me wrapped around her little finger. I had always been there for her. I hated that I had to stand on the sidelines and watch her deal with a disease that would affect her for the rest of her life.

I think Doneata took the news the hardest. She had been through so much with David and Larry, Jr. that she simply had a hard time digesting the fact that Mentora had diabetes.

After Doneata, Mentora, and I met with Dr. Lindsey, he gave us the facts of living with type 1 diabetes, and the change in lifestyle devastated Mentora. She hated shots, and the thought of living with needles for the rest of her life seemed unbearable.

Doneata took Mentora's journal to her while she was in the hospital. Mentora couldn't bring herself to write in it because she was afraid she might write something she would later regret. Doneata understood Mentora's feelings of sadness, but she went ahead anyway and placed the journal on the table beside Mentora's hospital bed.

Mentora later shared with Doneata and me some past entries in her journal. With tears in her eyes and a heavy heart, she kept seeing a recurring theme. She saw several times where she asked God to bring something into her life to prepare her for the future. While sitting there in her hospital bed, she realized that her diagnosis was God's answer. At that moment, she had peace and confidence that God would help her through this new trial of life.

Doneata and I both gave her a hug. Then she laughed as she said, "One thing I do know, I won't ever pray that prayer again!"

Litchfield was still trying to keep afloat. Doug Richardson presented the board at Litchfield with his next consideration: the filing of Chapter 11 bankruptcy. That option would give Litchfield protection by the court to restructure the outstanding debt and reorganize the company's current holdings.

The bankruptcy idea was put on hold for the time being. The primary concern with Litchfield Theatres filing Chapter 11 bankruptcy was that it had never been done before by a major theatre circuit. So the real question was, how would the film companies react to our filing bankruptcy? Would the film companies continue to supply top movies to a theatre circuit in bankruptcy in the highly competitive theatre industry? Or would they choose to sell their movies to the opposition theatre company that was on solid ground, financially speaking?

I started receiving calls from distributors. Their question was, "Well, Larry, what are you going to do? Are you going to stay and go down with the ship, or are you going to let us help you find another job?"

My pat answer was, "No, I'm here for the duration. I intend to stay as long as Litchfield Theatres needs me."

My colleagues in the business thought that was a loyal, but rather foolish, statement for me to make. However, I had information that I wasn't permitted to share with them. It wasn't a golden parachute, but I did have a parachute. The Board of Directors had met with Doug, Ulmer, Ken, and me. They rewarded us by offering us an admirable compensation package if we remained with the company until our services were no longer required.

Doug called one of the most important meetings of the year late one Sunday afternoon. There were five men in the meeting: Doug, Ulmer, Ken Martin—the chief financial officer, Tom Henson—our attorney, and me. The purpose of the meeting was to decide whether Litchfield Theatres should pursue going into Chapter 11 bankruptcy protection.

Doug and Tom did most of the talking. After two hours of going over facts and figures, Doug said, "Fellas, if Larry can obtain confirmation from the film distributors that they will work with us," Doug paused to glance my way, "then I suggest we move forward with the filing of Chapter 11 bankruptcy."

Doug then looked directly at me. "Larry, can you make a call to someone in distribution and feel him out as to how his company would react to our filing Chapter 11? Talk to him and get back to me, if possible, tonight." In frustration, Doug threw his pencil across his desk. "If the film companies won't continue to serve us top films, then we're dead in our tracks."

I left the meeting, went home, and called my good friend Bert Livingston. Bert was now living in Dallas and had recently been promoted to Senior Vice President, Southern Division Manager of 20th Century Fox.

Bert's wife, Janie, answered the phone and immediately recognized my voice. "Well, hi, stranger. Good to hear your voice." She paused, "Larry, Bert told me all about Mr. McKissick. I sure was sorry to hear about his untimely death."

"Janie, one never knows what fortune or misfortune tomorrow might bring—only the Lord knows."

"That's true. Well, I guess you want to talk to Bert."

Bert gave me a warm greeting.

"Bert, I apologize for calling you on a Sunday evening and taking you away from your family."

"Stop it! You call me anytime you want to. What's doing?"

"Bert, I have an important question to ask you. I have been in a meeting the past two-and-a-half hours with Doug Richardson and some other Litchfield executives. We are trying to make a very important decision that could ultimately decide the future of Litchfield Theatres. Doug asked me to contact someone in film distribution and feel him out as to his thoughts about what Litchfield is considering doing. He wants to know how Fox would respond to our . . ." I paused a moment, "well, our filing Chapter 11."

There was a moment of silence.

Bert asked, "Larry, where are you calling from?"

"I'm at home."

In his usual chipper voice Bert replied, "Okay, I'll call you back in a few minutes."

About twenty minutes later, Bert called me back. "Larry, guess who I just got off the phone with?"

"Silas Marner."

"Very funny; I was lucky enough to catch Bruce Snyder at home. I told him about our conversation."

"And?"

"Bruce said to tell you that 20th Century Fox's relationship is not with Litchfield Theatres, but with Larry Vaughn. As long as you tell me that your film rental will be paid as it has always been paid, then we don't care whether Litchfield Theatres is in bankruptcy or not."

"Oh, Bert, that is wonderful news! All it takes is one distributor to go along, and then I think everyone else will follow."

"Larry, Bruce and I want to see you guys pull it off. Whatever we can do to help, we're willing to do."

I thanked Bert for his support. I told him to thank Bruce as well. True friends are hard to find, and at that moment I felt very blessed to call Bert and Bruce my friends.

I called Doug and told him, verbatim, Bert's conversation with Bruce.

"And what is Bruce's position with Fox?" Doug asked.

"Why, Bruce is President of Distribution."

"Larry, that is exactly what I needed to hear. Now, first thing in the morning, call the rest of the companies, and then get back to me as soon as you have talked with everyone."

By 4:30 Monday afternoon, Frank and I had notified all the major film distributors of our intent to file Chapter 11 bankruptcy. Along with that notification, we had the assurance of all the companies that it would be business as usual, as long as Litchfield continued to make its film rental payments in a timely manner.

Late Monday afternoon, Doug, Ulmer, Ken, Tom, and I met. With the great news that all the film companies were supporting us, we were ready to proceed with filing Chapter 11 bankruptcy. Now that the immediate heat was off, we could roll up our sleeves and return to the business at hand. The board of directors talked with Doug about their concerns with our management team. One area we were weak in was operations. We had an excellent number two man in Ulmer Eaddy, but Ulmer needed help. So Doug hired Stephen Colson as President of Litchfield Theatres. Steve, being a former General Cinema executive, had excellent operational and management skills.

The theatres were now grossing beyond our wildest expectations. All the necessary pieces of the corporate puzzle were coming together to make it possible for Litchfield Theatres to come out of bankruptcy. Litchfield Theatres did a textbook turnaround and was out of Chapter 11 within a year. Things just couldn't have gone better for the company.

There were lots of big movies being released, and the film companies kept their word and gave us our share of the business. We were pounding our annual projections into the ground. Where a year earlier it had looked as if all was lost, we now saw not only a chance to maintain our current presence in the marketplace, but also an opportunity in the not-too-distant future to return to building theatres. It wouldn't be long at all before Litchfield Theatres, Ltd. would be back as a major player in the film industry.

FORTY

# MY SWAN SONG

*I came to a place where I realized what true value was. It wasn't money.*
*Money is a means to achieving an end, but it's not the end.*
– Robert Redford

AS I LOOK OUT THE window at the snow-filled clouds, I can't help but think about the snowstorm that is sure to come. The freezing weather gives a deeper sense of appreciation to my fresh cup of hot coffee. Even little Henry, my furry sidekick, lifts his head up. It is as if he too senses a storm nearby. He yawns, and then he edges closer to my side before returning to sleep. My memories of another time and another place are flooding my mind with thoughts of years gone by.

It seems so long ago now, when I made my decision to leave the industry. It was in the summer of 1994. I remember that I was amazed at how smoothly the merger between Litchfield Theatres and Regal Cinemas had gone.

It was that same year that I left the industry I had come to know and love for thirty-two years. Was it hard to leave? Yes, it was bittersweet. But what really made it so hard to leave was my film row family. I still smile when I think of how my friends in the business rallied around me.

341

When the news of the merger broke, my first call was from Bruce Snyder, the President of Distribution at 20th Century Fox. He said, "Larry, I just got off the phone with Mike Campbell, the CEO of Regal. I told Mike he better take you with him. You can expect to hear from him this week. And Larry, if Regal doesn't work, then we will find you something else."

After Bruce's call, I got the unexpected call of a lifetime. It's funny how things turn out sometimes. Curtis Fain, a branch manager with Universal Pictures, called and, from his tone of voice, I knew he was calling on an urgent matter.

"Larry, have I got some crazy news for you! You're never going to believe who called me and wants to hire you." He paused for emphasis and then said enthusiastically, "Ira Meiselman!"

I thought Curtis was joking. I started laughing, and finally Curtis interrupted my laughter by saying, "Larry, I'm serious. Mr. Meiselman wants you to come to work for him. I don't think he really cares what kind of money you want."

"Curtis, let me ask you a question. Why would a man whom I cost millions of dollars in a Miami courtroom want to hire me?"

Curtis chuckled. "Larry, I asked Mr. Meiselman the same question. He said, 'If Larry Vaughn can cost me millions when working for Wometco, then he can make me millions while working for me.'"

I thought to myself, "Well, it is obvious Ira puts his money above his personal feelings. I wonder if Fox is still off service with Eastern Federal because of the lawsuit? Ira must be in the doghouse with Fox or some of the other distributors, and he probably needs me to help mend some fences. I wish Art Hertz could hear this conversation. He wouldn't believe it—not in a thousand years!"

As I hung up the phone, I felt weak, as I knew I had just passed up a very big paycheck, along with a chance to live in Charlotte and make top dollar doing what I do best. No, I didn't particularly care to work for Ira Meiselman. But if I tied him up with a five-year contract making six figures a year with bonuses and expenses, I could very well expect to be financially independent by the ripe old age of fifty-two.

My final film-buying opportunity came from Cinemark Theatres, located in Dallas, Texas. Lee Roy Mitchell, the Chairman of Cinemark, was on an aggressive expansion program, and his buyer called me and asked if I would meet with them in Dallas. I gracefully thanked the man for the call but declined to accept the invite.

To walk away from my colleagues of so many years was not an easy thing to do. No doubt, at the time, many industry insiders were wondering why I would even consider doing such a thing. Well, here is the rest of the story.

I remember the initial meeting I had with Steve Colson regarding the Regal merger with Litchfield. We were thrilled that we would receive our payout once the merger was completed. Both of us would then be on a solid financial footing. Steve was toying with the idea of opening his own theatre. He asked me, "Larry, what are your plans?"

"The family and I are going to return to Greenville, South Carolina." I paused momentarily to give my next statement the attention it deserved. "Steve, I am going to retire from the film business."

"You wouldn't?" Steve asked in disbelief.

"I am afraid so. I told Doneata when we left Miami that Litchfield would be my swan song."

Steve was stunned at my statement. "But, Larry, what are you going to do?"

"Right now, I have no idea."

Steve's look of puzzlement begged for an explanation.

I tried to explain. "Steve, I don't want you to misunderstand my reason for leaving the business after the merger. It's not that I don't love this business. The Lord knows I do. Movies have been my life for the last thirty-two years. And what a wonderful life it has been! In addition, the junior executives I started out working with many years ago are today in the Who's Who of the industry. Those prominent men are some of my dearest and closest friends."

Steve interrupted, "That's exactly why I don't get it. You've made a very good name for yourself. Plus, you know everybody in the industry!" He frowned in disbelief as he vigorously asked, "Then why leave now?"

I held up my hand, "Steve, I love being a film buyer, but I am also a Christian, and my being a Christian is where the rub comes into play. As a Christian, I struggle with some of the movies coming out of Hollywood." I paused, "Obviously the film industry, like any other industry, needs good Christian men to give testimony of their faith in Jesus Christ. For me, though, the struggle has been too great. The hard part is, I will sorely miss my friends in the industry."

Steve just sat there and stared at me. He finally commented, "I heard about what you went through in Miami on *The Last Temptation of Christ*. You know, Larry, when *Last Temptation* played, I was employed at General Cinema, and they made a corporate decision, across the board, not to play *Last Temptation* in any of their theatres."

I frowned and said, "That picture just about put me in my grave!"

As I stood to leave his office, Steve stood, and then he walked over to me as he extended his hand. He looked me in the eye as he said, "Well, if you have a change of heart and wish to return to the business, I am confident there will be a film-buying job awaiting you."

It was obvious that Steve didn't understand my explanation. How could he? How do I explain the years of struggle I experienced in the industry as a Christian? Overnight, the screening room, where I watched anywhere from 200 to 250 movies a year, became a struggle for me. Even when I wasn't screening films, I had to put my thumbprint of approval on certain films that contradicted everything I believed. For me, it meant walking away from my dream job, a big paycheck, and dear friends in the industry. Although it was one of the hardest decisions I have ever made, the spiritual blessings have far outweighed the financial reward I would have gained.

During those last few weeks at Litchfield, I received many calls from the film companies concerning my future plans. Everyone was calling, wanting to know what I was going to do once the merger was final. What was one person's speculation turned into another person's fact. Most people thought I was going to open up my own film-buying and booking office and work out of South Carolina. Others thought I had stumbled onto something big in the Greenville area. Several individuals asked me if I were in need of investors.

I spent the last three days in the Litchfield office on the phone talking with many of the film companies, thanking them for the support they had given Larry Vaughn during the past twenty years and Litchfield Theatres during the past five years.

Late Tuesday afternoon, rather than wait until the last minute, I decided I would go ahead and take my personal items off the wall and clean out my desk. Before I began to put everything away, I took a long look around my office. There were many years of memories, with photographs of dear friends, actors, and actresses. I picked up the latest family picture, and marveled at how much each of my children had grown. I sat there behind my desk thinking, "This moment sure has been a long time in the making."

I sighed as I opened my desk drawer for the last time. I saw a business card lying there. I picked it up and saw that it was Foster McKissick's business card. I immediately remembered why I had that particular card in my possession. I laughed as I turned the card over. Sure enough, it was a worthless IOU for five dollars signed by Foster McKissick, given to me on one of those many days he found himself without lunch money. Foster was never one to carry cash. I couldn't help but smile when I saw his IOU.

I looked out the window of my office. I could see the sea oats gently blowing in the soft summer breeze. Behind the sea oats lay a pond—the epitome of tranquility. At that moment I saw a swan in its glory glide smoothly across the pond. On the other side of the pond, not too far away, were the sand dunes and the oceanfront homes at Litchfield by the Sea. I looked up at the sky. The clouds looked like ripples in the sea, as they peacefully passed overhead without so much as a small threat of rain. I breathed deeply, trying to absorb the moment into my very being.

I thought to myself, "God has been so very good to me. Even before I knew Him, He was watching out for me. Tomorrow I am starting a new life, but I will take with me some wonderful memories and friendships that took a lifetime to build."

I looked around my office. Apart from the furniture, it now looked dull and empty, as all those things that bring warmth and personality to an office were gone. There were nails on the walls, but no pictures; a desk, but nothing on it.

I put my boxes of memories and my briefcase into the trunk of my car. I stopped for gas and a Coke at a service station and then parked the car at the side. I then opened the envelope that Doug Richardson had earlier handed to me. Inside the envelope was my last paycheck—a paycheck that ended a career of thirty-two years in the motion picture industry.

Three months after I left the industry, I received a call from John Hersker, Paramount Pictures' Executive VP of Distribution, better known as one of Wayne Lewellen's trusted lieutenants. John was a dear friend and a twenty-year colleague. He asked me, "Larry, have you received your thank-you note from Regal Cinemas?"

Somewhat puzzled, I asked, "A thank-you for what?"

"Why, the play dates on *Forrest Gump*. It looks like you had *Forrest* booked everywhere Litchfield had a theatre." In jest, John continued, "Surely Mike Campbell sent you a thank-you note for all the play dates you gave him on the sleeper hit of the year!"

John's kind words brought back one of my last fond memories of film buying. In early 1994, Paramount un-veiled their summer lineup of mov-ies. Their big film of the summer—on paper, at least—was an Eddie Murphy film, *Beverly Hills Cop III*, which was scheduled to open in prime play time: Memorial Day weekend. Eddie Murphy, like Tom Cruise, was box of-fice gold and could guarantee a solid opening on any of his movies.

Paramount's second film of the summer was rumored to be a good film but, on paper, it didn't have the

*John H. Hersker, Larry's good friend at Paramount Pictures*

grossing potential of an Eddie Murphy film. The film was directed by Robert Zemeckis, who happened to be one of my favorite directors. I decided to take a chance and pass on *Cop III*, and instead go after Paramount's number two film, *Forrest Gump*. It was just a hunch, but I went after *Forrest Gump* in a big way. If I had been wrong, then Regal would have missed out on playing a big film . . . and on making a lot of money. But, in hindsight, I gave Regal a great going-away present, because I had *Forrest Gump* dated everywhere.

As it turned out, *Beverly Hills Cop III* was a major box office disappointment. And *Forrest Gump?* It was the sleeper hit of the year, and won the Academy Award for Best Picture.

Much has happened since I left the film business. My good friend, Victor Young, made a good life for himself. After he finished his tour of duty in the Marine Corps, Victor went on to graduate from the University of South Carolina. Today Victor is a successful businessman, is married to a lovely lady, Yvonne, and has three children.

In the late 1990's I went to Heyward Morgan's funeral. He opened a door of opportunity to me that most people can only dream of having the chance to go through. He poured an enormous amount of his life, energy, and money into mentoring me to be the man that I am today. Heyward Morgan was an entrepreneur and a visionary, and today I am a better man for having known him.

My brother Buddy and I made contact two or three times after our initial meeting. Buddy and Ann came to Mentora's wedding. We make it an annual event to call each other on Christmas Day.

Even today, when I watch an old Cary Grant film on Turner Classics, my mind goes down memory lane to my dear employer and friend, Eddie Stern. After all these years, I still miss him. Sadly, Eddie spent his last years suffering from Alzheimer's disease. But Eddie, like Heyward, lived a full life well into his eighties.

The last time I saw Art Hertz was in Myrtle Beach, where we had lunch at the Litchfield Country Club. Art came to Myrtle Beach on business and drove down to Litchfield Beach to spend some time with me. Art and Mike finally sold their theatres. After I left Wometco, I was told, through the grapevine, that Art called his key theatre personnel in and told them that if they would stay on with the company until the theatres sold, he would give them a year's salary as a bonus. Since the sale of Wometco, Art is doing just fine doing what he does best—making money.

My family has had many blessings and many challenges. I was diagnosed with cervical stenosis (a degenerative neck disease that, if untreated, causes paralysis) shortly after leaving the industry. Then a few years later I was diagnosed with colon cancer. The prognosis was not good: the doctors gave me only eighteen months to two years. But God gave me healing, and I am thankful to be here today. Lord willing, my best girl, the love of my life, Doneata and I will celebrate forty years of marriage this year.

David married a wonderful girl, Angie Downs, from Franklin, North Carolina, in 2000. We were told that David would never be able to have children because of his many years of chemo treatments for his leukemia, but God has blessed them with three wonderful boys, my grandsons: Adam, Andrew, and Austin.

Larry, Jr. met and married Shelby Anderson in 2005. Shelby is the girl of Larry's dreams. They have given Doneata and me a beautiful granddaughter named Rowan.

At this moment, I am sitting in my office. A loud roar on the TV has just interrupted my thoughts—the Fighting Irish just scored another touchdown. I would never have guessed that I'd be living a stone's throw from the campus of Notre Dame. How did I, a Southern boy who always cheered for any team that was playing against Notre Dame, end up being an Irish fan? Well, I guess I have my son-in-law, Jeffrey, to thank for that.

After graduating from college, Mentora fell in love with her knight in shining armor, Jeffrey Gratrix. They married in 2002, and the next thing I knew, Doneata and I were living in South Bend. The old saying, "when your daughter gets married, you win a son" certainly holds true for me. Jeffrey and Mentora have two beautiful daughters, my sweet granddaughters, Bellamy Doneata and Brinkley Mentora.

Obviously, I'm just brushing the surface. The years have continued with many ups and downs, as life tends to do.

I look out my window again. I see small snowflakes are beginning to dust the trees. The Scottish novelist, James Matthew Barrie, got it right when he penned the words, "God gave us memories so that we might have roses in December."

*I've thought of an ending for my book:*
*"And he lived happily ever after to the end of his days."*
– Ian Holm (as Bilbo Baggins), in *The Fellowship of the Ring*

THE END

# EPILOGUE

*A long time ago, I made me a rule. I let people do what they want to do.*
                                        – John Wayne, *Hondo*

FILM BUYING HAS CHANGED DRAMATICALLY since I left the movie business in 1994. My era was one of large auditoriums and fierce competition. There were few rules, and the few rules there were, no one paid much attention to. Those were the Wild West days of film buying, and the film buyer was known for showdowns and for keeping his guns blazing. Movies were booked by formal bids, behind-the-scene bids, by splits . . . or if all else failed by the luck of the draw.

When I left the industry, those days were already fading, and a new era of film buying was emerging. Long gone are the days when film buyers would meet to discuss all the movies to be released, and then split them up among themselves. The only time splitting didn't work is when a film buyer got greedy and wanted more than he deserved, or when a big movie stood out among all the other movies and everybody wanted that particular movie for his company. Then splitting would cease and the showdown would begin—bidding for the movie would prevail as the business of the day.

The film companies vehemently objected to theatre exhibitors splitting their movies. Some distributors claimed that split agreements were illegal restraints of trade under the Sherman Act. All film distributors took the position that since it was their studios that took all the financial risk in making the movies, they should have a say in where their movies played. In 1983, the Department of Justice agreed with the film companies and adopted the position that split agreements are illegal.

> *You see, in this world there's two kinds of people, my friend:*
> *Those with loaded guns and those who dig. You dig.*
> – Clint Eastwood, *The Good, the Bad and the Ugly*

Since then, film buyers have put up their guns, the smoke has settled, and a new unexplored frontier lies ahead. And while I am sure there are new challenges to face, the excitement of the old Wild West era doesn't exist today.

When I started my movie career in the 1960s, the largest theatres had at most two screens, but when I left the industry, my company only built multiplex theatres. The era of the large twin theatres with large auditoriums had to move aside in the mid-1980s to make room for the multiplex theatre. American Multi-Cinemas (AMC) was successful in spearheading the multiplex idea when they began opening their six-plex theatres (with six screens) throughout the United States. Then AMC pioneered the first megaplex theatre in North America in 1995. A megaplex theatre is a theatre with over twenty screens, where the multiplex theatre has fewer than twenty screens. In addition, there are now dine-in theatres, which offer the moviegoer a feature film while enjoying a wide range of chef-prepared menu selections.

Today when a film company makes a movie, they have invested, on average, upwards of one hundred million dollars in that movie. To try to make a profit on their gamble, the film companies have to have as many play dates as possible from the theatre circuits, as Wall Street investors expect the film companies to get play dates; it's a numbers game. The nationwide opening of a movie in theatres is the engine that initially drives the movie to the public for viewing. From its theatrical release, the movie then travels to DVD sales, pay-per-view television, HBO, Red Box, Netflix, iTunes, and lastly, network television.

*Yesterday is gone and we can't get it back.*
– Robert Duvall, *Lonesome Dove*

The term "bidding for movies" is a foreign term to a film buyer today. In this age, film buyers struggle with which movie gets the IMAX auditorium and which gets the 3D auditorium. The decision as to which movie plays in which auditorium trickles down to which movie has to play in the small auditorium. But all the movies released, with the exception of limited release films, play in one or more of the multiplex theatre's many auditoriums. With today's sophisticated movie tracking software and services, much of the film buyer's guesswork is taken out of play. Before a movie opens, the industry insiders can predict with almost pinpoint accuracy how much any given film will gross on an opening weekend. As for clearances, they are for the most part nonexistent today. There is little to no objection from film buyers when they date or play the same movie with another multiplex theatre, even if the theatres are located just a couple of miles apart.

Likewise, how a film buyer settles the film rental payment is entirely different today. In my era, film rental was settled on a theatre-by-theatre, picture-by-picture basis. Today, the large theatre circuits get the best film rental deals, and many of the small independent circuits of my day have been gobbled up by these larger circuits. So for any given movie, one film buyer can now sit down with one film distributor and make one film settlement for all of his company's two hundred play dates . . . all in one simple meeting.

*The old dreams were good dreams.*
*They didn't work out, but I'm glad I had them.*
– Clint Eastwood, *The Bridges of Madison County*

In 1976, my former boss and dear friend, Eddie Stern, had it right when he said, "Film buying is a special profession. We are part of a small select group that makes Hollywood happen. Larry, don't take this calling lightly."

I got the message. There was a place in time when I was one of . . . Hollywood's chosen.

# INDEX OF PHOTOGRAPHY

# ACKNOWLEDGEMENTS

I WAS HESITANT TO BEGIN this journey. Writing a book at any stage in life is no small feat. I lived the Hollywood life and had my story to share, but it was Mentora's enthusiasm and her dedication, coupled with her gift in writing, that enriched my story. Mentora sweetly prods, until the next thing I know, we are in the middle of writing a book together. Through this long process, we made memories that I will cherish always!

From the moment I met Doneata, I knew I wanted her to be mine forever. Almost forty years later, I realize that my instincts were dead on: she is the best thing that ever happened to me. Her fingerprints are sprinkled throughout our book. Doneata is my best friend and the love of my life.

I am also thankful to my son, Larry D. Vaughn, Jr., who was there for me on those days when I needed a good listener. And to my son-in-law, Jeffrey Gratrix, who was so supportive throughout the lengthy writing process. Jeffrey patiently loaned me his wife for months on end to coauthor this book with me.

To my good friends John Hersker, Bert Livingston, Bruce Snyder, Mark Gaines, Tony Rhead, Clark Woods, and to Lee Roy Mitchell, Founder of Cinemark Theatres, who were willing to take the time from their busy schedules to read the manuscript for suggestions, corrections, and accuracy.

To the Will Rogers Motion Picture Pioneers Foundation who, after my career in the industry ended, reached out and exhibited to me that the motion picture industry is indeed a family that cares for its own.

To our publishers, Sam Lowry and Tim Lowry, a special appreciation for their believing in the project. And to J.P. Brooks, our editor: he
is a gifted editor, and his insights and improvements made for a better
story. Also, I appreciate Hannah Nichols and the creative team for all
their work to make sure the finished product was above and beyond
my expectations.

L.V.

MY DAD WAS DIAGNOSED WITH cancer when I was in college. The prognosis was bleak: the doctors gave him just eighteen months to two years
to live. I hoped he would live long enough for me to meet the man I was
to marry, so my dad could walk me down the aisle. While some girls
don't have the opportunity to have their dad be a part of their wedding
day, I couldn't imagine making that important decision alone, without
my dad's stable hand to guide me. Now here we are, so many years later,
writing a book together. To say it has been an easy journey would simply
not be true, but I can't think of anyone I would rather go through this
process with than my dad. He is my mentor and my friend, and what
makes the process easy is we think alike. We make a great team.

My mom came up with so many great ideas for the book and worked
tirelessly to make sure every detail was right. She made phone calls, in-
ternet searches, and made sure we included certain stories. Simply being
the wonderful Nana that she is, and keeping my girls entertained so my
dad and I could work, was invaluable.

I am grateful for my loving, patient husband and best friend, Jeffrey,
who believed in our project and supported me in so many ways. I appreciate my sweet daughters, Bellamy and Brinkley, who give me so much
joy every day and inspire me to be a better writer. (They also played
nicely together on so many days so I could get my work done, which is
quite a miracle for two little girls who are nineteen months apart.)

True friends are rare indeed, and I am blessed to have such a friend.
Tracey Caison Ferguson prayed for me, called me, and sent me e-mails

and texts of encouragement. I couldn't ask for a better friend. (Plus she helped me keep my sanity through this whole process!)

I also appreciate my beautiful Aunt Mentora, and my good friend, Sally, for all their encouragement and support.

I am thankful for our editor, J.P. Brooks. He brought out the best in *Hollywood's Chosen*: he encouraged us to tell more of Dad's stories, and his insightful questions improved them. I appreciate Kendra Winchester and Anna Riebe and all their hard work on the final edit.

A special thanks to Sam Lowry for believing in *Hollywood's Chosen*, and to Tim Lowry for making it happen. Sam said that he hoped our experience would be a great one, and we could not have asked for a better publishing experience. I appreciate Hannah Nichols and the creative team and all their endeavors to make a beautiful finished product.

M.V.G.

# ABOUT THE AUTHORS

LARRY VAUGHN started ushering at his neighborhood movie theatre when he was fifteen and never looked back. Though he came from a poor, single-parent household, Larry's determination seemed to make anything possible—especially his dreams. Rising from lowly usher to Hollywood executive, Larry spent over thirty-two years in the film industry. Working with many box office hits, such as *Jaws, Star Wars, Rocky,* and *Forrest Gump,* Larry's star-studded success made him the man celebrities wanted to meet. Now, Larry is happiest being a celebrity to his six grandchildren. Larry, his wife, Doneata, and their dog, Henry, live in South Bend, Indiana.

larry-vaughn.com

MENTORA VAUGHN GRATRIX was born in Miami, Florida, and later lived in Myrtle Beach and Greenville, South Carolina. She and her husband, Jeffrey, currently live in South Bend and have two beautiful daughters, Bellamy and Brinkley, who offer plenty of inspiration for her love of writing.

For more information about
**Larry Vaughn &**
**Mentora Vaughn Gratrix**

*&*

*Hollywood's Chosen*

please visit:

*larry-vaughn.com*
*hollywoodschosen@gmail.com*
*@HollywoodChosen*
*facebook.com/hollywoodschosen*

...............................................

For more information about
AMBASSADOR INTERNATIONAL
please visit:

*www.ambassador-international.com*
*@AmbassadorIntl*
*www.facebook.com/AmbassadorIntl*